Misguided

Perry Bulwer has given us a real treasure, especially given that so few cult memoirs are written from a male perspective. He takes us on a wild and conflicted journey as a member of the Children of God, starting at age 16, living here, there, and everywhere – from Canada to Japan, China, the Philippines, and more. Readers will gain a vivid picture of life in a cult with worldwide spread, led by a pedophiliac narcissist. Definitely a book you will want to read!

— Janja Lalich, PhD. Author of *Take Back Your Life: Recovering from Cults and Abusive Relationships*

Misguided provides a detailed, heart-felt look inside the most notorious Christian sect to emerge from the spiritual counterculture of the 1970s. Perry Bulwer's memoir serves as damning indictment of the damage done when twisted prophesy meets blind faith.

— Don Lattin, former religion writer at the *San Francisco Chronicle* and author of *Jesus Freaks: A True Story of Murder and Madness on the Evangelical Edge*

Perry Bulwer has written a deeply personal and richly informative study that shows how a shy but smart (and rather religious) working class kid gets drawn into an emotionally and physically abusive cult, which was constructed around the often angry but always self-serving fantasies of a delusional but inspirational leader.

He weaves stories about his own psycho-emotional development within the cultural context of generational disillusionment about traditional politics and religion, both of which the cult leader prophesized would extinguish in an apocalyptic return of Jesus in 1993. That prophetic failure, plus Perry's eyewitness account of severe physical and mental abuse of the leader's granddaughter, contributed to his decision to leave, but twenty years of his own experiences of coercion, manipulation, and control haunt him long after he has renounced and debunked the cult's doctrines.

His struggles reveal that a toxic cult still can live in a person long after that person no longer lives in a malign cult. This highly readable account, however, is an impressive achievement that reveals a toxicity that Perry hopes all other spiritual seekers can avoid.

— Stephen Kent, Emeritus Professor, Department of Sociology, University of Alberta

Misguided

My Jesus Freak Life In a Doomsday Cult

PERRY BULWER

VANCOUVER
NEW STAR BOOKS
2023

NEW STAR BOOKS LTD
No. 107–3477 Commercial St
Vancouver, BC V5N 4E8 CANADA
1574 Gulf Road, No. 1517
Point Roberts, WA 98281 USA
newstarbooks.com . info@newstarbooks.com

The publisher acknowledges the financial support of the Canada Council for the Arts,
the British Columbia Arts Council, and the Government of Canada.
Nous reconnaissons l'appui financier du gouvernement du Canada.

Cataloguing information for this book is available from Library
and Archives Canada, www.collectionscanada.gc.ca.
ISBN: 978-1-55420-205-8

Cover design by Oliver McPartlin
Typeset by New Star Books
Printed and bound in Canada by Imprimerie Gauvin, Gatineau, QC
First printing September 2023

United Nations Convention on the Rights of the Child — Article 14

1. States Parties shall respect the right of the child to freedom of thought, conscience and religion.

2. States Parties shall respect the rights and duties of the parents and, when applicable, legal guardians, to provide direction to the child in the exercise of his or her right in a manner consistent with the evolving capacities of the child.

3. Freedom to manifest one's religion or beliefs may be subject only to such limitations as are prescribed by law and are necessary to protect public safety, order, health or morals, or the fundamental rights and freedoms of others.

Children have an inherent right to freely form their own thoughts and conscience, and choose their own religious beliefs, or have none at all, since freedom of religion necessarily includes the right to be free from religion. The concept of the "evolving capacities of the child" includes the moral principle of a child's right to an open future, which means reaching adulthood with the ability to fully exercise all their rights still intact. An open future can easily be denied to children through dogmatic indoctrination by misguided parents that prevents them from thinking critically and freely forming their own thoughts, conscience and beliefs.

When conflicts between parental and children's rights arise, the Convention sides with children. A parent's right to religious freedom does not give them the right to deny that same freedom to their child. As the U.S. Supreme Court famously ruled: "Parents may be free to become martyrs themselves. But it does not follow they are free, in identical circumstances, to make martyrs of their children before they have reached the age of full and legal discretion when they can make that choice for themselves."

Contents

Chapter 1
Gotta Serve Somebody

I believed God was speaking directly to me through the car radio the day I first heard Bob Dylan singing "Gotta Serve Somebody." The lyrics surprised me so much that I pulled over to the curb to make sure I was hearing them right. I didn't know that Dylan had converted to evangelical Christianity, so he seemed like an odd messenger for that clearly biblical message. Hearing those familiar words reactivated the dormant dogma I had been indoctrinated with. I immediately recalled a Bible verse I'd memorized seven years earlier, after I'd dropped out to follow Jesus with the Children of God:

> No man can serve two masters: for either he will hate the one, and love the other; or else he will hold to the one, and despise the other. Ye cannot serve God and mammon. (Matthew 6:24)[*]

It was August 1979, three years since I'd left the group while living in Asia, and two since my return home to Canada. Dylan's song sent me right back to the moment I first learned that scripture from a Jesus-freak street preacher. As he showed me those words from his pocket Bible, he pointed to the pulp and paper mill in the distance where my father worked, explaining that the factory represented mammon, a biblical term for money, material possessions and related greediness. I was an impressionable, immature sixteen-year-old in Grade 11, worried about my future and the lack of options the small, forest industry milltown held for me. Then that stranger appeared and offered me an alternative way of life.

My father, maternal grandfather and uncles all worked in the logging industry, either in the woods harvesting the trees or in the mills that processed the logs into lumber or paper. Even my mum worked in the plywood mill until she became pregnant with me. So, as I grew up, it seemed

---

[*] Cited scriptures throughout are referenced from the King James Bible

to me that there was an unexpressed expectation that I would wear the same working-class boots that most in my family and community did. As a teen, I dreaded the thought of following in my father's footsteps in the factory, becoming merely a cog in the machine. It was not a life I wanted, but I had no guidance from reliable mentors showing me other possibilities.

I felt trapped in that town, so when that evangelist offered me a way out of the valley into what I thought would be a life of freedom, I grabbed the chance to escape. Within weeks, I would become a COG of a different sort—a "Child of God"—but still controlled by the machinations of others. biblical truth did not set me free, as promised. Instead, I became a prisoner of Christian dogma, bound by spiritual chains.

Years afterwards, and just a few weeks before hearing that Dylan song, I came upon two Children of God who were passing through town on a proselytizing road trip. I offered them a place to stay for the night, and they turned my mind back to my former life as a disciple of Christ, trying to convince me to return to the flock. Now, listening to Dylan on the radio, I wondered if the song was another divine sign I needed to heed. Three months later, I would be back in the fold.

— — —

My hometown, Port Alberni, is nestled in a valley at the end of a forty-kilometre inlet from the Pacific Ocean that almost splits Vancouver Island in half. The Alberni Valley is where industrial logging started in British Columbia, with the first sawmill in 1860. Abundant employment opportunities in the forests, sawmills and the innovative pulp and paper mill built in 1946 attracted my mother's parents to move there from Manitoba with their six children. They had three more after the move. My father came alone as a young man from the Interior of British Columbia. My parents, Yvonne and Rod, married in 1954, and I was born the next year, at the height of the baby boom.

Port Alberni was also booming as the forest industry worked at full capacity to feed the huge North American demand for housing construction throughout the 1950s and '60s. By the time I reached my teens the town had one of the highest average incomes in Canada, and kids straight out of high school could easily get well-paying jobs in that industry.

Port Alberni is also known as one of the few cities in North America to suffer serious damage from a tsunami. The strongest earthquake ever recorded on the continent struck Alaska in the afternoon of Good Friday 1964, sending tsunami waves down the coast. Several hours later, a series of six waves, squeezed by the narrow Alberni Inlet, surged higher and faster until they slammed into the town over the course of seven hours. No one had anticipated such a catastrophic event that far inland, so there was no tsunami warning system in place at the time. The first wave hit shortly after midnight, but it was the larger second wave an hour later that caused most of the millions of dollars in damage.

We lived in a one-bedroom cabin on Falls Road, just outside city limits. We were on a hill above the Somass River, about five kilometres from where it empties into the Alberni Inlet, so we were safe there. My parents might not have been alerted to what was going on if my mum's sister hadn't called with the news. They woke up my sister Brenda and I, and we all went to my aunt's house nearby. My dad and uncle then went to check on one of my mum's brothers and his wife to help them and anyone else who lived near the river evacuate the flood zone.

There was too much excitement to sleep through this emergency situation, so I stayed awake, listening wide-eyed to radio reports with my mum and aunt as we waited for my dad and uncle to return. When they came back, they told us dramatic stories of how they went door-to-door at a motel on the riverbank to ensure everyone had been evacuated, and how they rescued my uncle and aunt from their flooded house, which eventually floated off its foundation and landed a block or so away. At one point, they saw in the distance a wall of water as high as the hood of their car headed toward them, so they quickly turned around and raced away. That surge was probably from the second wave.

Over the following week, I heard about other amazing escapes and rescues from the deluge, including family friends who fled their flooded home in a rowboat with their three young children. I saw up close the aftermath of the formidable, destructive power of nature. Fortunately, no one in Port Alberni died in that natural disaster, but my first experience with death did occur around that time.

Five months earlier, I was sent home from school after John F. Kennedy's assassination. I was in Grade 3 when the shocking news reached my little four-grade River Bend Elementary school that November 22 morning. The principal sadly explained that the US president had died and that out of respect, the school would close for the rest of that Friday. It was the first time I saw an adult cry. Over that weekend, I was fascinated by the constant television coverage of events, including the shooting of Lee Harvey Oswald, the first murder ever televised live, and Kennedy's elaborate two-day state funeral.

Those two momentous tragedies, the tsunami and assassination, had a significant impact on my young psyche, impressing on my eight-year-old mind the impermanence of life. Disaster or tragedy could strike at any time, and things could change in a moment. The tsunami also portended two pivotal, life-changing events that would wash over my world on two other Easter weekends, in 1966 and 1972. The first, involving two uncles, was a personally traumatic tragedy that triggered existential questions about death and the meaning of life. The second was my encounter with the Children of God, part of a wave of Jesus People who came to Canada from California and swept me out of my family's life.

— — —

A few months after the tsunami, we moved into a larger house near the main business and shopping area in the unaffected upper part of town. I had the upstairs bedroom to myself for a while, until we took in a boarder, my dad's co-worker who needed a place to stay until he could find his own. I moved into the other half of the second floor, which was more like an extra-wide hallway at the top of the stairs than an actual bedroom. There was no door, only a curtain, separating the two rooms. That remained my room when my mum's younger brother, W, replaced the boarder.

On the Easter weekend of 1966, I was part of a representative team of ten-year-olds in a hockey tournament in Victoria, the capital of British Columbia, on the southern tip of Vancouver Island. On Friday and Saturday nights, I billeted with an opposing player's family in Victoria, while my parents and sister stayed with my dad's uncle in Duncan, a small town about an hour's drive away. My dad and uncle drove in to watch my games. After the last one on Sunday, I returned to Duncan with them, sharing stories of the fun I'd had. But that happy holiday ended sadly with sudden, shocking news from home.

Early Monday morning, my mum took Brenda and me aside. There was obviously something wrong. Her eyes were all red and watery, and I could tell she was upset. She probably said more, but I only remember her crying out, "Your Uncle W has died and gone to heaven," as her tears flowed again. I had never seen her cry before. She hugged and comforted us, doing her best to control her grief. I don't remember crying myself. Maybe I was too numbed and confused by the news.

We drove an hour and a half back to Port Alberni in sombre silence. My parents decided to keep the car radio turned off so that we didn't hear any news reports. Unfortunately, a bratty kid who lived a few houses over must have heard those reports, or learned the news from his parents. When we arrived home, just as I was getting out of the car, he ran over and yelled: "Hey, Bulwer, your uncle killed himself, eh?" My parents quickly rushed us into the house, but it was too late. Those words would puzzle and haunt me for decades.

Over the course of that day and the next, as my aunts and uncles gathered at our house to grieve, I overheard parts of their conversations and learned that another of my mum's brothers, G, was in jail for killing a man in the same incident in which W had died. But everything I heard only led to questions that I never learned the answers to. I think my mum wanted to shield Brenda and me from those distressing details and the sorrowful mourning, so she arranged for us to separately stay with family friends who had children our ages. I stayed with former neighbours who had boys about my age. They kept me occupied and entertained, but no distraction could stop me from wondering if my uncle really had killed himself. If he had, why, and how was that connected to the other man's death?

I replayed my last memory of my uncle W over and over again. He had taken me shopping to buy some work gear for a new job he was starting the next day. As we passed a hobby shop, we checked out the window display. When he spotted walkie-talkies, he excitedly told me he would buy them for me with his first paycheque. After we got home, he discovered that his new work gloves were missing. I had carried the shopping bag they'd been in, and they must have fallen out on the way back. The shops were now closed, so it was too late to buy another pair. I felt embarrassed about it, and I knew he was annoyed, but he didn't get angry or scold me. I never got a chance to thank him for that kindness, or to say goodbye.

Brenda and I didn't attend our uncle's funeral. I'm not sure if my mum thought we were too young to be involved with that part of the grieving process, or if she was still trying to protect us from hearing details that might've come out in emotional conversations afterwards. I had watched Kennedy's three-year-old son taking part in his funeral, so I didn't really understand why I couldn't go to my uncle's. Later, my mum took us to his gravesite, where we knelt and prayed. It was my only opportunity to publicly express my grief, but I didn't cry. Instead, I internalized my emotions, which became a lifelong habit.

A few months later, in the summer of 1966, the first of two adopted Indigenous children came into our lives. Crystal, who was less than a year old, was a joyful antidote to the trauma of the tragedy that was still playing out. A year and a half after that, another infant, Jay, became part of our family. Life moved on, but I never stopped thinking and speculating about my uncle's death.

During my uncle G's homicide trial in October that year, I overheard more snippets of the story. My imagination filled in the rest. The trial was held in Nanaimo, so some of G's siblings and his wife carpooled the two-hour round trip each day. They often gathered at our house, so I eavesdropped when I could. I tried to piece together the few details I heard—there was a drinking party at my uncle E's house; a man I didn't know was shot and killed; when the police came, W was holding a gun; the gun went off and W died; G was arrested and held in custody in Nanaimo until his trial.

Knowing those details, the claim I'd heard from my neighbour that W had killed himself didn't make sense to me. I thought people only committed suicide when they were alone. Why would he shoot himself in front of a group of people, including his own brothers? Was it an accident? Did G accidentally shoot the other man, and did W then use the same gun to try and demonstrate to the police officers how the shooting had happened, only to have the gun accidentally fire again? I needed to tell myself some story, so that's what I imagined had happened—that both deaths were accidental. I couldn't believe my uncle deliberately killed himself.

Speculation and imagination based on those few overheard details were all I had to rely on for decades, because after G was sentenced to two years in prison for manslaughter, no one ever talked about what had happened. After more than fifty years of trying to make sense of that senseless tragedy, I finally discovered more details about it through newspaper reports of the trial I found on microfilm in a library archive. However, knowing those details still doesn't fully solve the mystery of W's death that my mind has mulled over for decades. Neither does his death certificate, which lists the cause as suicide. We will never know whether he fired the gun accidentally or deliberately, and if the latter, why. That unanswerable question leaves me unable to imagine W's state of mind as that violent tragedy played out.

Almost forty years after this happened, another shocking homicide-suicide deeply affected me. It also involved someone I had lived with briefly, in the Children of God.

— — —

After my uncle's death, life carried on normally, at least on the surface. I didn't show any overt signs of emotional distress or depression, but my mind was now fixated on spiritual questions. The Church was the only place I knew that had answers, so not long afterwards I became an altar boy, which reinforced the beliefs inculcated by my Catholic indoctrination.

My induction into Christian culture, which was the dominant ideology of the Canadian society I was raised in, began not long after my birth, when I was baptized in the Catholic church. Though I was obviously not aware of it at the time, that religious ritual was the first step toward the imposition of Christian belief on my immature mind.

I began attending Sunday mass before I started Saturday catechism classes at the age of six. Those classes ingrained fundamental Catholic doctrines through a set of formalized questions and answers. The word *catechism* comes from the Greek verb meaning "to echo." That's what all us little children did, echoed back to our priestly teacher the answers he taught us to specific questions. Instead of learning how to think for ourselves and ask the right questions, even if they had no answers, we learned answers that must not be questioned.

One of the first things I learned in catechism class was the importance of baptism, a ritual intended to remove the stain of Adam and Eve's original sin that disgraces all humans, which is a basic tenet of Christian belief. According to Catholic dogma, baptism is necessary for salvation, and baptism shortly after birth ensures an infant's soul is saved if they should die while still a child.[1]

After baptism, a child raised as a Catholic takes part in three other initiation rites: the sacraments of confession, communion and confirmation. Specific catechism classes prepared me for those rituals when I was eight years old. First came confession, a necessary repentance of sins before taking part in communion, a ceremony commemorating the Last Supper in which the faithful consume sacramental wine and bread, which Catholics believe is transformed into the actual blood and body of Christ. Confirmation was the ritual where I publicly confirmed my understanding of and commitment to basic Catholic doctrines.

It was frightening to learn I was a natural-born sinner, threatened by everlasting damnation if I didn't confess my sins.[2] I found it difficult to comprehend the concepts of sin and eternal life, whether in heaven or hell, but I didn't know how to question those beliefs. I simply accepted them as unquestionable truth not to be doubted, as I was trained to do. I was made a believer before I could think for myself, so I didn't learn how to, not even in secular school, where I also just accepted what I was told without learning the critical-thinking skills of doubting and questioning.

Catholic dogma deems children to be morally responsible, presumably capable of understanding the concept of sin and the need to confess, when they reach the "age of reason" at around seven or eight years of age. However, while the "age of reason" assumes a basic ability to understand right from wrong, understanding the complicated theology of sinning against a deity is much more difficult for an eight-year-old.

I was taught a simpler version in class, but the official catechism defines sin as "an utterance, a deed, or a desire contrary to the eternal law....Like the first sin, it is disobedience, a revolt against God...love of oneself even to contempt of God."[3] It also names some of the many different kinds of sins listed in the Bible, and distinguishes their seriousness by dividing them into two categories, venial and mortal.

My childish understanding of that dogma was simply that venial sins are less serious than mortal sins, which deserve the ultimate punishment of hell if one does not confess and repent. Breaking one of the Ten Commandments, which I was required to memorize, is a mortal sin. But within those commandments, some seemed far less deserving of hell than others, and I didn't even know what some of them meant.

To an eight-year-old, some things are obvious wrongs, such as killing, stealing or lying, but I didn't know what adultery was, or coveting your neighbour's wife or property. I was also confused about the commandment not to take the Lord's name in vain. My dad frequently said "Jesus Christ" when he swore, but he didn't go to church with my mum, sister and me, and never spoke to me about religion or his beliefs, so I didn't know if the commandments applied to him. If they did, he was a mortal sinner deserving of hell by constantly swearing, but another commandment required me to honour him. It was all very confusing.

My confusion followed me into the confessional, the mysterious booth where I confessed my sins to the shadow of the priest obscured behind the screened partition. Recognizing sin in my own young life was not so easy, but since I was a born sinner I must have had something to confess. I confessed things like fighting with my sister and disobeying my mum, but how much sinning can a child really do? So sometimes I made things up, in the same way I sometimes told fictional stories for show-and-tell in school so I wouldn't feel left out. Confessing my "sins" to the priest, who offered forgiveness and ordered me to say prayers as penance, made me part of the parish.

Purified by my first confession, I was ready to receive my first communion and be confirmed along with other children my age. Confirmation is an elaborate ritual officiated by a bishop. One by one, we were called by name to the communal rail that separates the altar from the congregation, accompanied by our adult sponsors who stood behind us. After a sermon and prayer, the bishop questioned us as a group, asking us if we believed in God, Jesus, the Holy Spirit and the Catholic Church, and we answered in unison, "I do."

Next, the bishop and priests performed the "laying on of hands," a biblical gesture representing the imparting of the gift of the Holy Spirit. They symbolically laid their hands on us by extending them over the entire group at once while the bishop prayed for the Holy Spirit to enter each of us.

The bishop then anointed us with chrism, a mixture of olive oil and aromatic balsam resin used specifically for the sacraments of baptism and confirmation. After blowing on the vessel containing the oil, symbolizing the Holy Spirit coming down to consecrate it, the bishop then dipped his right thumb in the chrism and made the sign of the cross on our foreheads with the oil, addressing each of us by name as he said, "Be sealed with the gift of the Holy Spirit." The catechism says this about that seal:

> By this anointing the confirmand receives the "mark," the seal of the Holy Spirit. A seal is a symbol of a person, a sign of personal authority, or ownership of an object. Hence soldiers were marked with their leader's seal and slaves with their master's.[4]

I was symbolically sealed as a slave to my Master's will, and marked as a soldier for Christ, a spiritual branding I took seriously a few years later when the Children of God recruited me to join their endtime army of Christian soldiers.

— — —

The next step in my Christian indoctrination was after I turned eleven and became an altar boy, assisting the priest during Mass. The tragic death of my uncle less than a year earlier had a profound spiritual effect on me. Not long after it happened, I began sleeping in his bedroom, in his bed. It was a bit spooky at first. I would lie awake, pondering the meaning of life and death, trying to make sense of his.

After his funeral, my mum and aunts were taking special catechism classes that I assume were intended to help them deal with their grief. I overheard them discussing a ritual a priest performed to spiritually cleanse my uncle E's house where the two shooting deaths occurred, purifying it with holy water and prayers. I also heard them discussing critical comments their brothers made about the Church when refusing to attend those classes. Those were the only negative remarks about church or religion I ever heard. If my dad, uncles or other adults in my life were unbelievers, they never talked about it with me.

Later that year, the head priest, Sigismond Lajoie, or Father Siggy as we called him, approached my mum and me with the idea that I become an altar boy. The notion of playing a part in Mass, wearing robes and assisting the priest, appealed to me. I always enthusiastically took part in the call-and-response prayers of the Catholic liturgy, and I especially loved singing hymns with their unifying, spine-shivering emotional power. Father Siggy's favourite hymn was "How Great Thou Art," which we sang at nearly every Sunday service. Perhaps Elvis Presley's 1967 hit recording of the song had something to do with that.

I joined a few other boys my age in weekly classes in the church basement, learning how to be a religious servant. We learned the meaning of the various elements of Mass, the names and purposes of the objects and instruments, the proper way to dress ourselves with white robes, how to assist the priest with his sacred vestments, and what our role was in ministering to the priest throughout the ceremony.

In those days, Latin was still used for some parts of the liturgy, such as communion, so we memorized the Latin phrases used to respond to the priest's prayers consecrating the wine and bread as the sacrificial body of Christ. Our classes also included practising our roles in a simulated Mass in the sanctuary where the altar rituals take place. It was like dress rehearsal for a theatrical performance.

As an eleven-year-old, I was eager to express my religious convictions and enjoyed being an altar boy for the next two years, but when I reached adolescence, my attitude toward the Church began to change. It didn't help that another altar boy got preferential treatment, picked by the priests to serve at weddings, where he would get tips from the couples. I was certain he got those lucrative assignments because, unlike me, he was from a "better," well-off Catholic family, with both parents attending and giving more financially to the Church. I was jealous and disappointed by what I perceived as the hypocritical favouritism of the priests. I was slowly growing disillusioned with the Church.

For my twelfth birthday, in 1967, I got my first album, *Sgt. Pepper's Lonely Hearts Club Band*. A few months earlier, in June, I'd watched the Beatles sing "All You Need Is Love" to hundreds of millions of people around the world, on the first TV show broadcast globally by satellite. It was the Summer of Love. The short-lived hippie movement had erupted earlier, in January, when thirty thousand people with flowers in their hair held the Human Be-In in San Francisco, and it ended that summer with the three-day Monterey Pop Festival.

The counterculture, anti-establishment, anti-war, pro-drug spirit of the '60s played a large role in my adolescence. I was attracted to the psychedelia of both the Beatles and the flower children, so I changed my greasy 1950s hairstyle to a Beatles mop top and started growing it long. A couple of years later, my psychedelic experiences on LSD would open the "doors of perception" to what I interpreted as the spirit world, leading me into the arms of Jesus freaks, the spiritual offspring of the hippies.

As I entered my teen years, I started to feel aimless and less connected, at home, church and school. Although I had decent grades in junior high school, report cards my mum kept show teachers frequently offering observations like "Perry does not produce at the level expected of him," "He has failed to come even close to his potential," and "Decline in evident effort recently." Some also commented that I was a class clown, distracted and distracting others, which sometimes got me sent out of the room.

I was distracted at church too, as I became increasingly bored with repetitive rituals that no longer inspired me or satisfied my search for a purpose in life. I didn't want to be an altar boy anymore, so I abruptly stopped serving when I was thirteen. I only continued attending Mass for another year, though I didn't stop believing.

I also stopped playing ice hockey around the same time. The violence and competitiveness, even at that age, had taken the fun out of the sport I'd loved playing since the age of seven. Hockey is almost a religion in Canada, and it was my dad's. Playing and watching the game was as much a part of my childhood as going to church was, so quitting was almost as life-changing as when I stopped going to church, which was a bigger surprise to my mum than quitting hockey was to my dad.

I gave her no indication of my decision beforehand, and there was no precipitating event like the broken nose I got playing my last hockey game. Although I had been thinking of it for a while, I decided suddenly one Sunday morning not to go to Mass with my mum and sister, as usual. She accepted my decision, and my dad had nothing to say either, since he never discussed religion with me. I never attended church again. I now found the hippie philosophy of peace and love more appealing than either hockey or church.

Not long after that, former Beatles guitarist George Harrison confirmed my decision in his song "Awaiting on You All" on the album *All Things Must Pass*. I didn't need the Church to be a believer. The Children of God would soon preach the same message to me: you don't need a church, all you need is love.

Chapter 2
California Dreamin'

In the summer of 1971, a couple months before my sixteenth birthday, I hitchhiked with my classmate Dave to California, where I had my first LSD experience. I'd first gotten high with a little help from my new friend two years earlier, at a junior high school dance. Dave brought a few cannabis joints, and we smoked them behind a classroom building bordering the forest. There were a few of us gathered there, but when Dave lit a joint and passed it around, a couple of them fled the scene of the crime. That was my initiation as a counterculture freak.

I didn't get very high the first time, but Dave befriended me after that because I was willing to experiment with drugs. From then on, we smoked cannabis most weekends. We usually bought small amounts sold in a matchbox for five dollars, which was enough for a few joints each. It was often low-quality, containing small stems and seeds, but still good enough to get us high. Occasionally, I skimmed small amounts from my uncle G's more potent but poorly hidden stash when I was babysitting my cousins.

Prohibited drug use popularized by the counterculture appealed to me more than the prevalent drinking culture. Alcohol had exacerbated the circumstances surrounding my uncle's death, and though that tragedy, and other alcohol-fuelled accidents where relatives were seriously harmed, didn't stop me from experimenting, my drinking experiences were unpleasant. I first got drunk with a few of my uncles when I was fourteen. I was fifteen when I got drunk with Dave from alcohol he'd stolen from his parents' liquor cabinet. Both times, I puked my guts out and had horrible hangovers, so I didn't drink much after that. I preferred cannabis, which made me feel good without making me sick and hungover. It was also easier to get than alcohol.

When Dave suggested hitchhiking to Disneyland during summer break between grades 10 and 11, I didn't need to be persuaded. Of course, the Disney destination appealed to the kid in me, but a trip to California excited me more. The 1970 documentary *Woodstock* had been released the summer before. I saw it twice. Although the hippie movement had died, to me that music festival epitomized the '60s counterculture generation. I thought hitchhiking to California would be a way to experience the ethos of that era. I wanted to escape the Alberni Valley, and my feet were itching with wanderlust, so travelling to the land of the hippies, even if they were gone, was a great adventure for me.

The horrific Charles Manson cult-murder trials were constantly in the news at the time, so I don't think my mum was too thrilled at the thought of her naive, inexperienced fifteen-year-old son hitchhiking thousands of kilometres to cult country. She said I could go but I would have to pay my own way, probably hoping I couldn't come up with enough money, and that would be the end of our potentially dangerous plan.

We optimistically estimated taking a total of eight days to hitchhike the four-thousand-kilometre round trip, but prepared for a three-week journey. Dave had relatives in San Jose, so we planned to stay with them for several days before continuing on to Disneyland in Anaheim. We didn't need money while at his relatives, and we intended to sleep rough under the stars while on the road, so we only needed money for food while travelling and tickets for the theme park. I estimated the minimum I needed for the trip was fifty dollars — forty for food and ten for tickets. Adjusted for inflation, that would be about $350 today.

As summer approached, I managed to scrape together the fifty dollars I needed from my weekly allowance, babysitting money and refunds from empty pop and beer bottles I collected from relatives. When my mum realized I was determined, she gave me another ten dollars to ensure I had enough. Dave had at least twice as much as me, and his parents said they would wire more if we got desperate, which reassured my mum. Despite any concerns she might've had, she knew she probably couldn't stop me from leaving on that adventure, just like she wouldn't be able to stop me from leaving home to join a new California cult eight months after I returned from that summer trip.

Our adventure almost ended before it started. Dave's parents drove us to the mainland and dropped us off near the Canada–US border. We were going to hitchhike on the other side, after we cleared US border control, but we were denied entry. The officer who turned us away said we needed written permission from our parents because we were minors. He also told us that hitchhiking was illegal on Washington's freeways, which we weren't aware of.

Undeterred, we walked back into Canada until we couldn't be seen by the border guards, and held out our thumbs. Two female university students picked us up. When we explained what had happened, they told us to lie this time and say we were Americans returning home to Seattle after visiting Vancouver. A different official greeted us in the car, which had Washington licence plates, and he accepted our story without checking our ID. The world was different then, and it was not unusual to be waved through the border after a few basic questions if there was no reason for suspicion. It wouldn't be the last time I lied when crossing an international border.

The girls dropped us off near the University of Washington campus. We slept there that night, hidden in some hedges. The next morning, we stood near an on-ramp to the Interstate 5 highway and quickly got a ride. We never had to wait long on the entire trip, whether we hitched on the I-5 or the spectacularly scenic Highway 101, which snakes along the Pacific coast from Washington to California. Most of the people who picked us up were friendly, longhaired freaks who happily shared their vehicles, homes, food and cannabis with us, impressed that two Canadian kids were making such a long trip. It felt a little like a summer of love to me.

We were very careful how we spent our money, buying mostly convenient food from grocery stores, such as bread, cheese, meat slices and other things that were easy to eat on the spot or carry with us. Sometimes, depending on where we were dropped off or spent the night, it was easier to buy a cheap meal at a diner. Most nights, we slept outside, but a few times we were offered a floor to sleep on. In Eugene, Oregon, we couldn't find an appropriate place outdoors, so when I spotted a Catholic church I suggested we ask for help. I told the priest I was an altar boy back home, and he let us sleep on the floor of a storage room. That wouldn't be the last time I took advantage of my Catholic heritage.

The next day, in Northern California, we were picked up by some enthusiastic Jesus freaks headed to Eureka. They invited us to go with them to their lighthouse. I thought they meant a real one. I didn't know that the word *lighthouse* referred to a common Christian symbol and was often used in the names of evangelical outreach ministries such as coffee houses and drop-in centres. I was intrigued by their gospel tracts and talk of a spiritual kingdom, and if I'd been travelling alone I might've been enticed to go with them. I only learned decades later that the lighthouse those missionaries referred to was a Christian hippie commune called the Lighthouse Ranch.[1] It was part of the Jesus People movement that started in California and was spreading around the world.[2] But Dave wasn't interested in religion. He was on his own mission to visit Disney's fantasy kingdom, so we turned down the invitation and got out when they turned off the freeway.

When we arrived in San Jose, we stayed almost a week with Dave's relatives in their large house in the suburbs. Sleeping on a soft bed was a relief after roughing it on the road, and they fed us well. We lounged about, swam in the backyard pool, played billiards, and watched TV channels we couldn't get back home. It was like being at a holiday resort. We couldn't smoke cannabis while we were there, but Dave's cousin knew the local drug scene, so she took us to an area where Dave easily scored several tabs of LSD from a street dealer. It was much easier to use that drug discreetly.

The hallucinations on my first acid trip were pleasantly mild, mostly a cool, fractal kaleidoscope of constantly shifting, swirling, pulsating patterns. Inanimate things seemed alive. At times, it got a bit more intense, like when we were making faces in a mirror and Dave's face seemed to melt like a surrealist painting by Salvador Dalí. We tried playing pool, but the balls wouldn't co-operate, so we went night swimming instead. Swimming underwater on LSD was such a sublime feeling of freedom that I almost forgot to surface, until my brain alerted me to breathe. Floating on my back, staring at the stars, I felt like I was drifting across the universe.

My second acid trip a few days later had an even more profound effect. Dave and I dropped a tab before heading to the Santa Clara County Fair with his relatives. The hallucinations had begun by the time we got to the fairground. With all the intense sensory input from the crowded, colourful sights and loud sounds of the midway amusements, it was an odd place to have a spiritual epiphany.

I was sitting alone on a bench, waiting for the others, when I became entranced by a large leafy tree that pulsated as if breathing. It suddenly started shaking and swaying like it was about to walk away at any moment. It seemed alive in a supernatural way. I thought I was seeing the life force in the tree and glimpsing another dimension, a spiritual world hidden from the physical one, which is how I interpreted the drug-induced experience for many years. That hallucination seemed to confirm my religious belief in that spiritual world.

When we finally got to Anaheim, Dave paid for a cheap motel room to ensure we got a good night's rest. We could only spend one day at Disneyland, so we wanted to be there from opening to closing. Although

I enjoyed the "Magic Kingdom's" attractions, they were not as mystical as my LSD trips. In a way, the fireworks finale that signalled the closing of the park for the night also signified the end of my childhood.

We started the long journey home the next day, but before we reached San Jose, I had an argument with Dave and we split up. I was still angry with him after we reunited at his relative's place, so without considering the risks, I stubbornly insisted on hitchhiking the rest of the way back to Canada on my own. Fortunately, the return trip was so uneventful that I can't recall many details.

A few weeks after returning from California, I turned sixteen and started Grade 11 at Alberni District Secondary School. I dreaded a dead-end life in the valley, but I was directionless and didn't know how to escape that future. In the previous three years, I had attended E.J. Dunn Middle School, where I was part of an experimental, student-centred learning program in an open-space classroom. Three classes were combined in one large room without dividing walls or the traditional layout of desks in rows. Our teachers taught collaboratively, and we studied in smaller groups according to our skill levels. We had most of the same teachers throughout grades 8 to 10.

Although that continuity was beneficial, and the learning style suited me, I don't recall being explicitly taught essential critical-thinking skills that would've better prepared me for the real world. That experiment ended when I was transferred to the high school and back to traditional class-rooms for my final two years. It wasn't the best move for me. It left me feeling even more unconnected and aimless.

I had no conversations with my parents, teachers or student counsellors about my future after high school. I seemed to have few options. It never occurred to me that I could go to university. As far as I knew, that was something only people from well-off families did. Because of that lack of foresight, I didn't see the necessity of most of my courses, and was unmotivated to study, so never achieved my full potential. I often skipped classes or got kicked out for distracting classmates or disrespecting the teacher. Occasionally, Dave and I dropped acid in the morning before classes and spent the day in school stoned.

My LSD experiences in rainy Port Alberni were not as fun as the ones in sunny California. A few times, I had anxiety attacks in dark, crowded rooms with heavy-metal music playing, like Black Sabbath or Deep Purple, and so fled to a quiet place to mellow out on my own. After hearing about a classmate taken to the hospital during a bad trip, I was reluctant to take

LSD again, but one night a friend suggested splitting half a tab with him. I thought that would have a milder effect, but I was wrong. My last trip was the worst.

It started at the Kingsway Hotel beer parlour. A year earlier, the legal drinking age in British Columbia had dropped from twenty-one to nineteen. After I turned sixteen, I'd gone to that pub with an uncle a couple times and the bartender hadn't checked my ID, so I thought I could get away with it again without my uncle. It was more about bragging rights than drinking, because I couldn't afford more than one or two beers. I dropped the half tab of LSD before I went in with two older-looking classmates and, surprisingly, we all got served. The pub was packed with the usual crowd of mill workers, loggers, longshoremen and fishermen. As the acid began to take effect, I felt the stubble on my chin and thought I was growing old on the spot, turning into a grey-haired old-timer like some of those around me.

While staring at a clock on the wall, I had this intense perception that time had slipped away, that I had wasted my entire life sitting in that bar. I panicked and headed for the exit, followed by my puzzled friends. Passing by the pool table, I pulled a cue off the wall rack and carelessly tossed it as I walked out the door. The guy it hit chased after me, lifted me in the air by my hair, and punched me in the mouth. For a moment, I was Alice Cooper hanging by a noose, a hallucination triggered by a calendar photo I'd recently seen of Cooper doing exactly that. As he punched me, my friends began screaming, "He's high on acid, don't hit him," so he dropped me and we took off.

A few other friends had been waiting for us outside, so we all crowded into a car and went to a classmate's party at his band's rehearsal space. No longer inhibited, I tried to make out with the girl squeezed next to me in the back seat, which was completely out of character. I was extremely self-conscious and too shy to even talk to girls I was attracted to. As soon as we arrived, I strutted around the room and began stripping off my clothes. When my friends saw me take off my shirt, they realized I was going all the way, so before I did they rescued me from myself and got me out of there.

I spent the next several hours mellowing out at a friend's house, waiting to come down from the high. I didn't want to go home until I was sure my parents were sleeping, so they wouldn't see my bruised, fat lip. Once home, unable to sleep while the drug continued its milder effects for a few more hours, I pondered the meaning of that troubling time-warp experience of growing older on the spot and spending the rest of my life in that bar. Was that my future? Did I really want to live a meaningless life, going nowhere on the same working-class treadmill as everyone else I knew? What else could I do? I didn't do LSD again, but my experiences had a profound effect.

Since its release in 1970, I had listened to George Harrison's highly spiritual triple album *All Things Must Pass*, over and over again until I had memorized most of it, including the hit songs "My Sweet Lord" and "What Is Life." Now, after my LSD experiences, contemplating the notion of the spirit world and the concept of time in relation to my mortality, I felt that the lyrics from that album meant more to me as I questioned the meaning and purpose of my life.

That wasn't the only spiritual music I was listening to. The rock-opera album *Jesus Christ Superstar* was also released in 1970, and I memorized that entire record too. Singing aloud along with those albums when no one else was home rekindled the inspiration that singing hymns in church had once sparked. I was super-excited to attend a theatrical production of *Superstar* that came to town toward the end of 1971, performed in the high school's thousand-seat auditorium. After the finale, in a reprise of the title song, audience members were invited onstage to sing along, and I didn't hesitate to join them. Though I'd stopped attending church a few years earlier, I was still spiritually stimulated by the gospel and willing to publicly profess my faith. Soon, scripture-quoting strangers would take advantage of that and misguide my youthful search for meaning and purpose.

Feeling increasingly disconnected from everyone, I was unable to express my fear of the future or discuss the deep existential questions I had with anyone. I became very introspective and stopped hanging out with friends on weekends. Instead, I went to movies or cafés alone. One Saturday night, I was in the Golden Dragon Chinese restaurant, drinking a cup of coffee at the counter, when a stranger sat on the stool next to me and struck up a short conversation about Jesus. He left a gospel tract before moving on to other customers. I didn't think much of it, but I must have said something that encouraged him to return later.

After he left, a former neighbour I hadn't seen in several years came in for a meal, so I joined him in a booth. While we were catching up on our lives, the stranger who'd spoken to me earlier returned with a companion. They walked straight to our table, as if they were looking for me. They appeared to be in their early twenties, with short hair and casual clothes, but the one I first met had such a glisten in his eye that at first I thought he might've been high. They asked if they could join us and, when they did, began to preach in a way I had never heard before.

I was far more interested than my friend, who left shortly after he finished his meal. Throughout our conversation, they showed me scriptures from their pocket Bible. We didn't have one at home, and the only Bible I saw at church was the one the priest read from during Mass. It never occurred to me that I could read it too; I thought that was something only priests did. Now, reading for myself what I believed were the words of God opened a new dimension to my spirituality, and made it more difficult to resist the evangelical message the two strangers preached.

Those evangelists captivated me until the restaurant closed. By then, they had hooked me, but couldn't reel me in, yet. I refused to say a simple prayer with them to invite Jesus into my heart, which they said would save my soul from hell. That confused me. I thought my soul was already saved by baptism, so I wasn't sure how their message fit with my Catholic beliefs. I told them I didn't want to be pressured by fearful threats of hell and needed time to think about what they were saying. They left me a variety of gospel tracts and illustrated pamphlets, which were specifically designed to attract young people, and invited me to visit them anytime. It was my first encounter with the Children of God, the beginning of a radical change in my life.

Chapter 3
He's Leaving Home

The Beatles song "She's Leaving Home," from their 1967 album *Sgt. Pepper's Lonely Hearts Club Band*, depicts the moment a teen runs away from home. Paul McCartney said the song was inspired by a newspaper report about a missing seventeen-year-old runaway, noting there were many at the time. In North America that year, the Summer of Love influenced tens of thousands of young people to leave home. Three years later, Joni Mitchell's Edenic call to "get ourselves back to the garden" in her counterculture anthem "Woodstock" expressed the essence of the era, as idealistic drop-outs from an alienating political and economic system dreamed of creating a peaceful, egalitarian society.

From 1967 to 1971, an estimated five hundred thousand young American dropouts experimented with alternative lifestyles and communities. In her book *Runaways: How the Sixties Counterculture Shaped Today's Practices and Policies*, University of Michigan professor Karen M. Staller describes the surge of teenage runaways sparked by the Summer of Love as a crisis that continued for several years, eventually leading the US Congress to enact the Runaway Youth Act of 1974.[1]

In the introduction to his award-winning book *From Slogans to Mantras*, Stephen Kent, a professor of sociology specializing in new religious movements, wrote the following about the '60s counterculture:

> The focus of this book is the cultural transition of American youth from radical politics to mystical religion in the late 1960s and early 1970s. I contend that young adults' attraction to an array of religious figures and practices in the late Vietnam War period was a direct response to their negative experiences with social—especially political—protest. When thousands of

youth went from chanting political slogans to chanting meditational mantras or prayers, this transition reflected the social and political frustrations and disappointments of a generation in despair....

Although people of all ages internalize such lessons and (re) interpret them according to their individual life experiences, class, sex, and race, it is for the young that such events can define the consciousness of a generation. Members of a generation are roughly the same age, which means that their social world affects many of them in a somewhat similar manner. Cultural events, including political ones, wash over members of a generation more or less at the same time, dousing people with information that they then must interpret and personalize. In particular, the years from about eighteen to twenty-six are crucial in the development of an individual's political and cultural consciousness....

Thus, the segment of the population that I am calling the 1960s generation consists of persons who were born anywhere between about 1937 and 1956 (and especially the college-educated among that group). Technically, at least, people in this age cohort would have been between eighteen and twenty-six years of age sometime during the period between Kennedy's assassination (1963) and Nixon's pardon (1974). Moreover, on a practical level, the experiences of political culture were cumulative for this age group, meaning that youth coming into political consciousness at the end of this era had a decade of symbolism and events to internalize and to interpret. A remarkable number of political and social events occurred during this period that affected youth, and each event added to the generation's collective experience of the society in which its members lived. Near the end of this period, another new phenomenon appeared: the emergence and popular appeal of new and alternative religious groups as a vital option in youth life and culture.[2]

I came of age during the cultural and political turmoil of the 1960s. As part of the first generation to grow up in front of the television, I quickly graduated from the innocence of cartoon violence to real-life political violence, starting with the first Kennedy assassination. Television rapidly expanded my view of the world. Watching Walter Cronkite's nightly newscasts with my parents exposed me to shocking scenes of war and social disorder. Numerous events in those turbulent times informed the development of my political and social consciousness, including the Vietnam War, political assassinations, police violence against civil rights and anti-war protesters, the Cold War and threats to the environment.

By the time I was a teen, the US had conducted two nuclear tests at Amchitka, Alaska, in 1965 and '69, and planned to conduct a third, its largest underground test ever. In 1970, activists in Vancouver trying to prevent that third test created Greenpeace and held a benefit concert there headlined by Joni Mitchell, to raise funds for a protest ship to sail to the testing ground. Her hit song that year about deforestation and pesticides, "Big Yellow Taxi," was part of my environmental awakening, as was Rachel Carson's 1962 book *Silent Spring.* In junior high school I wrote a photojournalism report on pollution spewed by the pulp mill in the middle of town.

There were numerous protests against the Alaskan nuclear tests in the following months, including in Port Alberni, where the threat of a tsunami generated by the underground blast was a real, relevant risk. My first political action was participating in that protest march shortly before the bomb was detonated in November 1971. Humanity was facing the existential threats of nuclear war and environmental destruction, while men were landing on the moon and the Beatles were singing that things were "Getting Better" and "All You Need Is Love." I didn't know if I should be hopeful or fearful, which added to my adolescent angst. Not only was my childhood ending, it seemed the world's end could be near too.

American physicist Spencer Weart described that source of teen anxiety in the 1960s in his book *Nuclear Fear:*

> The bombs, like death itself, had become part of the general background of living. What difference did it make to have this appalling danger as a normal way of life? Sensitive observers believed that it seriously disturbed young people at least. Well after the Cuban crisis a poll found 40 percent of adolescents admitting a "great deal" of anxiety about war, more than twice the rate found in older groups. A survey that said nothing about bombs, but only asked schoolchildren to talk about the world ten years ahead, found over two-thirds of the children mentioning war, often in terms of sombre helplessness. In 1965 a song lamenting that we were on the "Eve of Destruction"

became the first song on a political issue to become a number-one popular tune in the United States; the nineteen-year-old writer explained that he felt war like "a cloud hanging over me all the time."...By the 1960s, observers from Teller to Dr. Benjamin Spock of SANE were reporting talks with young people who said it was pointless to save up money or study when the world might end tomorrow. In 1982 a psychiatrist, summarizing decades of studies, said that the nuclear problem had left many young with a "sense of powerlessness and cynical resignation."[3]

Like the runaway teen in that Beatles song, I was living alone though living at home, increasingly alienated from my family, friends and community, wondering who I was, what I would do, where I fit in the world. I felt lost, but searching for purpose and meaning without the guidance of mentors made me vulnerable to manipulation by proselytizing preachers preying on immature minds. I was ripe for recruiting. As Kent's book describes, baby boomers who were older and more educated and experienced than me were being lured by gurus, preachers and prophets, giving up their socio-political activism to join new religious groups.[4] As a naive sixteen-year-old seeking existential answers, I was even more susceptible to that spiritual call.

My Catholic indoctrination trained me to believe without question. Even in school, I was influenced to accept the Bible as true. Reading a Bible passage and reciting the Lord's Prayer before classes started was still legally required in public schools when I was in elementary grades. Parents could apply for a conscientious exemption, but I remember only children of Jehovah's Witnesses leaving the classroom during that morning ritual. Christian culture pervaded society in other ways too, reinforcing my Catholic beliefs. It never occurred to me to doubt and question the authority of the Bible, so I couldn't unchain myself from that dogma on my own. I needed mentors to guide me, but instead, missionaries misguided me.

— — —

Reading Bible passages with those two Jesus freaks in the Chinese restaurant fascinated me, but I was confused when they asked me to say a salvation prayer with them. I told them I needed to think about what they were teaching me. Unfortunately, I wasn't taught the critical-thinking skills necessary to rationally analyze and evaluate religious claims. When I got home from the restaurant around 1 a.m., I stayed awake for another hour, reading the gospel tracts they gave me. Some were simply sets of scriptures on various subjects, but others were comics designed to attract youth.

One of those comics, titled *Mountain Men*, had a particularly effective message, given my state of mind. It portrayed a polluted valley town full of unhappy citizens seeking a way out of their drudgery and darkness. A group of mountain dwellers descends, calling the valley people to join them. The mountaineers throw a lifeline down to help pull those below up the steep slope to the mountaintop, where they find enlightenment and fulfilling lives. I read that simple metaphor as perfectly applying to my life in a pulp-mill-polluted valley town that I dreaded being trapped in for the rest of my life. I feared my future there, and now these missionary "mountain men" were showing me a way out. That tract included their evangelical call to obey Jesus's commandment to his disciples in Mark 16:15: "Go ye into all the world, and preach the gospel to every creature."

They had invited me to visit their home on River Road, so I decided to go later that Sunday afternoon to learn more about those mysterious missionaries. Their message had moved me to do something, but my head was all over the place when I got there. I hesitated on the side of the road, too nervous to knock on the door. Standing there, I suddenly decided to cut off my long hair. It was not something they suggested, but an impulsive gesture that indicated a desire to change my life. I had not cut it in four years, so it was a large part of my adolescent identity, and one of the few things in my life that I had control over. My aunt was a hairdresser, so before I changed my mind, I walked to her house and she cut it for me.

Everyone was surprised that I had suddenly cut off my hair for no obvious reason. I didn't give my parents any explanation, or tell them about the Jesus freaks I'd met. My behaviour was odd, but they had no other reason, yet, to be worried about me. A week later, Hezekiah, one of the guys I'd met that night in the restaurant, saw me in town and crossed the street to again invite me to visit them. He told me later that he had suspected my haircut was a significant sign. The following Friday evening, he spotted me in the Pine Cafe and invited me to join the two teen girls he was taking home for a visit. This time, I didn't hesitate.

Entering the small two-storey house was a bit strange because there had been a recent fire from the faulty wood stove. It had not caused structural damage, but the living room walls were blackened from smoke, and a strong burnt smell lingered. They were in the midst of restoring it, so we had to squeeze past furniture stacked in the kitchen to get upstairs where the rooms were still habitable. I was immediately separated from the two girls and taken into the room of a married couple, who I later learned led the commune of about a dozen people.

The husband, Japheth, was the other guy I'd met that night at the Golden Dragon. I was quite intrigued that he still had that same sparkle in his eyes, and I wondered if there was some mystical explanation for it. His wife, Hannah, was also in the room with their toddler and newborn. Seeing a mother and her children there helped ease my anxiety over being separated from the girls I came with. I later learned it was a deliberate tactic, to separate the "sheep" from the "goats," susceptible believers from skeptical doubters, so they could focus on converting me to their beliefs. Japheth and Hannah, who were from Anaheim, were among the Children of God members from the US who came to Canada after the group took over communes run by the Jesus People Army in Seattle and Vancouver.

Flipping through his Bible, Japheth showed me various passages that he said explained why I needed to say a salvation prayer with him. As before, I continued to resist him, since I already believed in Jesus and thought my soul was saved when I was baptised in the Catholic Church. I wasn't aware of a fundamental difference between Catholic and Protestant salvation theology. While both agree that salvation comes through faith and God's grace, Catholics believe God dispenses that grace depending on a faithful person's actions throughout their life in an ongoing process that ultimately leads to salvation, whereas Protestants believe God grants salvation instantly to professing believers on faith alone.

Protestants equate salvation to being born again, but Catholics conceive those two concepts differently. Although both denominations believe that being born again is a metaphysical reality, not merely a metaphor, Catholics and some Protestant sects believe spiritual rebirth happens through baptismal regeneration, while many evangelical Protestants insist being born again occurs only through a personal encounter with Jesus, separate from the baptism rite. That's why Japheth persistently tried to get me to say a salvation prayer. I had never heard the phrase *born again* before, so he overcame my resistance by having me read specific scriptures about it.

Other than in my first encounter with him, I had never held a Bible, let alone read it, so holding that holy book and reading the mystical words myself was a powerful spiritual experience. Japheth started by teaching me that the Bible is the literal Word of God, showing me the first chapter of the Gospel of John, which refers to God as "the Word," and Jesus as "the Word made flesh." I then read Chapter 3, where Jesus explains that to see the kingdom of God and live forever, a person must be born again by believing in him: "Except a man be born again, he cannot see the kingdom of God.... For God so loved the world, that he gave his only begotten Son, that whosoever believeth in him should not perish, but have everlasting life." (John 3:3, 3:16)

Japheth then told me that to be born again I needed to invite Jesus to literally come into my heart. He had me read Romans 10:9: "That if thou shalt confess with thy mouth the Lord Jesus, and shalt believe in thine heart that God hath raised him from the dead, thou shalt be saved." Next, he showed me Revelation 3:20, which depicts Jesus in the spirit world saying, "Behold, I stand at the door, and knock: if any man hear my voice, and open the door, I will come in to him, and will sup with him, and he with me."

He explained that confessing my belief by saying the salvation prayer was the way to open the door to my heart and invite Jesus in. I couldn't deny the words of God, but I was struggling to understand the theology. Japheth said it was not something to be understood intellectually, but simply accepted with childlike faith. He showed me Matthew 18:3: "Except ye be converted, and become as little children, ye shall not enter into the kingdom of heaven." That was the theme of one of their favourite proselytizing songs in those days: "You Gotta Be a Baby to Go to Heaven."

I finally yielded to Japheth's pressure and prayed what is generally known as the Sinner's Prayer. Unlike the Lord's Prayer, there is no formal version, so he led me through the essential elements. Praying aloud, I admitted I was a sinner, asked Jesus to forgive me, said I believed he died for my sins and rose from the dead, invited him to come into my heart and asked him to guide my life. Immediately after, Japheth showed me 2 Corinthians 5:17: "Therefore if any man be in Christ, he is a new creature: old things are passed away; behold, all things are become new." He told me I was now a new person, born again as a spiritual babe in Christ. I didn't have an epiphany in that moment, but it marked my conversion from Catholicism to evangelical Protestantism. The fundamentalist doctrine of biblical literalism would alter my life completely.

I couldn't stay away after that. Immediately after supper on school nights, I rushed to Japheth and Hannah's home for Bible lessons, often staying until 10 or 11 p.m. On weekends, I spent most of the day there. It wasn't only studying the Bible that attracted me. They always greeted me with holy hugs. My own family was not a huggy one, and I never saw people greeting others in public with a hug, as is fairly common today, so that simple gesture made me feel especially welcomed into their group. Singing songs of worship together, something I missed after I stopped going to church, was another unifying bond that also appealed to me.

Each night after their evening meal they gathered for what they called inspiration, where everyone held hands in group prayer, followed by prophesying, praising God, singing and circle dancing. There was a lot of rapturous raising of hands, hollering hallelujahs, thanking Jesus and speaking in tongues, which are supposedly actual languages of men or angels. It was all very unfamiliar, but infectious, behaviour. That freely expressive, charismatic form of worship was very different from the ritualized Catholic liturgy I grew up with. It was an entirely new, captivating experience for me.

The charismatic movement, which emphasizes the role of the Holy Spirit in Christian practice, spread throughout a wide variety of churches in the 1960s, and contributed to the development of nondenominational Jesus People groups, including the Children of God. They practised the Pentecostal belief that the spiritual gifts of the Holy Spirit bestowed on the first Christians "on the day of Pentecost," as described in the second chapter of the Book of Acts, are still functional today, and that Christians are expected to use them in their everyday lives.

Those spiritual gifts, specified in 1 Corinthians 12:8–10, include powers to heal, perform miracles, prophesy the future, communicate divine authority to others, instantly speak and understand foreign languages (speaking in tongues), and discern spirits. That last power includes: seeing actual spiritual beings; recognizing the difference between the actions of the Holy Spirit, an evil spirit, or the human spirit; and determining if someone is possessed by a demonic spirit. Accepting that those spiritual powers are real had a significant affect on my life as a disciple of Jesus, even though I didn't have any of them myself.

After I started preaching to classmates at school, some began to call me a Jesus freak. Even my history teacher teased me in front of my classmates when he saw me reading a pocket New Testament instead of paying attention to the lesson. None of that intimidated me or made me stop. I didn't tell my mum much about these strangers I was spending all my spare time with. I simply explained that they were teaching me the Bible, and showed her some of their gospel tracts. But when the sudden, unusual change in my behaviour continued for a few weeks, my parents became concerned enough to take action.

One day at school, I was called to the office and told my parents were waiting outside in their car. This had never happened before, so I immediately knew something was up. My dad didn't say a word, but my mum told me they were worried I was spending so much time with those strangers and asked if I would be willing to speak with a priest. I hadn't been to church in a couple of years, but I had nothing to hide and so didn't mind. I met with Father Mark Lemay, a younger priest I didn't know as well as Father Siggy. I was a bit apprehensive, not knowing what to expect, but he was very friendly and simply asked me to describe the people I was meeting with and what they were teaching me.

I didn't know much about the Children of God. They'd told me they originated in California as part of the Jesus People movement and had two thousand members in communes scattered across the US and Europe, but I knew nothing about their organizational structure or that the group was led by a much older, radical ex-pastor.

Father Mark was more interested in their message, so I explained that they rejected the church system and dropped out of society to follow Jesus, like his disciples did. They were imitating the lives of the first Christians by obeying his command to preach the gospel to all nations before his Second Coming. Their communal lifestyle was also based on those first Christians, as described in Acts 2:44–45: "And all that believed were together, and had all things common; And sold their possessions and goods, and parted them to all men, as every man had need."

That was a message Father Mark was very familiar with as a Franciscan priest. Perhaps as a way of helping me relate to him, and more readily accept his advice, he proceeded to tell me a bit about the Franciscan order he belonged to. It was founded in 1210 by Saint Francis of Assisi, who rejected the wealth and pompous rituals of the Catholic Church and created a medieval counterculture of dropout disciples based on a literal interpretation of Christ's commands. His band of brothers renounced material possessions and turned their back on worldliness to preach the gospel. They lived an itinerant lifestyle, roaming throughout Europe, relying on charity to survive.

When he became a Franciscan priest, Father Mark made various vows, including vows of poverty and obedience. The vow of poverty requires a priest to share all private possessions communally within their order, and to willingly surrender financial gains to their superiors for the benefit of the entire community—for example, the income from a book or work of art. The vow of obedience requires submission not only to God's will as expressed in the Bible, but to the will of superiors who stand in the place of God.

Certain similarities between the Franciscan order and the Children of God must've been obvious to Father Mark.[5] He would've understood their literal obedience to Jesus's command to give up everything to preach the gospel, and he lived a similar communal life, sharing everything in common with his brethren. He also seemed sympathetic to their criticism of churches in general, and admitted to me that he took issue with some aspects of the Catholic Church, but he hoped to help reform it from within.

It seemed to me that Father Mark was more inspired by my description of the Children of God than he was concerned about my involvement with them. Instead of discouraging me, my talk with him pushed me closer to the group. The only advice he gave me was to not make any sudden decisions that would upset my parents, but I ignored him and did exactly that. Ironically, it was this follower of Saint Francis, not a San Francisco flower child, who influenced my decision to drop out of society.

A couple of weeks later, during the Easter Holy Week of 1972, I watched a few of the Bible-based movies that aired on TV, as I did every year. That religious holiday, with its focus on death and resurrection, always aroused memories of my uncle's tragic death on Easter Sunday six years earlier. The power of film to bring Bible stories to life is probably why Father Siggy encouraged me to go see the 1966 film *The Bible: In the Beginning* when it came to town shortly after I became an altar boy, even though he had never instructed me to read the Bible itself. Other biblical films that usually aired that week included *The Robe* (1953), *The Ten Commandments* (1956), *Ben-Hur* (1959), *Barabbas* (1961), *King of Kings* (1961) and *The Greatest Story Ever Told* (1965).

After I became involved with the Children of God, the movies I watched that week were even more meaningful, and made me more susceptible to their teachings. The films reinforced my recent born-again experience, evoking strong emotions that moved me to make an impulsive decision to follow Jesus with the Children of God and drop out, not just from high school, but from society. A few days after the Easter weekend, I quit school, left home and family, and moved in with the Children of God. I was only sixteen years old.

Once I'd made that decision, I had to consider what to tell my mum. I rarely had conversations with my dad, so it was her I talked to about important things. The Children of God had taught me how to evangelize one-on-one and convince potential converts by sharing my personal testimony, emphasizing how Jesus had saved and changed me. Their own testimonies were mostly dramatic tales of drug use and depraved lives changed by Jesus. So I too created my personal salvation story, exaggerating the amount and kinds of drugs I used in order to convince my mum that the Children of God were rescuing me from potential drug addiction by providing me a purpose in life.

Before telling her, I packed all my clothes in the duffle bag I had used for my hockey equipment. The only other possessions I planned to take were my transistor radio and bongo drum. Both were Christmas presents from my parents. Throughout my childhood, I dreamed of playing the drums, and did play a rented snare drum in the junior high school band, but after seeing a conga drummer play with Richie Havens in the *Woodstock* film, I begged my parents for one. A conga was too expensive, but I was happy with the bongo. I intended to leave behind the only other things that were mine: my record albums and my expensive ten-speed bike. I had already given away my full set of *The Hardy Boys* mystery books to my long-time friends, twins Bob and Bill, after their Bible-believing grandfather burned all their books in a bonfire.

After dinner, while washing dishes with my mum, I told her my rehearsed salvation story, and said I was moving out to serve Jesus with the Children of God. She must have worried this moment might come. Confused and upset by my sudden decision, she didn't say much, but I saw tears trickle down her face. Perhaps she felt it was pointless to try and dissuade me, thinking it was better to stay friendly than to drive me away with anger and risk losing contact with me, so instead, she offered to drive me the two miles to their house. When we got there, I said goodbye and anxiously walked down their driveway to my new Jesus freak life.

Chapter 4
Revolution for Jesus

The Children of God were not expecting me when I showed up at their door ready to move in. They hadn't directly asked me to drop out and become a disciple, but they didn't have to. The scriptures they taught me were specific enough. According to the Gospel of Matthew, when Jesus saw two pairs of brothers fishing, he called to them, "Follow me and I will make you fishers of men," and they "straightway left their nets...immediately left the ship and their father, and followed him." (Matthew 4:17–22) They became his disciples on the spot, which required giving up everything in their life, including family: "So likewise, whosoever he be of you that forsaketh not all that he hath, he cannot be my disciple." (Luke 14:26–27, 33)

Jesus's followers, both those first ones and these latter-day disciples, took those words literally, leaving their lives behind without a second thought. Like my Franciscan priest, the Children of God believed that true discipleship required renouncing all worldly possessions and responsibilities, and leaving family to follow Jesus. If they could do that, then I could too. I was highly motivated to drop out and be a disciple with them, particularly by their belief that we were living in the endtime, the last days before Jesus returned.

I gambled my life that they were right, without realizing I was making that decision based on Pascal's Wager, a pragmatic but faulty philosophical argument that you should bet your life that God exists. The wager basically proposes that if God exists and a person believes that, then they will go to heaven, which is infinitely good, but if they don't, they will go to hell, which is infinitely bad. But if God doesn't exist, then whether they believe in God or not, their gains or loses are only finite. Therefore, it is a better bet to believe in God. I would later use that simplistic philosophy to deal with any ensuing doubts I had about God or the Children of God.

The dozen members of the commune were excited that I wanted to join them, enthusiastically greeting me with hugs and hallelujahs, but Japheth and Hannah were concerned about me moving in while I was still a minor. They told me that I would need to have my parents' permission, which worried me. Although my mum had implicitly permitted me by driving me there, I had no idea what my dad thought, and was extremely anxious about asking him.

What neither I nor my parents knew at the time was that the Children of God's short history up to then included many cases of outraged, fearful parents seeking law enforcement help to rescue their children from what they considered a dangerous cult. After the notorious Manson Family cult killings and trial, covered extensively in the media from 1969 to 1971, parental fears concerning a strange new religious group originating in California certainly seemed justified.

— — —

Throughout 1971, newspapers in California, Texas, New York, Ohio, Washington and elsewhere reported controversies concerning the Children of God's recruiting techniques. Worried parents accused the group of kidnapping, brainwashing, hypnotizing or drugging their children, holding them against their will, cutting off their connections, and shuffling them between communes to hide them from their families and authorities. Similar stories about the Children of God in Vancouver, Canada, appeared in a four-part series in the *Vancouver Sun* in January 1972, just three months before I joined the group.[1]

Those four Sun articles deal mostly with controversies related to the Children of God receiving government funding after the group took control of a well-established Jesus People Army's evangelical ministry in Vancouver consisting of two communal houses, a printing press shop, a bakery, an outreach coffee house and the use of a ranch and lodge. The opening paragraphs of the first front-page article in the series, titled "Teen Menace Feared: Amid Religious Sect Rivalry," give the gist of the series:

> A radical religious sect, which claims to convert young people from drugs to Christianity, is fast establishing itself in Vancouver.
>
> Anxious parents claim that the sect "brainwashes" the young, who disappear and are held incommunicado for weeks, even months.

The sect is the Children of God, whose activities and financing are being investigated by police and legal authorities in the United States. In Vancouver, however, it is being assisted by a provincial grant.

The grant, known as "the Gaglardi Grant", comes from the B.C. Government and totals as much as $2000 monthly. It is paid on the advice of a special advisory committee which consists of an official from the Children's Aid Society, Catholic Family and Children's Services and the special placement division of the mental health department....

The officials have approved payment as they sincerely believe the money is going to the Jesus People's Army and that it is being used in a well-organized educational and retraining program that brings former drug users back into school and society.

In reality, the Jesus People's Army was absorbed late last August by the Children of God; furthermore, no educational program exists.

Within the last two weeks there has been talk of a break between the two groups, yet both still seem to be somehow related, an impression that has been conveyed by words and actions by the local head of the Jesus Army, Russell Griggs.

At the core of the currently confused relationship between the two evangelical groups is a struggle for leadership over a vast, profitable army of young people seeking hope and salvation.

Griggs's opponent in the struggle is an American, David Berg, known to his followers as "Moses". There is more at stake than leadership of the 100-strong Jesus Army. As well as the monthly provincial grant of $1200-$2000 and the community "pot" of about 25 welfare cheques at $80 each, there is a thriving bakery, use—if not ownership—of a Chilliwack ranch and a lodge near Hope, and substantial regular donations from religious people who admire evangelical-style work.

For local parents of teenagers who have "turned on" to evangelical Christianity, first through the Jesus Army and now through the Children of God, the stakes are too high to be measured in such terms. They involve their children's future, education, job training, physical health and psychological wellbeing.

That first article goes onto to describe in detail the story of a mother's desperate attempts to rescue her seventeen-year-old son who suddenly dropped out of a prestigious school to join the Children of God. The second article in the series more closely examines the government funding scandal. The third tells the story of a worried, confused mother who gave her seventeen-year-old daughter permission to join because "she seemed so happy," but who also said, "She seems brainwashed and I think if she tried to leave there would be trouble." The fourth article, titled "Scripture Cards Back Breaking with Family," details a story very similar to mine, of a sixteen-year-old boy who also dropped out of high school to join the Children of God.

I doubt my parents read those articles, even though they subscribed to the *Sun*. The numerous negative details about the Children of God would certainly make any parent who read them suspicious about the group and wary of their child's involvement. So it's hard for me to imagine that mine knew about that very recent controversy in Vancouver, but didn't bother to discuss it with me once they became aware and concerned that I was involved with the same group.

Time magazine had also reported on the Jesus People movement and the Children of God prior to my involvement with them, but I doubt my parents read those articles either. The first *Time* article, published on June 21, 1971, was a cover story titled "The Alternative Jesus: Psychedelic Christ."[2] The cover pictured a hippie-like Jesus, haloed with the words "The Jesus Revolution." The report was about the Jesus People movement in general. There was only one reference to the Children of God: "Jeremy Spencer of Britain's Fleetwood Mac has joined the ultrarigid Children of God."

Even if my parents did read that article, they wouldn't have had any reason to associate it with me, although it would have given them insights on the strangers I got involved with less than a year later. The article opens with a "Wanted" poster depicting Jesus as a radical, followed by these first two paragraphs:

> He is indeed. As the words of this Wanted poster from a Christian underground newspaper demonstrate, Jesus is alive and well and living in the radical spiritual fervor of a growing number of young Americans who have proclaimed an extraordinary religious revolution in his name. Their message: the Bible is true, miracles happen, God really did so love the world that he gave it his only begotten son. In 1966 Beatle John

Lennon casually remarked that the Beatles were more popular than Jesus Christ; now the Beatles are shattered, and George Harrison is singing My Sweet Lord. The new young followers of Jesus listen to Harrison, but they turn on only to the words of their Master: "For where two or three are gathered together in my name, there am I in the midst of them."

Christian coffee houses have opened in many cities, signalling their faith even in their names: The Way Word in Greenwich Village, the Catacombs in Seattle, I Am in Spokane. A strip joint has been converted to a "Christian nightclub" in San Antonio. Communal "Christian houses" are multiplying like loaves and fishes for youngsters hungry for homes, many reaching out to the troubled with round-the-clock telephone hot lines. Bibles abound: whether the cherished, fur-covered King James Version or scruffy, back-pocket paperbacks, they are invariably well-thumbed and often memorized. "It's like a glacier," says "Jesus-Rock" Singer Larry Norman, 24. "It's growing and there's no stopping it."

A few days after that Time article came out, the Children of God published a response in a letter titled "Jesus People? Or Revolution!"[3] It's a transcription of a videotaped sermon by the group's leader, David Berg, although it used his pseudonym, "Mo," which was short for "Moses."

This is a Revolution! We are not compromising and conforming to the damnable System church! We are not conforming to the damnable Commercial System! We have dropped out economically! We have dropped out religiously, spiritually! And the only reason we stay at peace with the political System is because God's Word commands it for the sake of peace! We have dropped out educationally from the hellish, fiendish, Devil's own Satanic propaganda education—educational System!

You, the Children of God, are God's revolution for this hour and this day! You're it! You're the only ones I know in the world who are living like Jesus and His Disciples, who are not just talking about it, not just preaching it, but living it, living together in peace and in love and in joy and in witnessing and in Bible study and in prayer and in praise and in sharing a genuine, absolute and total change!

Almost from the beginning of the Children of God, a common call-and-response slogan in the group started with someone shouting, "Revolution!", and everyone else responding, "For Jesus!" as they each thrusted one arm in the air with a three-finger salute representing the Father, Son and Holy Spirit. It was a unifying gesture, one of several characteristics that set the Children of God apart from other groups in the Jesus movement.

Six months later, on January 24, 1972, Time published an article specifically about the Children of God titled "Whose Children?"[4] It came out just two weeks after the Vancouver Sun articles and two months before I joined the group. The article raises some of the same concerns about the group as those reported in various media throughout the US and Canada around that time.

> The Children of God are the storm troopers of the Jesus Revolution (TIME cover story, June 21, 1971), its most forceful and most criticized zealots....people who consider themselves good churchgoing Christians resent the purer-than-thou attitude—and the appeal it seems to hold for their children. Nonetheless, the group in some cases has had more success than parents in winning young people from drugs, casual sex and drifting. They also have potent precedents in St. Francis of Assisi and St. Thomas Aquinas, both of whom had to break with their families over their vocations....
>
> Some of the most vehement parental critics in California banded together in an organization called the Parents' Committee to Free Our Children from the Children of God—a movement that has since spread to other parts of the country. The parents' group charges, among other things, that the Children stoop to kidnapping, hypnotizing and even drugging to keep youngsters in the sect. The outcry has driven many of the Children from California; Ted Patrick, a San Diego aide to Governor Ronald Reagan, has accused them of trying to "destroy the United States."

One other media report about the Children of God that could have informed my parents and helped them prevent me from joining the group, if they had seen it, was an NBC Evening News story that aired on March 5, 1972, only a month before I dropped out.

> Don Oliver [reporter]: "About 60 of them live here in a run-down former church camp near Burlington in western Washington. [A year later I would briefly live in that commune.] They claim

a worldwide membership of about 2,000. They exist on donations of food and clothing and on the possessions of members. They say they teach converts useful skills, how to live in harmony. They say extramarital sex is forbidden as is the use of drugs. Many are married. They say their children are raised communally in an atmosphere of love. Lately, however, this colony has come under attack by some relatives of members who say that hate is preached here. That members are kept against their will, hypnotized, drugged. That parents are not allowed to visit their children."

...

Doris Peck [mother of member]: "And our ultimate goal is to free the children that have been taken in. The group is, we believe it is a subversive organization. They are told what to do and what to think. They have no will power."

...

Don Oliver: "Amid the confusion of claims and counterclaims, nothing is really certain in all of this but there are a couple of things that seem safe to say. Authorities have found no evidence that anyone is being held here against their will, no evidence that any drugs are being used here at this colony of the Children of God and since the people here are all 18 or over, they have the choice of remaining here whether their relatives think it is bizarre or not."[5]

My parents always watched the CBS Evening News with Walter Cronkite, so it is unlikely they saw that NBC report. It's possible they saw a similar report on CBS, but I doubt they did. Neither my parents nor Father Mark discussed with me any concerns they had about the Children of God, so apparently they were oblivious to all of these media reports and were as ignorant about the controversies surrounding the group as I was.

— — —

Japheth and Hannah were well aware of the controversy and hostility that followed the group wherever it went. After I showed up unannounced, ready to move in, they unexpectedly told me I couldn't stay with them without my parents' written permission.[6] They knew that recruiting a minor could attract unwanted attention from authorities, and were concerned my parents might file a complaint with the police.

After assessing my determination to drop out, Japheth decided to drive me home so we could ask for my parents' permission that evening. He knew that hostile parents in the US sometimes threatened violence, so he had Hezekiah, who was a large man, come with us for backup. Neither of them appeared intimidating, though. They both looked like the respectable guy next door, with friendly demeanours. Japheth also brought his toddler, probably to show he was a family man and to help ease any potential tension.

It certainly was a tense situation when we all entered my parents' living room. There was no aggression or raised voices, but it must have been extremely hurtful for my parents to hear these strangers, "fishers of men" who had religiously lured away their sixteen-year-old son, asking for permission to keep their immature catch. My dad was visibly upset, my mum was holding back tears, and my sister, Brenda, who had turned fifteen two months earlier, was probably distressed too as they tried to make sense of what was happening. My other siblings, Crystal and Jay, were too young to know what was going on, but they must have sensed the emotional turmoil.

When Japheth explained his concern about police involvement because I was a minor, my dad got angry and said the words that echoed in my head for the next two decades. "I'm so ashamed of him and what he is doing that I don't want anyone to know, so I won't go to the police," he snapped at Japheth. He refused to put it put in writing, but that verbal assurance was good enough for Japheth. I returned to the commune with him that night, where we were greeted by the others with hugs and hallelujahs for the good news. Mixed emotions made it difficult to sleep as I considered the heartbreak I'd caused my family, while also contemplating where my new life would take me.

I was a disciple of Jesus now, set free by the truth, or so I was misguided to believe by John 8:31-32: "If ye continue in my word, then are ye my disciples indeed; And ye shall know the truth, and the truth shall make you free." I never anticipated that the same dogma that supposedly set me free would come to control every aspect of my life. It narrowed my worldview, closed my mind, and broke my will. I was now a prisoner of God's will, as determined by my new spiritual superiors with their literal interpretation of the Bible.

Chapter 5
Indoctrination

My first night with the Children of God made it clear that I had left the comforts of a normal family home. Twelve adults and two children crowded into the single-family house. Half of the adults were Americans who came to Canada when the Children of God took over the Jesus People Army in Vancouver. The others were new recruits from around British Columbia. Everyone was in their early twenties, except for another teen a year older than me. The house had three bedrooms upstairs. Japheth and Hannah lived in the largest with their toddler and infant, and two single women slept in the smallest. Half of the single men slept on the living room floor, while I joined the others in the third bedroom, sleeping on the floor side by side in our sleeping bags.

After my momentous decision and the emotional events earlier in the evening, it was difficult to sleep that first night. I was awake when the guy next to me started snoring, waking the others. Hezekiah told me to reach over and pinch the guy's nose to make it stop. I hesitated to touch a stranger like that, but he insisted, so I obeyed. It was such a weird thing to do, but a fittingly bizarre start to my unconventional new life.

I didn't care about their living conditions or poverty. These modern disciples who rejected materialistic lives to serve God convinced me it was possible to live according to the Bible by literally following Jesus's instructions in the sixth chapter of Matthew: "Lay not up for yourselves treasures upon earth....Take no thought for your life, what ye shall eat, or what ye shall drink; nor yet for your body, what ye shall put on.... But seek ye first the kingdom of God, and his righteousness; and all these things shall be added unto you. Take therefore no thought for the morrow."

We lived a frugal lifestyle. No one had a job, although some of the Canadians probably received monthly welfare cheques. They never discussed financial details with me. As far as I knew, any money, food or items the group received were donations. Much of our food was donated directly by shops, which we picked up on regular rounds. We also scavenged still-edible food from dumpsters behind supermarkets.

We ate only two meals a day, a late-morning breakfast and an evening meal. When there was no donated food suitable for breakfast, we usually ate a porridge of chicken scratch, a mix of cracked grains that was sold as chicken feed, and so was cheaper than anything produced for human consumption. Dinner depended on what was donated or scavenged. One-pot meals like soups and stews were common since they could be made with almost any ingredient that was available.

I easily adapted to the simple meals, but not to the toilet paper rule. It wasn't listed in the official Revolutionary Rules;[1] it was more of a cost-saving requirement. We were instructed to use the smallest amounts of certain items that had to be purchased, such as tiny dabs of toothpaste and shampoo, and a three-square strip of toilet paper, wiping with one square at a time, folding it after each wipe. That never worked for me, so I always used more. It was the first rule I broke, though not the last.

Several days after I left home, I saw my parents pull into the driveway. Worried they were there to take me back, I hid in the backyard, but was soon called into the house. I expected to see another tense situation, and so was surprised to see my mum holding Japheth and Hannah's baby, and my dad apologizing to them for getting upset the night I left home. I don't know if they were acting on advice, or had realized on their own that they risked losing contact with me if our relationship was hostile. They offered to help us in small ways if they could, but I think they were probably more motivated by their fear I might disappear than by a sincere desire to befriend the Jesus freaks who spiritually seduced their son astray.

After they left, everyone burst into praise and thanksgiving. Japheth emphasized that this was an example of the power of prayer, since we had been praying daily that my parents would accept my decision to follow Jesus, and not cause trouble for us.

Over the next couple months, while I remained in Port Alberni, my mum occasionally brought us groceries. She also gave Hannah some used clothes and toys for her children. When a supermarket donated several boxes of frozen vegetables and meat, my mum made room in their freezer for it, since the commune only had a fridge. Afterwards, I frequently went home to retrieve some of that food and visit with my mum awhile, but always with a companion. One of the strictest rules was that no one went anywhere alone.[2]

While my mum was giving, my dad was taking back. I don't think he was happy that I had given things to the group that he had paid for, even if they were gifts to me. When Japheth learned I had left my ten-speed bike behind when I moved out, he told me to retrieve it on one of my visits with my mum. I think that irked my dad and provoked him to ask for it back. He also asked me to return my transistor radio because he wanted to use it in his forklift at work. We didn't listen to radio or watch TV, so the radio didn't matter, and though the bike was useful, Japheth decided it wasn't worth risking the relationship, so I gave both back. It saddened me when I thought about it later and realized that my dad had asked me to return my things, but had never asked me to return.

Other than my clothes, the only possessions I still had, though not for long, were the bongo drum and a quality wristwatch my dad gave me a couple years earlier, after he bought a new one for himself. Nothing was my own anymore. Japheth told me that a Children of God band in the US needed the bongo more than we did, so he sent it to them. A few months later, when I moved to another commune for the next stage of discipleship training, my new leader asked for my watch. He said he needed it more than I did, to keep everyone on schedule.

— — —

My indoctrination began the first morning of my new life, starting with a new name. Everyone had a biblical alias, which was their only name I knew. Japheth reminded me of the scriptures he showed me the night I prayed the salvation prayer, and explained that since I was born-again, I needed a new name to reflect the fact that I was a new person.

An alias not only reinforced the creation of my new persona, it also served a security purpose. Angry accusers and negative media reports sometimes attracted inquisitive authorities to investigate. By using assumed names, we could hide our true identities from each other, so that if we were ever questioned by officials, as I would be many times while living in foreign lands, we couldn't reveal the legal names of leaders or other members.

Japheth, whose namesake was Noah's son, told me to pray and choose a simple but uncommon Bible name that wasn't being used by others. So I searched through several long lists of names in the Old Testament and found my new name, that of one of King David's servants: "Over the camels also was Obil the Ishmaelite." (1 Chronicles 27:30) He is one of the most insignificant biblical characters, yet it seemed to me that being the king's camel keeper was an important job, which probably reveals something about my low self-esteem at the time.

I was still unaware that the Children of God had a leader, that his real name was David Berg and he considered himself a spiritual king, but in a very real sense I was becoming his servant. For the first three months, though, his true name and role was kept hidden from me, until they considered me indoctrinated enough to be trusted with his prophetic origin story.

On my second evening in the commune Japheth read us an essay he said was by a spiritual elder who often wrote the group letters of guidance. They called him Mo, short for "Moses," and I soon learned there were many more of these Mo Letters, which we read daily as part of our Bible studies.[3]

"Diamonds of Dust" was my first exposure to those letters. It's a short reflection on the common experience of watching dust particles sparkle in a ray of sunshine coming through a window. It's a simple spiritual meditation that paraphrases various Bible verses about serving God. The theme of the essay is that we are essentially nothing but a temporary dot of dirt, good only for reflecting God's light.

> The thinner you are, the more the light gets through. The less there is of you, the more the light shines through!…For they can sparkle so short a while, and then they're gone, like a man's life—like the grass of the field which today is and tomorrow is gone! For what is your life? It's but a vapour—a vapour that reflects His rays of light for a little while and then it's gone! You have no guarantee of tomorrow. You better sparkle now while you have the light, or you'll fade into oblivion and no one will know you even ever existed.[4]

Japheth then read the various scriptures cited at the end of the tract, including James 4:14, Psalm 14:2, 14:3, and Romans 3:10, 23. They emphasize that we are all unrighteous, filthy sinners and can do nothing good without God. The most descriptive verse says, "But we are all as an unclean thing, and all our righteousnesses are as filthy rags; and we all do fade as a leaf; and our iniquities, like the wind, have taken us away." (Isaiah 64:6) Japheth explained that the original meaning of the word translated as "filthy rags" was soiled menstrual cloth.

That belittling of any sense of self-worth became a constant refrain in my life. My old life had passed away, but I needed to continue dying daily by denying myself and giving up my life to follow Jesus, as he commanded: "If any man will come after me, let him deny himself, and take up his cross daily, and follow me. For whosoever will save his life shall lose it: but whoso-ever will lose his life for my sake, the same shall save it." (Luke 9:23-24)

I had little self-esteem before joining the Children of God, so it didn't take much to destroy what was left. Those scriptures were among the many Bible verses I was required to memorize as part of my daily indoctrination. Each of us had a three-by-five-inch index card listing ten sets of individual scriptures, four chapters, and a dozen psalms. We were expected to memo-rize at least two verses a day.

Those set-cards, as we called them, were the same ones referred to in the *Sun* article titled "Scripture Cards Back Breaking with Family." The first set of verses focused on personal salvation. Sets 2 and 3 were about forsaking self, family, possessions and worldliness in order to go into all the world to preach the gospel. Sets 4 to 9 more generally concerned various aspects of devotion and discipleship, such as obedience to the Word of God, and the power of prayer and faith. Set 10 was unique in that it consisted entirely of verses from the book of Daniel that concern a chronology of endtime events.

New members were referred to as "babes," a reference to 1 Peter 2:2: "As newborn babes, desire the sincere milk of the word, that ye may grow thereby." For the first three months, we were taught only the milkier aspects of Children of God dogma. That deliberately cautious approach to our indoctrination tested both our trustworthiness and readiness to read more controversial Mo Letters with meatier messages during the next three months of indoctrination. "For every one that useth milk is unskilful in the word of righteousness: for he is a babe. But strong meat belongeth to them that are of full age." (Hebrews 5:12–14)

By the time I was ready to memorize the last set of endtime scriptures, I had moved to a boot camp with other recent recruits where the next level of indoctrination introduced us to more specific, esoteric details of the Children of God's endtime message. For now, while I remained in Port Alberni, my three months of basic training focused on strengthening my faith and teaching me how to proselytize, or "witness," as we called it, a reference to the first Christians preaching the gospel: "Ye shall be witnesses unto me both in Jerusalem, and in all Judaea, and in Samaria, and unto the uttermost part of the earth." (Acts 1:8) Street evangelizing became my primary activity when I wasn't studying.

A typical day started with personal time praying and reading, then communal devotions before mid-morning breakfast, followed by house-hold chores. After that, I usually had a separate Bible lesson with one of the senior members. The rest of the day, most of us went witnessing in pairs. On weekends, we stayed out late into the evening, strolling the streets, searching public places for receptive people, just as those who found me had done.

— — —

About a month after I left home, as Mother's Day approached, Hannah had each of us make a card for our mums. Although only a few years older than me, she was a sweet and kind-hearted mother figure. She ensured that the other teen and I were given extra protein in our two daily meals, and a snack in between, just like pregnant women in the group were entitled to, because she recognized our bodies were still growing. Hannah had us send those cards as part of a public relations tactic the Children of God implemented after the first wave of negative media reports in the US claiming, among other things, that members hated their parents and were kept against their will. The strategy included letting members visit their families for Christmas and having them write regular letters to their parents. The message I wrote in my mum's card ended up in the local newspaper.

In less than a year in Port Alberni, the group had aroused fearful suspicions and concerns, especially in some local churches, which caught the interest of the local newspaper. To address criticisms and hopefully prevent negative publicity, Japheth and Hannah invited a reporter into the commune to see how we lived. They didn't permit her to question me alone, but they did suggest that she speak to my mum, which she did.

Soon after, on May 24, 1972, the now-defunct *Alberni Valley Times* published a front-page article titled "Sect Members Tell Their Side," with the subtitle "Under Some Criticism."[5] The accompanying photograph shows my profile in the foreground, seated in a circle with other members of the commune. Although the reporter interviewed my mum, and so knew our real names, she didn't identify her by name and only used my Bible name, perhaps because I was a minor. The article is only available on microfilm in Canada's national archive, so I've transcribed the full text here. It starts with the words I wrote in my mum's card.

> *One day I took, I took an honest look,*
> *I tried everything, I played every game in the book,*
> *And I saw there was nothing in this world to live for any more.*
>
> *Then one day, one day I heard about,*
> *A certain man, a man who could work things out,*

So I came to Jesus, you know
He came in and showed me the way.

Now all I want to do is serve Him
That others may know Him
And the power of His love.

This is one of the songs we sing in the Children of God. There is more to it, but this sums up my life. I really took an honest look. I certainly didn't try everything, but I did and knew enough things to realize that my life didn't and wasn't going to mean anything. But then I found Jesus, and He changed me. He showed me the way. Now I know what's really happening in the world. He showed me. I'm so grateful to Him. Out of thousands of kids he chose me to be His servant. I'm so honoured. And you as my mother should be honoured too. Other mothers can say: my son is a doctor or lawyer,[6] or my son lives in a mansion with two swimming pools. But you can say, my son lives and works for Jesus. It is something to be proud of. I love you.

A letter from a religious fanatic? No. A home-made Mother's Day card from a local 16-year-old boy who recently joined the local colony of the Children of God, a religious sect that has nurtured fear and doubts among some residents of Port Alberni.

"That's the first time my son has ever even acknowledged Mother's Day," says the mother of the boy. "And it's one of the few times he has ever said anything about loving me."

The lad, who has been with the sect just over three weeks, has adopted a name from the Bible, as all sect members do when they join the group. He is now known as Obil.

Obil was an average kid with average school grades and an average upbringing. He tended to be a bit of a loner, according to his mother, but had never got into serious trouble. What Obil's parents didn't know was that he was experimenting with LSD and methedrine for the past year.

"Obil was going over to this house run by the Children of God quite often, saying he was going to visit friends," says his mother.

"At first we didn't pay too much attention—you know how

it is with 16-year-olds — you can't always be asking them where they're going and what they're doing. But then he started going to the house more frequently, and we got a little worried, kept asking ourselves "Why?" Then one night he came into the kitchen and told me he'd been on drugs, had tried to quit them for three months, but had gone back. Then at least we had an answer as to why he was spending so much time with the Children of God. They've apparently helped a lot of kids on drugs."

"Obil finally decided to move in with the Children of God and become a member of the sect," his mother continues. "Everything just happened within three or four days, and my husband and I jumped to conclusions, I'm afraid. We condemned these people before we even knew them. We were afraid of what we didn't know anything about. But we just couldn't figure it all out—we didn't have any answers. We finally came around, figured if he's going to go, well, let him go. And we decided that we were going to try to understand his decision more. Then we went back and apologized to the Children of God for condemning them without knowing them. We go there to visit quite frequently now, and anytime we show up, we're welcome. Our son comes home when he feels like it, or phones us, and any member of the group is welcome in our home. As a matter of fact, we're letting them use our freezer to store some of their food.

"I can't see the sect being as bad as so many people say it is when anyone like Obil can be so happy."

Despite the testimony of this happy mother, the Children of God continue to be criticized by many local residents. Most of the unfavourable opinions appear to be based on second-hand knowledge, or on a series of articles that appeared on the front page of the Vancouver Sun in January.

During a visit to the tumbledown house on River Road, occupied by the 12 members of the local colony, the Children of God gave their side of it.

"We're not here to steal people's kids or cause trouble," says Hannah, a soft-spoken mother of two whose husband, Luke, heads up the local group. "We're people that have met Christ and have been born again. We're here to talk to people and tell them about Christ. So many people preach against things. Instead of preaching against everything, we've got a solution — Jesus. Instead of making a way for ourselves, we're trying to help other people."

Although most of the people in the colony have been involved with drugs at one time or another, they no longer use them. Neither do they condone drinking, smoking, or pre-marital sex.

During its three year history, the Children of God organization has gained a reputation for helping young people on drugs.

"We're not so much interested in being a drug rehabilitation group," says Luke, "as we are in preaching the message of Jesus. But if someone comes to us with a drug problem, we'll try to help him."

Luke was strung out on Speed and had ulcers when he joined the group. Now, he says, the ulcers and the drug problem are both gone.

"We've had kids come off heroin without any withdrawal symptoms, too," he said.

Despite its tumbledown tendencies, the house rented by the Children of God is spotless. Everyone in the colony does his or her share of housework during a one hour session each morning. Days are generally spent on devotional services, Bible readings and classes on various aspects of the Bible, the members say.

"We also spend a few hours each day out on the streets talking to the kids," says Hannah. "And on Friday and Saturday nights we make a special point of going to where the kids are and talking to them. But we're certainly not trying to steal young people from their families or anything like that."

Members of the local colony range in age from 16 to 26 years, but anyone under 17 years must have written permission from his parents before he can join the group.

"The consensus around here seems to be that we're sitting around waiting for kids to get out of school so we can convert them," says Luke. "That's simply not true. Sure, we have a lot of young people come over to visit, and we welcome them. But we're not trying to snatch them away from their families."

"These stories about kids being kept incommunicado for weeks on end, unable to see or talk to their families, aren't true," continues Luke. "And the ones about bodyguards and the like — that's just plain ridiculous. We're free to come and go as we please. This isn't a jail."

"As for the stories about kids phoning their parents at two or three in the morning and telling them that they're never coming home again, that they're going to stay with the group — well, that's just the way some kids react," says Hannah. "They just decide all of a sudden to serve Jesus, and sometimes they make the decision at weird hours."

The Children of God have only the bare necessities essential to sustain them. Communal life is maintained through the contributions of new members, who are expected to surrender all of their possessions and money to the sect when they join.

"Clothes, for instance," says Hannah. "Most people have more clothes than they know what to do with. When someone joins the group, he throws every piece of clothing he owns into the communal pot, and it is distributed from there to other members in outlying areas."

Food for the group is donated by various local merchants — Luke estimates that approximately a dozen of them are contributing now.

"Sometimes we're given crates and crates of the stuff — food that has nothing wrong with it, except that it's maybe a little too ripe or a bit stale for retail sales. It's amazing, the amount of food we've had donated."

Money, contrary to what many people think, doesn't come from the welfare offices.

"Any money we may need comes to us through the organization, which in turn gets it from new members or in the form of donations from parents. There are also occasional contributions from people interested in the evangelistic method of preaching," says Luke. "But really with the way we live, we don't need all that much in the way of money or material things."

Referring back to the adverse publicity about the group that has cropped up during the last few months, Hannah says, "Lisa Hobbs (who wrote the Sun series) talked to a couple of pretty strung-out people who weren't representative of the average person in the group at all. As a result, a lot of people have become wary of us. It's something we'll just have to keep working at to overcome, I guess."

Doubts about the group's sincerity and its objectives have been voiced by several local community leaders. And parents have begun to worry about whether their children will be the next to join the group, and possibly get tied up in some of the abominable activities they have read so much about.

The subject of the Children of God was brought up at a recent meeting of the local ministerial association.

"Our concern has come mainly as a result of efforts of the Children of God elsewhere," says Lester Goertz, president of the association. "Our main concern is that their objectives and the aftermath of what they are pursuing is not desirable. They have completely disassociated themselves from responsibility—none of them hold outside jobs. Sure, one person like the local lad can join and be happy. There's at least one happy person in any religion. But what we're thinking of is the group's overall objectives, and what they've reportedly been doing in other cities. The association hasn't, however, decided to make any moves concerning the group."

Rev. Goertz said he has not been out to the house on River Road and that he was basing his opinions on the series that ran in The Sun a few months ago, and information that he's heard from other people.

Father Mark Lemay and Rev. Len Jenner agree that most of the bad things circulating about the Children of God have been based on rumour and the Sun series.

"I haven't had much contact with them," says Father Mark, "but from what I've seen and heard, they seem like a sincere bunch of young people trying to get a message across. I can't see anything wrong with that."

Bob Baird, Reverend at the West Coast Mission on River Road, has been out to visit with the group on occasion.

"They're pretty defiant of some of the articles that have appeared recently in newspapers in Vancouver and the U.S., all right. But there doesn't seem to be any trouble caused by them yet—let's just wait and see what happens."

The reporter refers to Hannah's husband as "Luke," but it was definitely Japheth she interviewed, since she identifies him as the head of the commune. Although there was another member there named Luke, I doubt it was her mistake. It is more likely Japheth deliberately deceived her. They were trying to portray the Children of God in the most positive way, so he probably wanted to use a less unusual name.

The group's spokespersons often misled reporters by misrepresenting facts and giving false impressions. For example, Japheth claimed that the Children of God's message and lifestyle alone helped some heroin addicts quit cold-turkey without any medical detox treatment, and that they had no withdrawal symptoms. However, while saving addicts was a great public-relations story that generated goodwill and donations, it was a deceptive claim. Many members' anecdotes of addiction were purposely exaggerated, including mine.

The reporter accepts that the group has a reputation for helping addicts quit drugs, and quotes my mum to imply that I was one of them. Although it's true I occasionally used cannabis and LSD, I certainly wasn't addicted to them, and I had never used methedrine (methamphetamine/speed), as the reporter stated. But the night I left home, I told my mum I was using drugs, including speed, and couldn't quit. I wanted her to think the Children of God saved me from addiction. That salvation myth helped her make sense of my decision, and she simply repeated what I told her to the reporter.

In the article, Hannah and Japheth also distorted the facts when they deceptively denied accusations that the Children of God encouraged youth to abandon their families.[7] Yet there I was, living proof of that. Among the verses I was required to memorize were Matthew 10:35–38. We referred to hostile parents as "Matthew 10:36ers":[8]

> For I am come to set a man at variance against his father, and the daughter against her mother, and the daughter in law against her mother in law. And a man's foes shall be they of his own household. He that loveth father or mother more than me is not worthy of me: and he that loveth son or daughter more than me is not worthy of me. And he that taketh not his cross, and followeth after me, is not worthy of me.

Interestingly, Father Mark is quoted in the article as having a favourable view of the Children of God. I don't know if he was aware I had joined the group when he gave that interview. He doesn't admit meeting with me a few weeks earlier, but he seems to reference my conversation with him. The reverend who had visited the commune was aware I had joined, but Japheth and Hannah wouldn't allow him to speak with me, probably to prevent him from interfering with my indoctrination.

An important fact not mentioned in the article is that I dropped out of high school midway through Grade 11 to join the Children of God. It's an odd omission, considering all the concerns parents and pastors had about their children being led astray by the group. Although the head of the ministerial association criticized the group for shunning social responsibilities and paid employment, he said nothing about their rejection of the education system. Neither did the reporter, even though the recent *Sun* series reported stories similar to mine of teens dropping out of school.

If the reporter had been allowed to interview me, she would've learned that several days after joining the group, I returned to school to clean out my locker. I didn't intend to talk to anyone, but a couple of my teachers saw me as they came out of the staff room. Knowing I hadn't been in class recently, they asked me what I was doing. I told them I was quitting, which surprised them because I wasn't the typical student who dropped out. They asked me if I was willing to talk to the guidance counsellor before I left.

I had never spoken to him, or received guidance from any teacher before. No teacher ever told me that I had the intellectual potential to do almost anything I wanted, pointed out all the possible options, and encouraged me to pursue a university education. Perhaps more importantly, my educators hadn't taught me the critical-thinking skills required to recognize and resist irrational religious dogma. Though I did talk to the counsellor that day, his inadequate advice was far too late.

— — —

With the benefit of hindsight, I recognize a few things that could've prevented the Children of God from taking advantage of my childhood Catholic indoctrination to manipulate my teen naiveté. A public-school education emphasizing critical-thinking skills that taught me how to think, not just what to think, would've equipped me to examine and dispute the religious beliefs instilled in me. And a reliable mentor could've helped me with that process, advising me before I made the misguided decision to drop out of society.

My parents were confused and worried about the influence those religious strangers had on my behaviour, but they didn't know how to handle the situation and didn't have many options to turn to for help in our small town. Although they had my best interests in mind when they sent me to a Catholic priest for counselling, Father Mark was influenced and blinded by his own religious dedication, so his poor advice pushed me toward the Children of God, not away from them.

What I really needed was a nonreligious mentor such as a teacher or some other knowledgeable adult to take me under their wing and counsel me after I became involved with those religious radicals. A counsellor like that could've cautioned me not to make an uninformed, rash decision to drop out of society with total strangers; helped me ask the right questions about the group and their beliefs; and encouraged me to examine religious claims I had always simply accepted as truthful by considering criticisms of Christianity, before I completely surrendered my life and future to that dogma.

A mentor could've prompted me to ask Children of God members direct, essential questions, and helped me determine if their answers were explicit enough to satisfy any doubts or concerns. They could've also helped me do some fact-finding about the group. Although that was more difficult in the pre-Internet era, it was certainly possible, especially since the Children of God were already notoriously controversial by that time.

There were many newspaper, magazine and television reports about the Children of God I wasn't aware of, including recent ones in nearby Vancouver just a couple months before I met them. A mentor could've helped me search for reports directly from media outlets or other sources, such as library newspaper collections. I could have learned to seek the opinions of various religious leaders and secular counsellors regarding my involvement with the group, and even to ask the police if they were aware of any complaints or crimes involving them.

Perhaps the most important thing a mentor could've taught me was to be skeptical when presented with a truth claim of any kind, including those by religious authorities, and to always question the reliability of the source and consider the empirical evidence for the claim before accepting it. What I needed was a mentor's voice of reason urging me to question claims about God and the Bible that I had always blindly believed on faith. If I had learned to examine and doubt those beliefs inculcated in me as a child, and reinforced throughout my adolescence by cultural influences, I probably would've been more wary of proselytizers who inter-preted the Bible literally, and not so easily persuaded to make the irratio-nal, emotional decision to give up my life and devote it to following Jesus with them.

I didn't have a mentor to give me that kind of guidance, but might not have needed one if I had been taught critical-thinking skills. If I'd known how to challenge the long-held beliefs passed on to me by doubting, questioning, considering criticisms and rationally analyzing evidence objectively— instead of just passively accepting religious ideas, assumptions and claims— then I might've been able to overcome my childhood indoctrination, protect myself from religious fanatics, and make a more logical, informed decision about my future.

Something else I wasn't offered at school that could've prevented priests and preachers from misleading me was a basic course on comparative world religions that examined a variety of religious beliefs. Though generally aware of the major religions, I didn't know there were thousands of other religions around the world. I never considered the fact that their mutually exclusive beliefs couldn't all be true. I also wasn't aware that each of the main religions have incompatible branches and sects, and that Christianity has thousands of divisive denominations. I didn't even understand the basic differences between Catholics and Protestants. I simply believed what I was taught, that Christianity was true, and I wasn't aware of any reason to doubt it.

Teaching children the tenets of just one religion as if it is the only truth is indoctrination, but teaching them about the basic beliefs of various religions that all claim to be true is a metaphorical inoculation that immunizes them against religious fervour. Comparative religion lessons in the social studies curriculum could've taught me to think critically about the subject by asking essential questions like: How do we know if God or gods exist? How does someone decide which religion has the truth? Why did I believe Christianity's truth claims, but not those of other religions? And if Christianity is the only true religion, as its proponents proclaim, which version is the correct one, since many denominations insist they are the one true Church?

A teacher who prompted me to ask those and other questions, and discussed the relationship between religion and science, could've helped me comprehend how the incompatibility of all religions means they could all be false, including my own, since they can't all be true. The uncertainty created by those queries might've caused me to doubt not only my Christian faith, but my belief in God.

I didn't have the benefit of a course or teacher like that, but a short, simple essay by the famous philosopher Bertrand Russell titled "Why I Am Not a Christian" could've had the same effect if I had read it.[9] That widely published essay is a transcript of a lecture he gave in 1927. In the first half, Russell questions the existence of God by arguing against "the Catholic Church...dogma that the existence of God can be proved by the unaided reason." He analyzes and rejects some of the Church's main arguments for God's existence. In the second half, Russell discusses some of the moral defects in Christ's character and teachings.

That essay would've given me many reasons to doubt the rationality and morality of what the Church had taught me, and what the Children of God were now teaching me. I'm certain it would've armed me with arguments that enabled me to resist their persuasive proselytizing and prevented me from giving up my life for a religious cause. It might've led me to reject religion altogether. Unfortunately, I wasn't aware of it, and didn't have any religiously skeptical adults in my life willing to share their own doubts with me, so it never occurred to me to question my religious beliefs.

— — —

One of my teachers who saw me cleaning out my school locker accompanied me to the guidance counsellor's office and asked him to speak with me. When I told him I had left home to serve Jesus and didn't need more education to do that, he looked puzzled and took a moment to look at my school record. I doubt he'd ever had a student tell him that. He suggested I take time over the summer to reconsider my decision, probably assuming it was just a pie-in-the-sky fantasy I would soon give up.

Since there were only two months left in the school year, and I wasn't failing my classes, he said I could go straight into Grade 12 if I came back in September. Unfortunately, that guidance counsellor didn't guide me by discussing the value of higher education and the opportunities it would provide me. In fact, no teacher or any other adult had ever discussed with me the possibility of going to university. I just assumed that it was both financially impossible and beyond my intellectual ability, and so didn't see it as an option.

Less than three months after I joined the Children of God, Japheth told me I was moving to a new commune, joining other recent recruits for more basic training. The Port Alberni commune shut down not long after I left. I visited my family briefly that Christmas of 1972, which was the last time they would see me for about four years.

Chapter 6
The Endtime Prophet

After the Children of God took over the Jesus People Army's Vancouver operations in 1971, they spread around British Columbia. On Vancouver Island they set up communes in the capital city, Victoria, and in Nanaimo, before arriving in Port Alberni. In the summer of 1972, a couple months after joining, I moved to a new commune on the outskirts of Nanaimo, set up as a boot camp to train recent recruits.

A supporter gave the group the use of an old, vacant farmhouse in an undeveloped forested area just off the island highway north of the city. With no immediate neighbours, it was the perfect place to house a large number of Jesus freaks and mould our minds into endtime Christian soldiers fighting a spiritual war. Although conditions were rough, we were expected to "endure hardness, as a good soldier of Jesus Christ. No man that warreth entangleth himself with the affairs of this life; that he may please him who hath chosen him to be a soldier." (2 Timothy 2:3-4)

After a major cleanup and minor repairs, the long-neglected farmhouse was livable, and large enough to house the married leaders, all the single sisters, and some of the single brothers. The rest of us slept in a cabin that contained nothing but several bunk beds and a wood stove in the centre. The house had electricity, but no working indoor plumbing. We got our drinking and cooking water from a well with a hand-pump.

The old outhouse no longer worked, so until we finished digging a new one, we used a designated section of the forest as our toilet. We would dig a small hole in an unused spot, squat over it, and then bury the waste. One of the leaders explained this was a biblical practice based on one of the rules Moses made for the Israelites as they wandered the desert for forty years: "Thou shalt have a place also without the camp, whither thou shalt go forth abroad: And thou shalt have a paddle upon thy weapon; and it shall be, when thou wilt ease thyself abroad, thou shalt dig therewith, and shalt turn back and cover that which cometh from thee." (Deuteronomy 23:12-13)

Sometime after we started using the new outhouse, several people became seriously sick. Apparently, their symptoms indicated hepatitis, but I don't think anyone got a professional diagnosis or medical care. Fortunately, the weather was warm enough for the sick to be isolated in a rickety old barn. The leaders were unsure if the sickness was caused by our fecal matter in the forest, or if they had built the new outhouse too close to the well and contaminated it. We stopped using the well and got our drinking water from the closest neighbour, who let us fill containers from his outside tap. For bathing, the leaders went to town to use a community centre's facilities, while the rest of us walked a trail to a spot on a lake nearby where we were out of sight of anyone who might object to a bunch of hippies soaping up there.

Another poor decision by the leaders was to place a compost heap too close to the house. It might've been okay if it had been maintained as a properly layered compost, but it wasn't, so instead of odourlessly decaying into soil, it became an unbearably stinky, rotten garbage pile that attracted pests. A couple of us were tasked with moving the mound to a pit we dug at the bottom of the small hill the house was on. I constantly gagged at the stench and sight of squirming maggots as we shovelled the mushy mess onto a wooden sled, pulled it down the grassy slope and buried it in the pit.

Odd jobs like that kept us busy when we were not studying the Bible and Mo Letters, or assigned to other tasks. There was a rotating schedule for routine things like cleaning, helping in the kitchen, or accompanying the driver who made regular rounds in town to pick up donated food. We also took turns going witnessing into town, or on road trips up island. My most memorable trip was with five others in an old bread-delivery van to witness to a thousand or more hippies living on the beaches between Tofino and Ucluelet on the wild west coast of the island.

The only route there took us through Port Alberni, where we stopped for a brief visit with my family. At Long Beach near Tofino, we camped rough right on the beach, which was still allowed in those days. It was August, so we were able to watch the spectacular shooting-star display of the annual Perseid meteor shower while lying on the sand around a campfire, with a soundscape of ocean waves.

After several days of witnessing and passing out tracts to the hundreds of hippies camping on that beach, we travelled to the eastern side of the island to witness at an outdoor folk music festival in Comox. During a break between performances, our two guitarists were permitted onstage to play some of our more lively gospel songs, while the rest of us started a large circle dance with audience members. Afterwards, we passed out literature.

The next day, we headed to nearby Campbell River. While we were parked at a shopping centre, the police spotted our distinctive black van and interrogated us about our activities in Tofino. There had been a double murder on the beach around the time we were there. Beach dwellers interviewed by the police described the suspect as a Jesus freak. He disappeared, leaving all his possessions. Some evidence, including a biblical alias written in a Bible, suggested he might have been involved with the Children of God. The officers questioned each of us, but we knew nothing. The perpetrator eluded capture for thirty-seven years, until he was killed in a US police shootout.

Sometimes we didn't need to leave the Nanaimo commune in order to witness to people. We had a sign on the highway directing curious passers-by to our "farm," where they could find free food and Jesus. It was usually long-haired freaks or other travellers living on the cheap who took the bait and showed up at our gate. We did feed their bodies, but that was just a means to an end, which was feeding their souls with scripture, served with songs.

One day, four of my uncles and aunts showed up unexpectedly. I don't know if my parents had asked them to check on me, or if they were just curious to see how I was living. I hadn't spoken to them since I'd become a Jesus freak, so I wasn't sure how they would react to our religious fanaticism. I was pleased to see each of them engage in friendly discussions about our beliefs and lifestyle. I don't know if they were believers or not, but they joined in our circle as we prayed and sang songs. Our joyous fervour for Jesus was infectious.

They left friendly, but before they did, my uncle G took me aside. Among other things, he asked me about my sex life, which embarrassed me. I was a virgin and had never even dated or kissed a girl. I told him honestly that we didn't date outsiders or even each other, and sex outside of marriage wasn't allowed. If two members wanted to get married, they needed permission from leaders before pursuing their relationship.[1]

Uncle G found that hard to believe. I think he assumed that given our countercultural, communal lifestyle we would be as promiscuous as hippies. He told me he didn't think it was natural to abstain from sex, but I was sexually naive and so had no answer to that other than to point out that Catholic priests were celibate. Perhaps I was a late bloomer, had a low libido, or was just very shy and awkward with girls I was attracted to, but I was kind of relieved I didn't have to deal with dating.

I had now finished my first three months of basic training, studying the Bible, memorizing the set-card scriptures and reading Mo Letters that prepared us for the next stage of indoctrination. After that test period, new members were ready for a deeper dive into the group's dogma, which included learning Mo's real name, David Berg. We were permitted to read a series of letters that revealed he was God's final endtime prophet. Study sessions now focused on Berg's origin story, his doomsday warning message for a wicked world, and a timeline of specific biblical endtime events that Berg predicted would culminate with Christ's return in 1993.

— — —

It wasn't just Berg's radical Christian message, but his autocratic control of the Children of God through a chain of command that made them different from the Jesus People Army, some of whom rejected the merger of the two groups because of his leadership role. Berg believed he was the final endtime prophet, the fulfillment of Old Testament prophecies that refer to a king named David living in the last days before the Second Coming of Christ.

Berg's writings contain much militaristic imagery depicting spiritual warfare, and references to his role as the monarch of a spiritual nation. An early Children of God publication was called the *New Nation News*. His kingly claim may seem to be just a metaphor or figurative fantasy role-playing, but to Berg it was all very literal. When he described himself as a spiritual king of a spiritual nation, his vision extended into the real world. Berg believed that he and the Children of God were Christ's chosen cadre who would help Christ reign over heaven on earth for a thousand years, a period known as the Millennium.

To convince his followers that certain scriptures referred specifically to him as the last true prophet before the Second Coming, Berg created an origin story that started with a deliberate comparison between himself and John the Baptist. The first chapter of Luke portrays the prophet who prepared the way for Jesus as being filled with the Holy Ghost while in his mother Elizabeth's womb. Berg made a similar claim, setting himself up as a latter-day John the Baptist preparing the way for Jesus to return. Berg wrote:

> It was prophesied many years ago that I was filled with the Holy Ghost from my Mother's womb....My mother had dedicated

me to the Lord before I was born, and she prayed for a name, and the name the Lord gave her for me was the name that some of you know—David!...commissioned by the Lord to serve Him even before I was born![2]

Berg's founding myth sets him apart as someone special, not only named and filled with the Spirit before his birth, as John was, but born with an innate ability to hear God's voice speaking directly to him. Within a couple sentences Berg leaps from being "dedicated *to* the Lord" by his mother to being directly "commissioned *by* the Lord" before his birth. He appropriated God's ordination of the Old Testament prophet Jeremiah to claim he was similarly chosen by God to fulfill a foreordained endtime plan: "Before I formed thee in the belly I knew thee; and before thou camest forth out of the womb I sanctified thee, and I ordained thee a prophet unto the nations." (Jeremiah 1:5)

Just as John the Baptist's ministry was supposedly prophesied in the Old Testament,[3] Berg's personal mythmaking required a direct connection to biblical predictions in order to establish himself as God's prophet. So Berg boldly announced to his followers that he was the fulfillment of various Bible passages predicting the rise of a new King David who would lead God's children in the last days. Several publications[4] set out a chronology of events in Berg's life that culminated in his claim that he was predestined to be God's endtime prophet with the ability to precisely predict Christ's imminent return. He claimed God revealed to him in 1970 "the exact number of years with their dates and events between now and the Coming of Christ."[5] Among other things, he specifically predicted that he would die in 1989 and Jesus would return in 1993. Berg died in 1994.

Born in 1919 in California, Berg spent the 1920s and '30s learning to be an itinerant preacher like his parents, travelling and preaching with them in churches and evangelical revivals. His mother, Virginia Brandt Berg, was one of the first females to host a gospel radio program. She eventually became a well-known evangelist with the Christian and Missionary Alliance in Miami. Her claim that she had suddenly been miraculously healed after five years of paralysis from a car accident attracted thousands to her sermons. Although members of her family disputed her account of the accident and claim of paralysis,[6] Virginia continued to exploit her faith-healing story throughout her career.

After a decade pastoring and preaching at churches around Miami, Virginia returned to independent, itinerant evangelism, preaching in churches and revivals across the United States. David remained by her side as her assistant for another ten years or so. Working closely with his mother since childhood, Berg learned all the tricks of the evangelistic trade, from spiritually inspiring showmanship, sermonizing and gospel singing to fleecing-the-flock fundraising.

In 1941, Berg was drafted into the US Army, but was discharged in 1942 for health reasons. Later, as part of his mythmaking, he took a cue from his mother and claimed that he too had been miraculously healed while on his deathbed, after promising God he would serve him full-time if he lived.

Berg wrote that in the late 1940s, while struggling to establish his own evangelical career, three complete strangers in different churches laid hands on him and prophesied over him. Each person cited the same scriptures in Chapter 3 of Revelation, about "the key of David," which Berg interpreted as referring literally to him. He says that he broke down crying after the third time "that I had received this exact same prophecy—each time by someone who never had seen me before, and did not even know me—so I knew that it was God speaking! That somehow this passage was peculiarly for me personally, and that it was to be fulfilled in my own life in some way."[7]

Berg married in 1944, started a family, and by the end of that decade was the pastor of a small Christian and Missionary Alliance church in Arizona. After a couple years, the Alliance expelled him over doctrinal disputes and an allegation of sexual impropriety with a seventeen-year-old church member, though Berg denied it. Now with four young children, he followed the same path his mother took after she left the Alliance church and started a non-denominational ministry. Critical of the church system, which he considered ineffectual and hypocritical, he became an itinerant evangelist, living in a travel trailer with his family, preaching around the US while relying on donations from friends and strangers sympathetic to their mission.

According to Berg, a few years later, while he was praying to know God's plan for him, he was told by God to open his Bible randomly and read the first passage he saw. He opened to the second chapter of Ezekiel, where the prophet learns that his purpose is to preach a warning message to the rebellious Israelites, God's people. Berg wrote:

> In 1952, I received the call of Ezekiel, which definitely confirmed my ministry against the churches, their failures and hypocrisy. I'll never forget that night as I stood there in the darkness telling God I'd done what He'd asked me (which was to drop out of the System)—now what did He want me to do! And suddenly

He drew my attention upward toward a blinking red light atop a tall radio antenna, saying, "I want you to be like that red light atop My Broadcasting Antenna, beaming My Warning Message to the world!" And I climbed in my little trailer where the six of us lived in a tiny room just 14 x 7 feet and asked God in prayer what He meant, and He told me to open my Bible and read the first passage my eyes fell upon and it was the call of Ezekiel, in Ezekiel Chapter 2. And the Lord told me this was to be my message also, our message against the so-called Christians and churches of today, praise the Lord![8]

During that period on the road in the 1950s and into the mid-1960s, Berg also worked as a travelling salesman for a Los Angeles televangelist, Fred Jordan, promoting his *Church in the Home* program to TV stations around the country.[9]

The next event in Berg's origin story came in 1961. He wrote: "The message of Jeremiah was revealed to us in December of 1961 when I was very ill, and God said this was to be our Message from now on — the Doomsday, Endtime Warning Message. This message is God's final warning to a doomed nation (America) and His pattern of action for His Prophets during such a time as its fall."[10] Jeremiah was another Old Testament prophet, like Ezekiel, who warned the Israelites that they faced punishing destruction because of their disobedience and rejection of God.

Four years later, Virginia Berg claimed to have received a similar doomsday message. In 1965, she told her son that she had received a prophecy that warned of the impending destruction of "the Great Society" (President Johnson's description of America) by "the Author of Confusion" (the Antichrist), followed by a "Great Confusion," a reference to the period of "great tribulation" mentioned by Jesus as one of several endtime events preceding his Second Coming.[11] Berg published that prophecy in a one-page pamphlet referred to as the "Warning" tract, which included numerous scriptures supporting its doomsday message.[12] It was one of the tracts Japheth gave me the first time I met the Children of God.

In 1967, Berg received another prophecy pointing to passages in the book of Ezekiel that he said revealed God's plan for him, this time from a woman he called "a precious prophetess, Sister Gunn."[13] He wrote that she was so excited by a prophecy she had received about him that she drove a three-thousand-mile round trip to tell him in person. She told him God had revealed to her that he was the endtime leader of God's people described in Ezekiel Chapter 34 and specifically named in Verse 23: "And I will set up one shepherd over them, and he shall feed them, even my servant David; he shall feed them, and he shall be their shepherd."

A few years later, Berg received other prophecies directly, and from others, claiming that references in the books of Ezekiel, Jeremiah and Hosea to a latter-day King David appearing after the restoration of Israel were scriptures specifically speaking about him and his endtime ministry.

> Thus saith the Lord God; Behold, I will take the children of Israel from among the heathen, whither they be gone, and will gather them on every side, and bring them into their own land:...And David my servant shall be king over them; and they all shall have one shepherd. (Ezekiel 37:21, 24)

> But they shall serve the Lord their God, and David their king, whom I will raise up unto them....in the latter days ye shall consider it. (Jeremiah 30:9, 24)

> Afterwards shall the children of Israel return, and seek the Lord their God and David their king; and shall fear the Lord and His goodness in the Latter Days. (Hosea 3:5)

Berg believed the phrase "latter days" used by those prophets made it clear they were predicting a future king named David, since the Old Testament King David supposedly reigned hundreds of years before their prophecies. Berg also believed the Middle East war described in Ezekiel 38 as occurring "in the latter years" (Verse 8) and "in the latter days" (Verse 16) was the same one depicted in the Bible's final book. Revelation 16 describes an endtime battle at Armageddon (Megiddo, in northern Israel) that occurs right before the Second Coming.

Like other apocalyptic Christians, Berg searched for biblical signs of the endtime. One of those signs was the restoration of Israel as a nation. The same prophetic passages in Ezekiel and elsewhere that Berg believed foretold his endtime ministry also predicted that the people of Israel would one day return from the foreign countries they were exiled to and become their own nation again. Berg wasn't alone in believing that prediction was fulfilled when the modern Jewish diaspora returned to Palestine and David Ben-Gurion proclaimed the establishment of the state of Israel in 1948. Berg believed that event signified the Second Coming was imminent, as promised in Psalm 102:16: "When the Lord shall build up Zion, He shall appear in his glory."

In 1966, a year before receiving the Ezekiel prophecy from Sister Gunn, Berg's mother continued encouraging her son's prophetic mission when she prophesied that God had given him the understanding of the prophet Daniel "to know the number of the years unto the End of Desolations." Virginia's prophecy included a reference to Daniel 9:2, which revealed that number to be seventy years. Berg wrote that his mother's prophecy referred directly to him as "the one called David by Divine Anointing," and that "the Lord kept calling me 'thou, O Daniel', and said He was going to reveal the number of years, as He had to the prophet Jeremiah, but I never connected that with the revelation we got later—a couple of years ago at TSC—That 70-year revelation regarding my prospective age."[14]

His mother's prophecy said Berg would know the specific timing of endtime events leading to the Second Coming. In 1970, Berg received a numerological prophecy concerning his own lifespan that corresponded to the seventy years in his mother's prophecy. In 1972, he connected their two prophecies and published "The 70-Years Prophecy of the End," believing that his life coincided with those endtime events and he would play a crucial role in them.

In this Mo Letter, he explains that while he was very ill, he asked God how long he would live. Much like a medium claiming to hear a message from a spirit, Berg describes hearing ten distinct sets of seven knocks, meaning he would live seventy years. There was a pause after the seventh set, which he interpreted as his life having two separate stages, forty-nine years followed by twenty-one years.[15] His first forty-nine years ended in 1968, which was the year he formed the Children of God. The next twenty-one years ended in 1989, the year he thought he would die.

In that same Mo Letter, he discusses other prophecies and biblical numerology, and tells a story about having his future told by a palm-reading "gypsy" who predicted Berg's second wife, Karen Zerby, would live to the year 1993. Berg said he had a vision of her being raptured in the Second Coming, so he interpreted the palm-reader's prediction as the year Jesus would return. He said that fit with other prophecies indicating that his predicted death in 1989 would happen before the period of great tribulation Jesus said would occur prior to the Second Coming.

Working backward from the year 1993, Berg tied the prophecies about his own life to specific biblical prophecies concerning the endtime. Like other Christian eschatologists who study theological theories about the end of the world, Berg was convinced that various chapters and verses in Daniel, Revelation, Matthew and elsewhere provide a chronology of events leading up to the Second Coming. Daniel's visions, dreams and apocalyptic prophecies are particularly pertinent because they specify a timeline that Berg interpreted literally as describing the final seven years before Jesus returns.

According to Berg's interpretation of these scriptures, the beginning of the end starts when a warrior prince, generally referred to as the Antichrist, invades recently restored Israel and signs some kind of international covenant or peace treaty. Midway through those last seven years, the prince breaks the covenant, resulting in three and a half years of what Daniel refers to in Chapter 9 as a period of war and desolation.

Jesus referred to the same period as the great tribulation when his disciples questioned him about the end of the world. In Matthew 24, Jesus mentions numerous endtime events that would signal his imminent return, and then cites Daniel's prophecies: "When ye therefore shall see the abomination of desolation, spoken of by Daniel the prophet, stand in the holy place…then shall be great tribulation.…Immediately after the tribulation of those days…shall appear the sign of the Son of man in heaven.… And he shall send his angels with a great sound of a trumpet, and they shall gather together his elect." (Matthew 24:15–31)

Berg was convinced he now knew the specific years when certain endtime events would occur. He was confident enough in his predictions that he published "The 70-Years Prophecy of the End" with the designation "GP," meaning he permitted the general public to read it. He wanted the world to know he was the endtime prophet predicting the end of the world. And to make it very clear exactly what he was predicting, he summarized the sequence of events leading to the Second Coming:

1. The Restoration of God's true Israel—the Children of God—began in 1968 or 1969.

2. We should begin hearing something about the Anti-Christ and his rise to power soon, and certainly not later than the early 1980s.

3. He would therefore have to confirm the Covenant about 1985.

4. 1985 therefore, would be the beginning of the Seventieth Week of Daniel 9.

5. This would be the Last Seven Years of world history and the reign of the Anti-Christ.

6. The Tribulation would then have to begin about the end of the year 1989.

7. The Lord would then come exactly 3-1/2 years later, sometime during the first half of 1993![16]

A month earlier, in February 1972, Berg told his followers that his sermons and letters were the very "Voice of God Himself" and were required reading for at least two hours a day. He wrote: "You, my dear children have an appointment with me every day, and you'd better not miss it, or you're going to be sorry! To ignore the Word of the Lord through His Prophet is to ignore the Voice of God Himself....As throughout all time, God has always required His People to follow and obey His chosen Mouthpiece, His Prophet, His man of God, His chosen Leader, Shepherd, or King!"[17]

Within fours years of founding the Children of God, Berg declared that he was personally named in the Bible as the prophet-king who would lead God's people in the endtime, that his word was God's word, and that Jesus was coming back in 1993. After six months of indoctrination, I believed him. I hadn't learned to think critically about claims like these, and it was even harder to doubt or question them when the information presented to me was supported by the moral authority of the Bible, a holy book I believed was absolutely true, as many do. My indoctrination ensured I didn't doubt the Bible, or Berg.

I learned that doubts were devilish. When the devil tempted Christ, he tried to make him doubt his messianic mission, repeatedly taunting him to prove he was the Son of God: "If thou be the Son of God..." (Matthew 4) Doubts showed a lack of faith, as illustrated by the disciple known as Doubting Thomas, an epithet used in the Children of God to ridicule and denigrate doubters. Although Jesus had instructed his disciples to "neither be ye of doubtful mind." (Luke 12:29) Thomas needed proof before he would believe the other disciples when they told him they had seen and spoken to Jesus after his resurrection. He only believed after seeing for himself and sticking his fingers in Jesus's wounds, and Jesus chided him for doubting, saying those who believe by faith without seeing are more blessed.[18]

Like a good soldier, I was expected to obey dictates; disagreements were not tolerated. My indoctrination not only denounced doubts, but also discouraged independent thinking. A common chant around the Nanaimo boot camp was "When you think, think, think—You'll sink, sink, sink—Because you stink, stink, stink." I quickly learned to squelch my doubts and bury them in the back of my mind. No longer thinking for myself, and conditioned to groupthink, I was convinced by Berg's endtime prophecies that Jesus was coming back in 1993. That belief kept me committed to Berg's doomsday mission.

According to the book of Matthew, Jesus told his disciples the end would only come after the gospel was preached to the entire world: "And this gospel of the kingdom shall be preached in all the world for a witness unto all nations; and then shall the end come." (Matthew 24:14) I would soon flee the impending destruction of America and become a missionary spreading Berg's endtime message in Asia, eagerly waiting for Jesus to return.

Chapter 7
Fleeing Babylon the Whore

The Children of God in the US and Canada began fleeing to foreign mission fields in 1971, heeding Berg's doomsday warnings about the impending destruction of America. That same year, Don McLean released his album *American Pie*, and the title track became a number-one hit in 1972. McLean had long refused to explain the meaning of the song or confirm interpretations of its many cultural allusions, but in the 2022 documentary "American Pie: The Day The Music Died", he does say many of the lyrics are autobiographical and he rejects various interpretations by others. He also says he was reflecting on the decline of America when he wrote it.

Berg's interpretation of the lyrics twisted the song's metaphors to fit his doomsday message. In the Mo Letter "Bye, Bye, Pie," Berg said the broken church bells and the children screaming in the streets represented the Children of God decrying the ineffective church system and warning of God's abandonment of America, which he claimed was depicted as the Father, Son and Holy Ghost taking the last train to the coast when the music died. He wrote that the song was "an uncanny prophetic parable about the death of America," and he connected it to his 1961 "Message of Jeremiah" doomsday prophecy:

> It not only mourns the passing of America, but also the death of a lost generation and the end of their music of hopefulness! In fact, I am sure that the inspiration of this ballad of gloom goes far beyond the significance the composer dreamed! The kids understand its spirit even if they don't comprehend the meaning of the words. It's like the lamentations of Jeremiah over the ruins of Jerusalem. It's youth's lament over the death of America and the music that died with her and her lost generation....

> This song reminds me of what God gave us about America in "America the Whore," as Babylon in the Bible, Revelation 18:21,22: "Thus with violence shall that great city Babylon be thrown down and shall be found no more at all! — And the voice of harpers and musicians and of pipers and trumpeters shall be heard no more at all in thee!"[1]

Two months before that letter, Berg published "America the Whore," claiming that the US was "tottering and reeling on the brink of economic and political disaster, about to fall to her doom, a perfect picture of the certain self-destruction of corrupt Capitalism by its own selfish weakness and rottenness and cruelty, as predicted by both Marx and the Bible!... and when she falls, the whole world capitalistic System is bound to fall with her!"[2] Many Mo Letters in that period contained similarly extreme anti-American diatribes warning of the nation's impending destruction, and pushing members still there to flee to foreign fields.

At the end of the summer of 1972, I moved to the Victoria commune on the southern tip of Vancouver Island. Shortly after, we started selling illustrated Mo Letters on the street for the first time. We tested the waters with basic ones that had a simple salvation message, like "Diamonds of Dust"[3] and "Mountain Men,"[4] but soon we were selling Berg's doomsday warnings too. After I moved to Vancouver a few months later, I walked down busy city streets holding the provocative cover of "America the Whore" at the eye level of passing pedestrians, asking for donations for that anti-capitalist pamphlet.

Berg now believed it was more important for us to deliver his message than it was to try and win souls individually. Since the beginning, the group's primary proselytizing method had been one-on-one preaching. Whether witnessing in teams of two, or in groups using singing, dancing or free food to attract people, the goal was to convert individuals. Personal preaching was effective and led to over two thousand full-time members in the first four years, but Berg thought it was inefficient evangelism, too slow for reaching the world with his urgent endtime predictions. He also thought he was a better preacher than his followers, so he wrote a series of letters that changed the emphasis of our street ministry from saving souls to selling Mo Letters. He wrote:

> We'll win very few compared to the millions to whom we'll witness. But we're more responsible to give them all God's message than we are to win them, for only His Spirit can win.

We can only witness!…Have you shared [the Mo Letters] with your friends? Have you passed them to the kids in the park? Have you asked for donations to print more?…Reprint or translate in every language and give His wonder working words to the world![5]

Tell those kids I can do my own preaching. I don't need them to do it for me, and I think the Letters do a better job than they can. All I need is sweet, bright-eyed happy kids to get it into their hands.…Be God's newsboys! Witnessing is our main job, not winning. We can't possibly reach enough people in our personal witness.…That's why God has given me the burden to get these kids out on the road and sell literature.[6]

In Children of God jargon, witnessing became "litnessing," since literature was now doing our preaching for us. It was more lucrative too. Instead of just passing out free gospel tracts, every member could now make money on the street by asking for donations in exchange for a pamphlet. Litnessing quickly became a primary source of income for members in most countries. It was profitable for the prophet too. All communes tithed at least ten percent of their income to Berg and his administrative team.

At the end of November, I moved to Vancouver. The commune was in a semi-industrial area of South Vancouver, a few blocks from the Fraser River. The very old, two-storey wooden house had an unfinished basement and a rickety shed, which were infested with rats attracted by the boxes of donated or scavenged fruits and vegetables we stored in them. The house had barely enough room for the twenty or so members there, though the number constantly fluctuated as people left for foreign mission fields, and new recruits moved in.

As Christmas approached, the leader advised those of us with families in the province to go visit them over the holidays. Though partly a public relations ploy to convince critics we were not brainwashed captives, it was also a test of commitment that weeded out those who were weak in faith and not fully dedicated disciples. Not everyone who went home for Christmas returned to the group. It was the first time I'd gone anywhere alone since joining about nine months earlier.

Once I was on my own in Port Alberni, without the constant peer pressure from other members, it was the best opportunity anyone would have to try and persuade me to drop out of dropping out and return to normal life. With each move to a new commune, I was getting farther away from my family. That visit was the last chance for someone to offer me guidance and suggest alternatives to life with the Children of God. I might've been susceptible to such persuasion.

I stayed two weeks, which was longer than I had planned. Perhaps I was just enjoying the comforts of home, or maybe I lingered because subconsciously I hoped someone would intervene and discuss my future with me. I participated in my family's holiday rituals and visits with relatives, but I don't recall having any meaningful conversations.

One discussion I unsuccessfully attempted to have was with Father Mark. The leader of the Vancouver commune knew from the *Alberni Valley Times* article that Father Mark wasn't hostile to us, unlike other Christian leaders, and I told the leader my story about how Mark had compared the Children of God to St. Francis when he counselled me. Just a few months before my visit home, Berg wrote that the Children of God had much more in common with Catholics than Protestants.[7] So, following Berg's direction that we develop good relations with Catholics, the leader told me to visit the priest while I was in Port Alberni.

When I went to the church, a priest I didn't know had me wait in the rectory's dinette. After several minutes, he returned to tell me that Father Mark was not well and I couldn't see him. Just moments earlier, I'd glimpsed him down the hallway, passing from one room to another, so I thought it was curious he couldn't at least say hello. It's possible he was prohibited from speaking to me, perhaps because he failed to dissuade me from joining the Children of God, or maybe because he was going through a crisis of faith. A few years later, my aunt who worked as a housekeeper for the priests told me that Father Mark had left the priesthood and become a youth social worker in Victoria.

My saddest memory of that trip is of my seven-year-old sister, Crystal, coming upstairs to talk with me. It breaks my heart to realize now that she craved brotherly affection, but instead I offered her pie-in-the-sky by praying with her to ask Jesus into her heart. I broke my fraternal bond with my other siblings, Jay and Brenda, too. It hurts to know they must've all been confused and distressed by my sudden disappearance from their lives. I regret not being a supportive big brother they could've leaned on, but I was blinded by faith at the time, so couldn't see the emotional harm my religious zealotry caused them and my parents.

When I returned to Vancouver, I telephoned the commune from the bus depot. I expected an excited response welcoming me home, but the woman who answered didn't know me. There was a constant shuffle of members moving between communes, and she had moved in while I was away. I momentarily felt lost between worlds, not truly known by either my real or religious family, and feeling that no one cared whether I came or went, but I quickly squelched those seconds of doubt. The stranger on the phone told me the group's bus was parked downtown on Granville Street and I could meet up with the litnessers there. Some of them knew me, which helped me fit back in immediately.

When I wasn't litnessing, I worked mostly in the kitchen, learning how to prepare meals from scratch for twenty or more people, using whatever was donated or scrounged from dumpsters. We often got more than enough free food to feed ourselves, so we used some of it in our street evangelism. On weekend evenings, we parked our converted school bus on the Granville strip, one of Vancouver's busiest shopping and entertainment areas. A sign outside our bus advertised free food, usually peanut butter and banana sandwiches, and our gospel music played over external speakers. Songs and sandwiches were lures we used to try to hook people on Jesus.

In the summer of 1973, we took the bus to one of the last hippie be-ins in Stanley Park, an event that had been held annually since the first one there in March 1967, modelled on San Francisco's Human Be-In of that same year. We set up on the edge of the festival, passed out sandwiches, sang songs and witnessed to anyone interested. The Hare Krishnas were there too, also giving out free food to the tie-dyed crowd. I often encountered them around Vancouver, doing the same things we were. Though we had different religious messages, our proselytizing methods were similar: using music and food to lure people, selling literature on the street, and setting up evangelistic missions abroad. I would next encounter Hare Krishna members on the streets of Japan, and one in an immigration office where we were both being interrogated.

— — —

In April 1972, Berg and his secretary moved to England. By then, some members had set up a few communes in Europe and Latin America. Around this time, Berg wrote "The Great Escape," describing a dream in which a fast-approaching storm threatened a luxuriant land, while a group of shepherds and sheep huddled for safety. He interpreted the storm as God's impending destruction of America and said the dream was a warning from God.

> As Jeremiah warned God's people in his day, if we do not escape now, some of us will be swept away with God's Judgments on

the wicked! Nevertheless, He has promised us that in that day, when His Rod of Judgment descends upon America, there will be a very great Harvest of souls, so some of us will have to stay behind to rescue those poor lost sheep in that day. These were no doubt those shepherds huddled together with their sheep in little places of refuge in the midst of the storm, like our farm and ranch Colonies, where you should now be storing food, and be sure of an independent water supply and even provisioning animals and wagons for transportation while others flee!

Meanwhile, while the escape routes are still open and fairly easy to cross, as many of you as possible who are ready with your passports should be moving on to higher ground of the other nations we must reach.[8]

Children of God members in Canada and the US had two options in response to Berg's doomsday warnings: flee from the impending destruction of America to mission fields in the Eastern and Southern hemispheres, or stay behind in refuges ready to endure the chaos of war and witness to the survivors. Berg's warning had his desired effect. At the end of 1973, there were well over two thousand Children of God members dispersed to forty countries, living in about 140 communes. I was thinking of heading north to Alaska with a brother who had hitchhiked from the US East Coast with that destination in mind, but leaders had other plans for me. At the end of that summer of '73, they sent me south across the border to Burlington, Washington, about a hundred kilometres from Vancouver.

In a Mo Letter dated November 1971, Berg described the commune in Burlington as the group's largest at the time, with over two hundred people living there.[9] Vancouver had over a hundred members, though not all living in one location. Three months later, an *NBC Evening News* report described the Burlington commune: "About 60 of them live here in a run-down former church camp."[10] There were only about thirty people left when I moved there, and most of them were following the others overseas. The camp was in the process of shutting down, not only to obey Berg's warnings to flee America, but because of negative reactions from the local community. According to Berg, those "attacks of the System" included two members being kidnapped from the camp.[11]

Berg told us to expect that kind of persecution and explained numerous reasons why it was a good sign.[12] The apostle Paul said those who "live godly in Christ Jesus shall suffer persecution" (2 Timothy 3:12), so we considered it a badge of honour. It was also motivation to move to friendlier fields.

Jesus told his followers, "When they persecute you in this city, flee ye into another." (Matthew 10:23) While we still occupied the camp, though, we continued the extra security measures in place there.

The compound's main building had a large central room for meals and meetings, an industrial-sized kitchen and storage rooms, several bedrooms that leaders and other married couples used, and an office. A separate building had men's and women's washrooms with multiple toilets and shower stalls. Scattered around the property were numerous cabins of various sizes, with bunk beds where the singles slept, divided by gender. There was also a large two-storey house close to the compound's gated entrance. It was used as a nursery school, and some of the children and their caregivers slept there. Its enclosed front porch held a guard post with an intercom connected to the office. A sentry kept watch there day and night, ready to warn the camp when enemies were at the gate. Every evening after lights out, two males conducted a security sweep of the entire compound. I was on the rotating schedule for both of these security jobs.

I often visited that child-care house when I had free time. I knew one of the single sisters, Nekoda, from the Nanaimo commune. When she first arrived at that boot camp, with the fringes of her buckskin jacket and her long hair flowing as she joyfully bounded across a flowery field, beaming with delight, I was instantly attracted to her. The rule against dating, and my shyness, prevented me from expressing my attraction, but now that we were reunited in Burlington I tried to spend as much time at the child-care house as I could.

I often delivered meals to the girls and would stay to help them with their chores. I cleaned, washed dishes and even hand-rinsed pails of poopy cloth diapers, preparing them for laundering. Sometimes I played with the toddlers so their minders could get other things done. I enjoyed that because it wistfully reminded me of playing with my two youngest siblings.

One of those toddlers led me on the exodus out of doomed America. Benjamin was the son of Amos and Abigail. I played with him when I visited the nursery, so he grew fond of me. I'd first met Amos in Victoria when he came on a supervisory visit in his role as area leader. While there, he conducted a communion ceremony as described in Matthew 26, which was the first one I'd participated in since leaving the Catholic Church. It wasn't a regular ritual in the group, but it was more intimate and meaningful than what I experienced in church. My first re-enactment of the Last Supper with other fully dedicated disciples, living according to the Bible, strengthened my spiritual bond to them.

I looked up to Amos after that, perhaps partly because of the solemn, priestly role he played in that ceremony. He'd once been a Protestant youth pastor in Texas, and was one of Berg's earliest followers. So were Caleb and Lydia, who were also living in the Burlington commune.[13] Caleb and his brother Arnold were Berg's first two followers. Lydia was a minor when Berg married her to Caleb in 1968. They were now the regional leaders of North America, so their wish was my command.

People were gradually moving out as the commune's closure neared. One day, Lydia called me to her room to discuss the leadership's plan for me. She told me they had a more important mission for me than staying behind in British Columbia or Alaska. They needed me to help Amos and Abigail move to Hawaii, which was a staging ground for members on their way to the Asia-Pacific region. They had a couple of kids older than Benjamin, and an infant too, so they needed a child-care travel assistant. Since Benjamin was comfortable with me, Lydia said I was the best person for the job. I didn't have much choice, but with winter setting in, tropical Hawaii did sound more appealing than icy Alaska. I was also excited to take my first flight.

I soon moved with Amos's family, his secretary and several others to a small former seniors' nursing home in a Seattle suburb, rented for the two months before our flight at the end of December. I took care of Benjamin most days, but I also visited a commune in the city a few times for weekend litnessing blitzes. The house had a printing press in the basement, so we freely distributed large numbers of Mo Letters, mainly ones with a dooms- day warning message about the approaching comet Kohoutek, which was expected to appear the same week we were leaving the continent.

On March 7, 1973, the Czech astronomer Luboš Kohoutek had discovered a comet passing through the solar system. Scientists speculated it would produce a spectacular display as it passed by Earth at the end of December. Anticipating this effect, various news media, including *Time* magazine, described it throughout the ensuing months as the "comet of the century," until its unimpressive arrival.[14] Encouraged by these media reports, Berg proclaimed his own ominous prediction. He wrote a couple of letters[15] about the coming comet, before predicting in the Mo Letter "40 Days!" that the United States would be destroyed forty days after Kohoutek appeared.[16]

In a subsequent letter, "The Comet Comes," Berg discussed an arti- cle headlined on the cover of the British magazine *Saga*, "The Christmas Comet: Omen of Peace — or Doomsday Messenger?" The article confirmed Berg's beliefs about comets being harbingers of historically important events. Relying on the article's questionable scientific and historical claims, other pseudo-science, such as predictions by well-known astrologers, and his own numerology, Berg agreed with the author that the discovery of the comet was a sign that significant political, social and environmental events were occurring around the world even before it was visible to the naked eye. Berg also believed that the predictions by astrologers matched his own endtime prophecies:

> All of these predictions coincide almost exactly with the interpretations of Bible prophecy and our own personal revelations in recent years which place the Second Coming of Christ about 1993 after all these foregoing events. What an amazing correlation of the forecasts of scientists, astrologers and prophets alike![17]

Although Kohoutek was a little brighter than most comets and visible to the naked eye, it didn't come close to being the comet of the century as expected, disappointing most observers, though not Berg. He simply reinterpreted events after the fact, explaining in the January 1974 letter "The Comet's Tale" that because the Children of God had warned the world with his message, God didn't need the comet's tail to be a visual warning sign of doomsday.[18] Whether the comet had been observable or not, he insisted it was related to all the momentous world events that preceded its arrival, and to the ones he predicted would follow.

Before leaving for Hawaii, I helped distribute those doomsday warning letters around Seattle. We passed them out freely to pedestrians and placed them on car windshields in shopping-mall and stadium parking lots. Some of us went to a Washington Huskies college football game and passed out stacks of letters inside the stadium, while two others unfurled a banner with a doomsday message on it and ran along the sidelines, until we were all escorted out. We did the same thing at a SuperSonics NBA basketball game.

The Seattle commune also advertised the forty-day doomsday message on a prominent billboard in the city, and produced a simple television advertisement featuring an ominous voice-over and showing covers of various Mo Letters, along with contact information. That TV ad aired on a late-night Saturday music program popular with young people. It was exciting to see our message broadcast like this, knowing that others were doing similar doomsday publicity stunts around America.

I participated in another thrilling one on the day I left for Hawaii with Amos and his family. Amos had prearranged for a television reporter from Seattle's most popular evening news program to come to the nursing home to interview and film the Children of God fleeing America. On the morning of our flight, a few days before the end of the year, the reporter interviewed Amos and filmed us packing our vehicles. The TV crew then followed us to the airport, filming our motorcade, which included other members just there for the camera. With the camera rolling, the reporter followed us inside to the check-in counter, and then to the waiting area, where we sang the doomsday song "The Message of Jeremiah," written by Children of God member Russell McClelland, known as Jeremiah Singer in the group.[19]

When we arrived in Hawaii later that evening, we learned that the final scenes of the news report showed our exit through the boarding gate and the plane taking off. Caleb and Lydia, who'd moved to Hawaii several weeks before we did, excitedly told us that the report's dramatic scenes of the Children of God's departure from doomed America had been rebroadcast around the country.

Chapter 8
Revolutionary Sex

After arriving in Honolulu, we drove directly to Wai'anae, a small town fifty kilometres away, where Caleb and Lydia had moved after they left Burlington. Although I was still in the United States, Hawaii was the start of my foreign adventures. It was the farthest from home I had travelled, and now separated by an ocean, with no money of my own, I had no easy way to return to Canada if I wanted to. I wasn't considering going back, but I was still uncertain about where I was headed, which made me anxious.

Berg's Comet Kohoutek warnings predicted America's destruction, presumably by war, so he had encouraged members in North America and Europe to move to the Southern Hemisphere and Far East, where repercussions of war might be less severe. All the members living in Hawaii, or passing through, were eventually heading to those regions of the world. A couple nights after our arrival, my anxiety erupted in a panic attack when I was jolted awake by the sounds of explosions in the distance. Disoriented, my mind racing and heart pounding, it took a minute to overcome my foggy confusion, remember where I was, and realize the bombs bursting in the air were fireworks. Hawaii wasn't under attack. It was New Year's Eve.

Amos and Abigail were planning to move to Australia soon. Although my Canadian passport would have made it easy to get a visa there, they didn't need my help with that trip. Amos told me that because I was single, I would be more useful in Hong Kong, which was also part of the British Commonwealth at the time. He said the plan was for me to eventually help a team set up a commune there, but until they were ready for me, I was going to Japan. Litnessing was very lucrative there, so they needed more members to take advantage of that.

I soon moved to a commune in a Honolulu neighbourhood and waited for the leaders to arrange my travel plans. Using a front organization, they were able to get missionary discounts for flights to Seoul, South Korea, which was much cheaper than a direct flight to Japan, even counting the additional cost of getting from there to Tokyo. While waiting for the documents I needed for the clergy discount, I spent the next month or so litnessing in Honolulu and smaller communities nearby. A few times, I went on hitchhiking trips around the island of Oahu, sleeping rough on secluded beaches.

While I was in Hawaii, the US was in the midst of an oil crisis due to a six-month embargo imposed by the Organization of Arab Petroleum Exporting Countries. Gasoline shortages led to rationing and long lineups at every gas station. There were shortages of other consumer products too. We believed the developing crisis was part of Berg's predictions playing out, which increased our urgency to flee that paradise in peril because of its large military presence. I would encounter similar shortages in Korea.

In February 1974, I left Hawaii with two American members who were travelling to Japan with me. Arriving in Seoul, I experienced my first culture shock as a stranger in a strange land. South Korea was ruled by a military government facing political and economic troubles. The country was dependent on imported products, and so was suffering severe shortages due to the oil crisis. As the plane descended from the night sky, I saw few lights in the eerily darkened city. Inside the airport terminal, and outside on city streets, there were heavily armed soldiers everywhere. With most street and building lights turned off to conserve energy, there was a dystopian atmosphere as the taxi driver sped into the dark heart of the city.

We stayed overnight in the Seoul commune, then took the train to Busan on the south coast and the ferry to Shimonoseki, Japan. From there, it was about a six-hour trip on the bullet train to Tokyo. Viewed from the window, the modern cities we passed through could easily be mistaken for ones in the West, but the rice paddies, tea fields and bamboo forests of the countryside reminded me that I was in the Far East. That was even more obvious inside the train, surrounded by people who looked and sounded foreign to me. But I was clearly the foreigner now, a *gaijin*, literally an "outside person," or "outsider."

The Tokyo commune was in an old wooden house in the Ikebukuro district, and already overcrowded when the three of us arrived. For the few nights I was there, I slept in a closet used to store futon mattresses during the day, since there was no space left on the floors. On the first morning, jet-lagged after the long journey, I was surprised to learn that I had to sell some Mo Letters before I could eat breakfast. It was inconvenient to cook for everyone in the tiny kitchen, so most of us ate our meals in restaurants, paid for by selling pamphlets.

My partner wrote down the romanized Japanese phrases for "Good morning" and "A little donation, please," and by the time we got to a nearby litnessing spot I had them memorized. It didn't take long before we had enough money for breakfast, which my companion chose and was unlike any I'd had before: *katsudon*, a breaded pork cutlet with scrambled egg and vegetables over a bowl of white rice.

The Tokyo commune was too crowded to stay in, so within a few days I left on a two-month road trip with a Californian called Brother Sun, after a hymn by Saint Francis.[1] He was a few years older than me and had been in Japan for a few months. He knew enough basic Japanese to get around, aided by a dictionary. The leaders who assigned specific territories to the litnessing teams travelling around the country sent us to cover the cities of Okayama and Hiroshima, and all the smaller ones in between.

On the first night of the journey south, we stayed with the Little Sisters of Jesus in their small Catholic convent.[2] Children of God members had befriended that community of nuns in various countries after Berg instructed his followers to nurture relationships with Catholics. His daughter Faithy met with their founder, Little Sister Magdeleine, in Rome and accompanied her to an audience with the pope.[3] As a result of that relationship, the convent in Japan had previously put up other travelling teams for the night. After dinner and a conversation with the mother superior, the nuns set up futons for us on the floor of a small classroom. Before dawn, a nun rolled in a trolley with toast and tea, and bid us adieu.

When we arrived at our first destination, we left our backpacks in a train station locker and immediately began street litnessing. We needed money for meals and a room in a youth hostel, which was the cheapest accommodation. As it turned out, though, we often didn't need to pay for a hostel. It was quite common for people we met on the street to invite us home for the night when they learned we needed a place to stay. They usually fed us too.

People were generally receptive to foreigners asking for donations for pamphlets, so we sold a lot of Mo Letters working the streets all day. We couldn't carry all the letters we needed for that two-month trip, so the Tokyo team resupplied us by sending boxes of pamphlets by freight train ahead of us to our next destinations. We stored them in a station locker and replenished our litnessing bags as needed.

Litnessing was more lucrative in Japan than in the US and Canada, especially for Brother Sun, who was more confident and outgoing than me. His pockets quickly filled with coins, so he had to go to a bank more often than I did throughout the day to change them into bills. Once a week, we sent most of the money we made back to the leaders in Tokyo by postal money order. We kept only enough to pay for transportation, meals, public baths, laundry and youth hostels. There were other road teams all over Japan, doing the same thing.

After more than two months on the road, we returned to Tokyo. The two leadership couples in charge of the Japan mission had recently moved into a newly constructed high-rise building in the same Ikebukuro district where the commune I landed in was. They lived in apartments on the ninth floor, and their staff in one below that. They also rented an entire floor that was eventually turned into offices and a large meeting space. One of the couples needed a child-care helper for their toddler son, so I moved into the staff apartment. That situation led to my first sexual experience.

— — —

Before I joined the Children of God, I was quite awkward around girls. I didn't have female friendships and was too shy to talk to girls I was attracted to, so I never danced at school dances, dated or had a girlfriend. One time, my high school friend Dave set up a blind date for me with his girlfriend's friend. He didn't tell me, though, so I wasn't expecting them when they showed up at his place. Soon after they arrived, Dave and his girlfriend disappeared into his room. I was extremely uncomfortable in that situation, alone with a girl I didn't know and wasn't attracted to. Embarrassed, unsure of how to act or what to say, I panicked and ran out the door without a word.

Soon after that, I joined the Children of God, so I never developed the social-emotional skills that teens and young adults typically learn through dating rituals. Members were forbidden to date or have sexual contact of any kind outside marriage, which required a leader's approval. However, unknown to all but his inner circle, Berg had been living a sexually permissive lifestyle secretly behind the scenes, while imposing those strict rules on most of his followers.

Berg eventually began to relax these rules by publishing his boundary-breaking beliefs on sexuality in a series of letters. He began grooming his followers to accept his unorthodox sexual doctrines in "Revolutionary Sex," in which he emphasized the godly naturalness of nudity, masturbation and sexuality in general, and criticized religious dogma that saw sex as shameful.[4] Some passages foreshadowed later letters that opened the door to almost every kind of sexual activity.

A couple of years earlier, Berg had written two letters with explicit sexual advice for married couples only.[5] Although, in one of them, he briefly discussed the issue of singles masturbating, he didn't encourage it, saying marriage was preferable.[6] But in "Revolutionary Sex" he enthusiastically endorsed masturbation, referring to it fifty-four times. I was at the Burlington commune when it came out. We all gathered to read it as a group, which we didn't do for every Mo Letter. It was also unusual that one of the female leaders read it to us, perhaps because of the subject matter. Single members, including me, were particularly relieved by that letter.

My limited sex education began in elementary school when Grade 7 students watched a basic birds-and-bees sex-ed film on the human reproductive system. Our parents were expected to participate, so the lesson was held during the evening. Boys and girls watched it separately from each other and from our parents, who were also separated by gender. We remained separated for the question-and-answer session afterwards. No one raised their hand except my friend Bill, who asked what a boner was. Everyone giggled. The instructor explained the biological process, but didn't discuss how an adolescent could handle an erection. The film contained no practical guidance like that. Mentioning masturbation probably would've caused some parents to protest.

Many parents are uneasy about having the sex talk with their children, so participation in this sex-ed program was intended to help parents initiate that conversation. On the short drive home, my dad asked me if I had asked any questions after the film. I suspect that was what the adults' instructor suggested parents ask as a way to break the ice. When I said I didn't, he replied snidely: "So you think you know everything, eh?" His sarcastic put-down was typical of the way he talked to me. Instead of teaching me, unconstructive criticisms like these pushed me away from him. I didn't reply. We drove the last couple blocks in silence. That was the extent of our sex talk. Sex, like religion and education, was something my dad never discussed with me.

Similar biology lessons in junior high school also inadequately educated me, so I remained mostly ignorant about sex. For example, I didn't know what a wet dream was, so I was confused and embarrassed when I started having nocturnal emissions. I couldn't hide the evidence from my mum, so she explained masturbation to me, without using the word. The Catholic Church considers masturbation a sin, so my mum was either unaware of that dogma or simply ignored it. Her attitude suggested it was normal, but I still felt a bit shameful masturbating, so learning from Berg that God was okay with it was a great relief. He also explained wet dreams in "Revolutionary Sex," which was the first time I heard that expression.

In that letter, Berg described the sexual liberation movement spreading throughout society as a good thing in that it was ending "taboos and inhibitions and abnormal guilt complexes," but said it went too far in other ways. He criticized "liberationists [for] going to the opposite extreme of total promiscuity and permissiveness in any form whatsoever, with anybody, any time, any place, and any how, in any way, or everywhere, with everybody!" However, in the same paragraph, Berg declared the Bible prohibits only four forms of sexual activity—fornication, adultery, incest and sodomy—but that God made "many exceptions, allowances and tolerations" for all of them except homosexuality.[7]

As well as homosexuality, Berg absolutely condemned abortion and birth control. He believed God's divine demand in Genesis to "be fruitful and multiply" was the best way to increase his followers. He urged members to have as many children as possible, and start their sex education young: "Children should be taught the same: That there is nothing wrong with their bodies and nothing catastrophic about masturbation, but that all are perfectly normal, necessary, natural and God-given physical functions, but that our bodies in no respect must ever be abused or misused or overused, or exposed or used in such a way as to offend or hurt others."[8]

Berg also approved of adolescents marrying when they reach puberty and are capable of sexual reproduction: "If child marriage is wrong then why did God make girls able to conceive and bear children at such an early age if it is wrong for them to marry at such an age?"[9] Polygamy is another biblical custom Berg approved of in that letter, and he implied that adultery was okay too.

Berg had not yet revealed to regular members his personal sexual life, so it never occurred to me that he was justifying his own adultery and use of prostitutes when he wrote: "If you'll even take a look at Bible history, you'll make the shocking discovery that most of God's greats had oodles of wives, women, mistresses, harlots and what have you, as well as multitudes of children!"[10] A year later, he described details of his promiscuous sex life when he was on the road without his wife during his previous life as a travelling salesman for an evangelical TV show, writing that he often picked up women or went to strip joints and brothels.[11]

In a prophecy titled "The Old Church and the New Church," Berg cryptically referred to an affair with one of his young followers.[12] Dated August 26, 1969, it was the first official Mo Letter. The prophecy targeted Berg's wife, their oldest daughter, and others in his inner circle who resisted his sexual promiscuity. Although it didn't name them, they knew exactly what the metaphors and coded language meant. However, when I first read the letter, I simply thought it was about the Children of God rejecting the church system. I didn't understand the innuendo, double entendres and hidden meaning in the prophecy until sometime later, when I learned the story behind Berg's relationship with his secretary.

Soon after forming the Children of God, Berg had several young lovers among his entourage, whom he referred to as his wives. He favoured his secretary Karen Zerby, known to members as Maria.[13] As the transcriber of his sermons and prophecies, she was a conduit to his followers and remained his constant companion. In effect, she was the co-leader and took control of the group when Berg died in 1994.

When Berg took Zerby as his de facto wife, he was still legally married. Jane Berg, known as Mother Eve[14] in the group, objected to her husband's adultery and bigamy. At least one of their four children, Deborah,[15] also questioned his new marital arrangement, but Berg insisted that his relationship with Zerby was God's will. He used the old church/new church prophecy to justify that relationship, to condemn Jane and Deborah for their disobedient resistance, and to prevent their dissension from spreading.

In the prophecy's double metaphor, the old church applied to both the Christian church system and to Berg's old wife, Jane: "They claim to be Mine — My wife, My Church — but the relationship is in name only.... Therefore is this hypocrisy and not a marriage. This is pretense and not love."[16] On the other hand, the new church applied to both the Children of God and Berg's new bride, Zerby: "My infant Church...My Revolutionary Children...I will have a new bride who will love Me and obey Me and do My will....Therefore do I...give her a place above all the maidens."[17]

That purported prophecy is the first documented example of Berg usurping God's voice as his own to justify his questionable behaviour. From then on, Berg's prophecies featured prominently in the Mo Letters, conveniently sanctifying his beliefs and doctrines, no matter how extreme or extra-biblical. He not only believed God spoke directly through him, but also claimed he was clairvoyant, could channel spirits, and visited the spiritual realm. Zerby recorded all his dreams, visions, séance communications and spirit trips, which she transcribed into letters that included his discussions about them with her.

For the three years after that first Mo Letter, most of Berg's writings focused on his anti-American doomsday warnings and endtime prophecies, and on organizational matters as the rapidly growing group spread around the world. He continued to praise the virtue of monogamous marriage during those early years, but by 1972 he had radically denounced conventional marriage. Four months before he published "Revolutionary Sex," Berg wrote the letter "One Wife":

> God's in the business of breaking up little selfish private worldly families to make of their yielded broken pieces a larger unit—one family! He's in the business of destroying the relationships of many wives in order to make them One Wife—God's Wife—The Bride of Christ!…God breaks up marriages in order that he might join each of the parties together to himself. He rips off wives, husband or children to make up His Bride if the rest of their family refuses to follow! He is the worst "ripper-offer" of all! God is the greatest Destroyer of home and family of anybody! God does more to break up marriages than anybody!…Partiality toward your own wife or husband or children strikes at the very foundation of communal living…Whatever's best for God and His Family is what's right! Amen?[18]

"One Wife" did more than just promote communal group marriage. Like the old church/new church prophecy, it was also a general warning to obey God's will as defined by Berg, or risk losing your spouse or children. He was a master manipulator, playing people as pawns to move as he pleased for his or the group's benefit, not their own. After that letter came out, leaders used it to justify separating spouses from each other, and parents from their children, usually claiming it was for organizational reasons. It was common for couples to be split up so that one of them could join a leadership team without their spouse or children. But forced separations were also used to punish people who got out of line, or in some cases to satisfy a leader's own selfish lust.

The "One Wife" doctrine was exactly the opposite of what Berg dishonestly wrote about marriage in the group just a few months earlier, in an open letter addressed to relatives of members: "The marriage relationship is considered valid and sacrosanct and solemnized with the Holy vows of biblical betrothal!…children are in the same house with their own parents most of the day…we have much more family life, love and fellowship, than the average worldly home of today."[19]

That letter was a public relations ploy in response to negative media reports about Berg and the Children of God. He claimed it was the true story of his personal family and the founding of the group, but it is more of an unreliable hagiography than factual history. In order to portray himself and the group in the best possible light, he left out crucial details about his life and beliefs that were certainly controversial. He outright lied about some things, as he did with his claim about marriage.

The next two pivotal letters that unleashed the Children of God from traditional Christian sexual morality came out in early 1974. First, "The Little Flirty Fishy" introduced the practice of religious prostitution. A few months later, Berg wrote "The Law of Love," which was the foundation of all his sexual doctrines. With these and related letters, Berg ended the restrictions against extramarital sex within the group and sex with non-members.

In "The Law of Love," Berg twisted New Testament scriptures that speak of sacrificial love and describe the first Christians' communal lifestyle.[20] He applied sexuality to those verses about giving up your life for others and sharing everything in common with fellow believers. After that, the word *sharing* became a euphemism for sexual intercourse, whether it was sex between singles, couples spouse-swapping or having sex with singles, or members having sex with outsiders, which became known as "flirty fishing." Berg asked his disciples:

> Are you willing to lay down your life, or even your wife, for a starving brother or a sister?…For, as Jesus said, "If any man would come after me, let him deny himself and take up his cross and follow me." (When hiking, that bed roll you carry on your back could become your cross!) "For whosoever saveth his life (or wife?) shall lose it, but whosoever loseth his life (or wife?) for My sake and the Gospel's, the same shall save it!"…That is the ultimate ideal in total sharing, total giving, total forsaking all, total freedom, total living, total loving and total liberty in the total love of God![21]

Three years later, in a follow-up letter to "The Law of Love," Berg cited a few dozen Bible verses and wrote: "According to the Scriptures there is therefore no longer any law against sex that is done in Love, God's love, and hurts no one: It is no sin, neither adultery nor fornication!...God's only law is Love! We are totally, utterly free of the old Mosaic law."[22]

— — —

In 1970, fearing legal actions by hostile parents and authorities, Berg and Zerby started living in hiding, secluded from their followers, constantly on the move, their location known only to trusted leaders. They moved to England in 1972. The group's publishing and financial operations also moved there that year, but Berg and Zerby remained isolated from their followers who were now setting up communes in Europe.

By 1973, members were selling Mo Letters on London streets, and had a new evangelical ministry. In a rented venue they called the Poorboy Club, they entertained people with skits, songs and dancing.[23] They attracted people with a live band that played the group's gospel music. Among the musicians was Jeremy Spencer, a British rock star who dropped out of the original Fleetwood Mac to join the Children of God while the band was on tour in California in 1971.[24]

Meanwhile, still secluded from their followers, Berg and Zerby were experimenting with their own new way of witnessing and winning souls by wooing people they met at social clubs. Berg first revealed the unorthodox proselytizing method in the letter "The Little Flirty Fishy," which he wrote in January 1974 while living in a London borough. As he did with other controversial practices and doctrines, Berg used a prophecy to introduce his latest sexual revelation to his followers. The letter is mostly a prophetic metaphor based on Jesus's call to his first disciples to "follow me and I will make you fishers of men." (Matthew 4:19) Berg expands that metaphor, describing Zerby as bait used to sexually lure and hook men for Jesus.

The first paragraph simply states that after Berg and Zerby spent a night out socializing with friends (who were unaware they were leaders of a religious group), Berg received a prophecy about their interactions. There is also a section in which Zerby asks Berg whether the various people they met that night, both male and female, were spiritually receptive or not. They leave the setting of that social event to the imagination of the reader, but the message was clear: flirty fishing, or "FFing" for short, was a new witnessing method meant for members to practise too.

> Help her to catch men, be bold, unashamed and brazen to use anything she has, O God, to catch men for Thee! — Even if it be

through the flesh, the attractive lure, delicious flesh…the bait, impaled on Thy hook, torn by Thy Spirit, O Lord, crucified on Thy cross, Jesus!…Are you even willing to be bait on God's hook or in His trap? Would you do anything for Jesus to help your Fisherman catch men, even to suffer the crucifixion of the hook or the danger of the trap? How far would you go to catch men? All the way? May God help us all to be Flirty Little Fishies for Jesus to save lost souls.…Amen?[25]

The fledgling FFing ministry began to flourish a few months later, when Berg and Zerby flew to the tourist hot spot Tenerife, the largest of Spain's Canary Islands, on March 13, 1974. Berg eventually wrote dozens of letters about all aspects of FFing, pushing it as a primary proselytizing method, and a source of support and income. However, as they were always careful to hide their location, from authorities as well as most of his followers, it wasn't until Berg and Zerby fled Tenerife in 1977 that they fully revealed the story of their sexual experiment.

Although the Mo Letters that focus on FFing date from January 1974 onward, most of the early ones weren't published for members until 1976 or later. One of the few that was, other than the original "Flirty Fishy" prophecy, was "Beauty and the Beasts," written one month after their arrival in Tenerife. The letter doesn't disclose that location, but it does reveal Berg and Zerby were FFing in dance clubs and bars.

Berg describes their first FFing experiences as experiments: "we are always pioneers and we have to learn and experiment and experience first before we can lead the Children. We're like the shepherds going ahead of the sheep."[26] They first went to hotels and clubs catering to tourists, but the beauty-and-the-beast parable occurred to Berg while at a dance club frequented by locals. He directed Zerby to dance with specific men, one of whom he describes as a "poor labourer who doesn't get much love, and that her tender gentle love for him is even greater by contrast, because he is so rough and ugly and really hard to love."[27]

Berg left no doubt about what the fishing metaphor in his prophecy meant in practice when he described sexual intercourse as the ultimate hook. Showing God's love by expressing love for others is the cornerstone of Christianity. According to Jesus, it's the second of the two greatest commandments.[28] But Berg insisted that sexuality is also an expression of God's love.

It's clear in "Beauty and the Beasts" that Zerby had already had sex with several men. Berg cautions her that not all "fish" deserve to go all the way and swallow the "bait." When she asks if it's fair to tantalize them, but leave them unsatisfied, he replies: "Sex isn't everything!" Nevertheless, Berg ends the letter by saying:

> We've shown the world every other kind of love, and the world knows we try to help them and meet their needs. We've given them shelter and food and clothing. We've given them training, truth and triumph! Now we're even going so far as to give them other forms of physical love, even sexual love, to minister to one of their final and greatest natural needs![29]

In England, Berg and Zerby had remained incognito while experimenting with FFing, but that changed in Tenerife. Emboldened by the success of their sacred sexual seductions, they brought their personal assistants and a dozen or so women to join them there. Wearing a cape and carrying a cane, Berg behaved more like a flamboyant pimp than a preacher, appearing in clubs every night surrounded by a harem of "hookers for Jesus."[30]

It didn't take long for journalists to discover the scandal. The German magazine *Stern*, Spain's *Interviú*, and America's *Time* published articles that included a photo of Berg surrounded by his heavenly harlots, with Zerby seated next to him.[31] Most of Berg's followers had never seen him or Zerby, in person or in a photo. The group's censorship of information in that pre-Internet era ensured that many, including me, did not see those media reports either.

Berg mistakenly believed they were winning powerful friends through FFing who would support and protect them, but the local Catholic bishop became concerned by the group's flagrant behaviour, leading civic authorities to investigate and summon Berg to court. He made one court appearance, but fled the island before further legal action.[32] However, all that was in the future. I hadn't yet learned about this new sexual ministry when I landed in Japan in early 1974.

Chapter 9
I Felt the Earth Move

When I was on that two-month road trip with Brother Sun shortly after arriving in Japan in 1974, Tokyo headquarters not only shipped us resupplies of literature for litnessing, but also mailed us copies of Berg's latest letters to general delivery at the central post office of the cities we visited. One of the new ones we received was "The Little Flirty Fishy." Soon after, Brother Sun had his own flirty fishy experience, though I'm not sure who was fishing whom.

We usually started litnessing as soon as we arrived in town and continued into the early evening if we were staying in a youth hostel. We stopped earlier if we got an invitation to stay with someone eager to practise their English, or who enjoyed the novelty of entertaining westerners.

While litnessing, we usually split up to take advantage of different street corners, train station entrances, or ends of covered pedestrian streets. We were often out of sight of each other, so we prearranged a time and place to meet for lunch and dinner. One day, while alone, I met a Danish woman who was married to a local and was happy to encounter another foreigner. After chatting awhile, she asked me if I liked sake. I had never tried it, so she bought two hot glasses of the rice wine from a nearby vending machine and we sat on a mall bench. I was surprised that you could buy alcohol like that and drink it openly in public. Before she left, she gave me her phone number and said Brother Sun and I could sleep on the living room floor of her apartment. That evening, after a meal of steamed baby clams that her husband had harvested, he lit a joint and offered it to us, but we politely declined. Drugs were strictly forbidden in the Children of God, and drinking wasn't part of our lifestyle either, at least not for non-leaders. Other than a few sips of ritual red wine during occasional communions, the only alcohol I'd had since joining was a glass of wine at a wedding in the Burlington commune.

After drinking sake that first time, I realized alcohol loosened my inhibitions while litnessing, which I wasn't as good at as Brother Sun. I lacked his confidence and ability to communicate, but a little liquid courage helped me, so I began to take short breaks to down a glass of sake or beer. It was easy to buy alcohol even when there was no vending machine around. Though only eighteen years old, two years under Japan's legal drinking age, I was never asked for ID when I bought it in a store or restaurant, perhaps because I was a foreigner.

I'm not sure if Brother Sun drank like I did when we were separated, but one day while alone he also met a woman who offered us a place to stay for the night. He came looking for me, excitedly explaining that after giving him a generous donation for a Mo Letter, she invited him for coffee to talk more, and showed him erotic photos of herself. We met her later and she took us to what I assumed was her home, where we would stay for the night. I also thought she was single because of the intimate photos she showed Brother Sun, so I was puzzled to see a man there when we arrived.

After a brief conversation I didn't understand, Brother Sun explained that she was going to put us up in a hotel. She changed into classier clothes and we left in a taxi without her companion. When she checked us into the hotel, the staff seemed to know her, so I thought she might have been an employee with authority to give us a free or discounted room. Considering how it turned out, though, she may have been a flirtatious bar hostess known as a *kyabajō* (cabaret girl), or an exotic dancer.

Before leaving us, she gave Brother Sun the room key and money to buy dinner and have our laundry done. She said she would return sometime after midnight and instructed him to leave the door slightly open for her. Later that night I woke when she entered the room. Pretending to be asleep, I watched as she crept into Brother Sun's bed and had sex with him, half-hoping she would hop into mine next. She didn't. It finally occurred to me what her motive for helping us was.

While Brother Sun's intention was to hook her soul with his flirty fishing, it seems she flipped that script by luring him with a similar seductive strategy. A Japanese sexual euphemism describes her flirtatious behaviour with him. The word *gaijin* means "foreigner," so the phrase *gaijin hantā*, or "gaijin hunter," refers to Japanese who are attracted to foreigners as preferred partners or sexual conquests. She apparently considered Brother Sun the latter. I would have my own encounter with a gaijin hunter, not in a hotel but in a hospital, on another road trip months later.

After she left early in the morning, Brother Sun and I didn't talk about what had happened, but he did include his sexcapade in the weekly report of our activities we sent to the leaders in Tokyo. Soon after, we received a letter from them in which they reprimanded him and ordered him to apologize to me. They implied that he was wrong to have taken "The Little Flirty Fishy" letter literally and gone all the way. However, in that letter, Berg asked his followers: "How far would you go to catch men? All the way?" That was an obvious reference to sexual intercourse, so it seemed to me that Berg would've approved of Brother Sun's behaviour. I was confused when they made him apologize. I wasn't sure if it was because he had sex with her, or because I was in the room at the time.[1]

The weekly reports each road team sent to Tokyo headquarters included statistics on the amount of literature we distributed and how much money we made, most of which we sent to them as a postal money order. We sold so many Mo Letters that we had to change the coins that quickly filled our pockets into bills several times a day. That year, an article in the now defunct *New Times* magazine described how lucrative litnessing was.

> Litnessing team members have quotas to meet each week.... If they reach their quota or do better than the others, they are listed as "shiners"... If they fall below the quota, they are to feel ashamed.... The Staten Island colony, one of the most profitable for litnessing, gets out up to 40,000 Mo letters a week, taking in about $4,000. That adds up to $200,000 a year. To be conservative, about half that goes for printing costs and colony support, such as food and clothing. The other half, or $100,000, goes abroad, where the leadership decides how to spend it. If all the 300 colonies around the world did as well as the one on Staten Island, that would mean the total take going abroad into central headquarters would amount to about $30 million annually.[2]

My litnessing stats were not very impressive compared with most others. I was considered a "shamer" according to Berg's letter "Shiners? — or Shamers!"[3] so after Brother Sun and I returned to Tokyo, the leaders kept me there to help them. Two American couples were co-leaders of the Japan mission: Medad and Shiloh, and Abby and Laadah, whose toddler, Jephthah, was the first Children of God baby born in Japan.[4] I moved into their headquarters to help take care of him and do whatever else was needed. Since I was helping with their child, I interacted mostly with Abby and Laadah, who were parental figures to me, like Japheth and Hannah had been. Laadah similarly mothered and monitored me, as during this period of living with them I was often on my own. Later, in a different home, she bought me a new set of clothes and a watch, and taught me cooking skills I utilized throughout my life in the group.

Abby and Medad were Vietnam War veterans, a combat helicopter pilot and door gunner, respectively. In February 1972, they attempted to establish a mission in what was then Saigon, South Vietnam.[5] Laadah arrived soon after to help them, but it proved too difficult to remain in the country with the raging war ramping up, and the resistance of US military authorities to their proselytizing among soldiers. In May that year, all three left for Japan to set up a commune there.

Both couples were now living on the ninth floor of a newly constructed apartment building in the Ikebukuro district of Tokyo. I moved into a small apartment below theirs, sharing it with a few other staff members and temporary visitors. They also rented half of another floor that had a large open area for group fellowships and weekend proselytizing parties modelled on the London Poorboy Club. We attracted potential converts with posters and flyers inviting them to an evening of live music, dancing, skits and English conversation.

Most days, I helped take care of Jephthah. I usually took him to a small playground nearby, but sometimes, when I had him for longer periods, we went on short subway trips to explore other areas of the city. I often carried him in a baby backpack, and everywhere we went I heard women around me cooing "*Kawaii*" ("cute"), delighted by his smile and curly blond hair. He was a happy kid, and I enjoyed my time with him, but I was happier about not having to spend endless hours selling on the street or worrying about where I would sleep.

When I wasn't helping Laadah with Jephthah, I was on standby in case she or the other leaders needed me for odd jobs and errands. Because of my irregular schedule, I was often alone, even for meals. Unlike commune members I'd lived with before, we didn't all eat together. Litnessing teams bought meals while they were out, and the rest of us ate in nearby restaurants. Sometimes I ate with another staff member or one of the leaders, but I didn't mind eating by myself because that enabled me to order sake. I was such a frequent customer at my favourite mom-and-pop restaurant, the owner greeted me by name.

I befriended other neighbours too. On the block beside our building, there was a small convenience store. I quickly made friends with the owner, who often invited me into his home in the back for tea. The leaders allowed that as a way to maintain a friendly relationship with the neighbourhood. He had an extensive record collection, mostly American jazz and classic country, which he enjoyed playing for me on his high-end stereo system. A few times, he invited me to join him and his wife for dinner.

At one of those meals, he introduced me to his niece, Keiko, who had recently moved to Tokyo to attend school. She lived in her own apartment a short walk up the narrow lane that separated the two blocks. She was about my age and irresistibly cute, so I was instantly attracted to her. Although her basic English was better than my very limited Japanese, her uncle still needed to translate some of our conversation. He knew we were Christians, though not much else about us, but he didn't object when I invited her to one of our weekend parties.

The first time she came, I asked others to witness to her because I wasn't confident I could communicate well enough to lead her to Jesus. Near the end of an exuberant evening of spiritually inspiring singing and dancing, one of the hosts led our visitors in a group salvation prayer. Caught up in the infectious enthusiasm, Keiko joined in. She was probably still emotionally aroused when I walked her home soon after.

Outside her building, I said goodbye and reached out to give her a habitual holy hug, a non-sexual, brotherly love embrace we used as a greeting or when departing. Before I joined, I never saw people, including my own family, hug like that. It wasn't part of Japanese culture either, so while I naively intended my hug as a purely spiritual gesture, Keiko interpreted it differently. Tightening our embrace, she suddenly started kissing me, taking my breath away.

I succumbed to the sensuality spreading from her soft lips and tongue, and we continued kissing for several minutes before I left. That was the first time I had kissed a girl, and I was infatuated by it. After the next party she came to, instead of walking her straight home, I took her to the rooftop of our building. Alone, we passionately kissed, caressed and cuddled for half an hour, though that romantic moment backdropped by Tokyo city lights seemed timeless.

I wasn't sure how Abby and Laadah would react, even though I was eighteen years old, so I didn't tell them about those two make-out sessions. If they had known, they might not have given me permission when Keiko invited me to go out with her and her friends for a meal and a movie. They did allow me, but as it turned out, I don't think it was because they were encouraging me to flirty-fish Keiko and initiate an intimate relationship with her.

I also don't know if Keiko, or her friends, intentionally chose the movie, 1968's *Romeo and Juliet*, which was re-released in 1973. The love story, and particularly the bedroom balcony scene, fuelled my desire and inspired me to find a way to be alone with my Juliet. I had to be as sneaky as Romeo to make that happen without anyone knowing.

Fortunately, I wasn't as closely supervised in that commune as in previous ones. A few times, I had the staff apartment to myself when the others were out of town on a litnessing road trip or some other mission. When that happened, I could go out late at night without anyone noticing, so the next time I knew I would be alone, I arranged a secret rendezvous with Keiko at her place. Around midnight, when I was certain the leaders and other members in the building were asleep, I snuck out and hurried up the lane. As soon as Keiko opened the door, I was in her arms. Words weren't necessary.

I was ignorant and inexperienced, so I followed her lead. After locking lips in a steamy make-out session for a while, she set up her futon on the floor. When she began undressing, I did too. We lay on the futon, our naked bodies entwined, and resumed kissing, but I wasn't exactly sure how to initiate penetration. Hoping she would make the first move and guide me, I waited too long and ejaculated prematurely.

I didn't know if this was her first attempt at sexual intercourse too, or if she was more experienced and so perhaps disappointed by my awkward performance. I left almost as quickly as I came, self-consciously embarrassed, though not enough to stop me from trying again.

I had no intention of telling Abby and Laadah about this sexual tryst with Keiko. Mindful of how Brother Sun was reprimanded for his flirty-fishing sexcapade, I was sure they would disapprove. Keiko was also trying to keep our affair a secret from her uncle. She was worried her nosy neighbour might tell him if she saw or heard me coming and going late at night, so she came to my place the next time I was alone for the weekend. However, considering the almost Shakespearean way we were discovered, we were apparently star-crossed, just like the playwright's forbidden lovers.

We had just started to make out, playfully rolling around on the floor semi-clothed, when the floor itself began to rock and roll. It wasn't us making the earth move, it was an earthquake! When an earthquake strikes, it can take several seconds for you to realize what's happening. Our sexual arousal probably also delayed our reaction as the building began to sway, until things started falling off a shelf.

We jumped up and dashed to the window, sticking our heads out to see what was going on. Abby and Laadah were doing the same thing in their apartment directly above. Looking down, they saw two heads where there should have only been one and called out to me. Caught in the act, I didn't know how to react. Keiko left, and I never saw her again.

Abby and Medad interrogated me the next day. I confessed to secretly meeting Keiko alone several times, without going into all the details. They insisted on knowing those details, though, specifically wanting to know if we had sex, and worrying about negative consequences for our mission if I had impregnated her. I didn't know if conception was possible with that one clumsy attempt to copulate. Too embarrassed to explain what had happened, I simply shrugged, so they asked me directly if I'd ejaculated inside her. I felt humiliated describing my first sexual experience to them. Although it is possible for pregnancy to occur without penetration, they seemed relieved, but still scolded me for my secrecy.

The leaders became more concerned about the situation when Keiko's uncle told them he was aware of our illicit liaison, probably by hearing from her elderly female neighbour. Keiko's parents didn't live in Tokyo, so her uncle was acting as her guardian. When the leaders learned that her father was a policeman, they worried he might cause trouble if he found out and disapproved of Keiko's involvement with us. They thought it was too risky to allow me to continue my relationship with her, so to cool things down they banished me from Tokyo.

I soon left on a road trip to Shikoku island, where my next sexual encounter got me into more trouble. My partner and I were staying in a youth hostel in the city of Komatsushima when I woke up in the middle of the night with the worst abdominal pain I've ever experienced. I suffered for hours, barely enduring the agony, waiting for the day to start. My worried partner told the hostel manager, who suggested I go to the Red Cross hospital, which, fortunately, was right across the street. My partner insisted I go, but I resisted at first, reluctant because of my indoctrination.

Berg taught that God allowed sickness to punish us for our sins or to test our faith. He made it clear from the beginning that going to a doctor showed a lack of faith and trust in God's healing power. One of the earliest Mo Letters was "Faith and Healing," published in 1970. It concerns Japheth and Hannah, the leaders of the Port Alberni commune I originally joined. They were among Berg's earliest followers, and that year were living with him and about 150 others on a ranch near Thurber, Texas. Called the Texas Soul Clinic, it was owned by Berg's former employer, televangelist Fred Jordan.[6]

In that letter, Berg describes the difficulty Hannah was having in birthing her first child. Most of the children born in the group had been home births, but the women who assisted with those were not prepared to deal with Hannah's situation. Her labour began three weeks early, and after three days there was no sign of progress. Hannah was exhausted and getting weaker, and her midwives were increasingly concerned that they didn't have the experience or equipment to deal with a difficult case that might require surgery and an incubator for the baby.

Berg describes visiting Hannah on the third night and encouraging her with Bible verses to keep trusting God. He expresses disappointment that Japheth, Hannah and her helpers were all losing faith that the child could be born naturally, without professional medical assistance. He uses the example of his own refusal to go to a hospital when he had appendicitis to criticize their decision to finally take Hannah to the hospital.

> That's what I did with that attack of appendicitis. I just told God, "Lord, I'm not going to do a thing."…Some people play "chicken" with God! They figure if God doesn't do it, they'll go to the hospital at the last minute! This is not faith! Faith never considers the hospital! Faith knows God will do it!…What kind of faith do you have? How far are you going to go with God?[7]

I didn't know if God was punishing me for my sins or testing my faith. Regardless, hours of excruciating pain eventually overpowered my fear of failing God. I agreed to go to the hospital. After an examination in the emergency ward, I waited unbearably long for the blood test and X-ray results, moaning, groaning and pacing around the waiting area.

When I finally saw a surgeon, he explained I had an infection, probably in my appendix, but he couldn't know for certain unless he opened me up. He gave me the option of trying antibiotic medication first to see if that helped. I told him I couldn't pay for either treatment, but he said to forget about money for the moment. I was delirious from the intolerable pain and desperate for it to end, so I asked him to make the decision for me. He sent me straight to surgery.

As they wheeled me into the operating room, I was dreading both the surgery and the consequences of disappointing God and my leaders. The kind nurse who prepped me must have noticed how nervous I looked, because she comforted me by holding my hand as I went under. Afterwards, the doctor told me he'd operated just in time, as my infected appendix had been close to rupturing. If it had, it could've caused serious problems, even death, if left untreated. My indoctrination almost prevented me from getting that treatment. Pain probably saved my life.

I spent the next few days recuperating in the hospital. When I was well enough to walk around the ward, I recognized an attractive young woman in another room down the hall. She had been in the waiting room when I was pacing around, and would smile at me each time she caught my eye. She'd seemed unusually forward, like she was flirting with me, but I was too distressed at the time to engage with her. Now I noticed a male visitor in her room and assumed he was her husband or boyfriend.

Later, when I walked by again, she was alone and waved me over. She didn't speak much English, but the few words and phrases each of us knew in the other's language were sufficient for simple small talk. I had memorized some of our gospel songs in Japanese, so in an attempt to witness to her, I offered to sing one for her. She suggested we find some place where we wouldn't disturb the other patients in her room. Naively, I let her lure me to a vacant area on another floor.

When she led me to a nook with a bench, the last thing I was expecting was a bit of nookie. Soon after I started to sing, she suddenly reached through the front of my hospital robe and began stroking my penis. Shocked, I stopped singing. She then started sucking it. I didn't know that oral sex was something people did, so I was stunned, unsure what to do and worried someone might come along, but too aroused to resist. After I ejaculated in her mouth, she tried to kiss me. Disgusted by that, I pushed her away and hobbled off as fast as I could, feeling conflicted and ashamed that I'd let it happen.

My partner visited me while I was recovering to tell me he had informed Abby and Medad, and they had arranged for him to pay my medical bill. After that, I never saw him again. I assumed he went to the nearest commune, in Osaka, but when I went there after I was discharged, I learned he'd left the Children of God and returned to the United States. I feared that my situation had contributed to his backsliding, which added to my guilty conscience over the surgery and sexual encounter.

According to Berg's dogma, God allowed my appendicitis for a reason, so Abby and Medad came down from Tokyo to find out what that was. Suggesting I was out of God's will in some way, they pressed me to confess. In my fragile state, as I faced another interrogation about sex so soon after the first, it didn't take much pressure to break me.

If God was testing my faith with the illness, then I failed him by having surgery. If he was punishing me, I wasn't sure why. It was like I was back in the Catholic confessional booth, childishly trying to think of some sins I must've been guilty of. I couldn't think of anything I'd done to displease God before my illness that Abby and Medad hadn't already dealt with in Tokyo. Needing to confess something, though, I told them about the gaijin hunter in the hospital.

This time, they didn't need to worry about a pregnancy or angry relatives, so they didn't condemn me for having oral sex with a stranger, but I wasn't off the hook. After condemning any sins I might have committed, including causing my partner to stumble and backslide from God's will, Abby and Medad said they were concerned that my pattern of problematic behaviour when not closely supervised was a security risk. My tendency to get into trouble could endanger the mission, so to prevent that and punish me, they said I had to return to North America. I considered this a kind of death sentence, given America's imminent destruction.

They told me I needed to raise the airfare myself through litnessing, which seemed to me like asking a condemned man to make the rope he would be executed with. I had no choice, though, so while still sore with stitches I hit the streets to sell literature. Perhaps my success at quickly raising the required cash proved to them that I had repented and submitted, or maybe they had just been bluffing, because they commuted my sentence, allowing me to stay in Japan. I remained based out of the Osaka commune for a few more months, until I was arrested by an immigration officer.

— — —

I got into trouble again when I went on a visa trip to South Korea and got lost in Seoul. My visa for Japan was only valid for six months, so before it expired I had to leave the country in order to get a new one. I followed the footsteps of other foreign members who renewed their visitor visas by taking an overnight ferry to Korea, then returning to Japan a few days later. South Korea had a large and rapidly growing Christian population, so Koreans were generally receptive to the literature we passed out. That summer of 1974, the team in Seoul needed extra help with a special outreach opportunity, so I ended up staying about a month.

In 1973, Seoul had hosted Billy Graham's largest-ever evangelical "Crusade," attended by more than three million Koreans over five days.[8] Now, in August 1974, there was another massive evangelism conference at the same location in Seoul.[9] It was organized by Campus Crusade for Christ, which had sponsored a similar spiritual festival in Texas called Explo '72.[10]

The Texas event was considered the Christian version of Woodstock, which Jesus People groups and the Children of God attended.

The evangelistic gathering in Seoul was more churchy, and we were not authorized to distribute literature, but that didn't stop us. Our four teams of two mingled with the multitudes, stealthily passing out as many Mo Letters as we could before we were stopped. We kept on the move, with one eye out to avoid officials, but they soon became aware of us. I saw one team being escorted off the grounds. The rest of us continued until we were all eventually caught and evicted.

The commune was located on the outskirts of Seoul. It was a long bus ride to the busiest commercial areas, so sometimes litnessing teams stayed in the city for a night or two in a cheap Korean-style inn. I went one weekend with five others. We split into three teams to cover more territory. Late Saturday afternoon, while following the flow of the throng, I wandered away from my partner. I wasn't worried, as I knew how to find our prearranged meeting place for dinner.

When I took a break to have a beer in a small bar, a young, off-duty US serviceman struck up a conversation. He told me he was an intelligence officer. I wasn't exactly sure what that meant, so I didn't try to witness to him. He bought me a couple more beers, and by then I was feeling good enough to make bad decisions. Ignoring my own dinner plan, and the consequences of going AWOL from my mission, I accepted his invitation to buy me a meal.

We took a short taxi trip to what turned out to be a strip club near the US military base in the heart of Seoul, where we were soon joined by his friends. I was a clueless Canadian kid completely out of my element, partying with a rowdy crowd of American soldiers. Increasingly intoxicated, and mesmerized by titillating topless dancers, something I had never seen before, I lost track of time until I was out of it.

I had forgotten about the midnight curfew that had been imposed during the Korean War and continued under the current martial law. As closing time neared, and soldiers stumbled out of the strip joint with girls on their arms, I suddenly realized I had no idea how to get back to the inn where my companions were. It was too late to take a bus back to the commune, and I hesitated to use my litnessing money for an extremely expensive taxi to the suburb. I had to get off the street, though, so I decided the leaders would prefer I pay the fare than be arrested.

I hopped in a cab, relieved I was safe, until I realized the driver had no intention of taking me all the way. After driving about fifteen minutes, he suddenly stopped, pointed to his wristwatch and refused to go farther. I begged him to keep going, but he wouldn't budge, explaining in broken English that he had to be off the street too. Refusing to pay him, I stepped out of the cab, stranded on a dark, deserted street.

To avoid the police, I got off the main road and stumbled down a side street, searching for a spot where I could wait out the night. Out of nowhere, a woman appeared and started talking to me. I couldn't understand her, so she grabbed my hand and tried to tug me along with her. I resisted at first, unsure of her intention, but she was insistent and I had no other options, so I followed her down a lane toward a dim light, thinking maybe she was taking me home. She brought me to an open window where a man sitting at a counter asked me if I wanted a room. I couldn't understand the signs in Korean on the wall behind him, but the situation seemed sleazy.

I was reluctant to spend my money on a questionable room if it wasn't necessary. I didn't want to return to the commune empty-handed; it was going to be hard enough to explain my disappearance to the leaders. I gave the man a couple of Korean Mo Letters, and tried to explain that I was a missionary and couldn't afford a room. I asked if there was somewhere I could sit for a few hours, but he didn't seem to understand me. It was a warm summer night, so I decided to just squat on a spot across the lane and wait until buses started around 4 a.m.

The man in the window could see me sitting out there. Half an hour later, he called me over. He must've realized I intended to spend the night in the alley, and took pity on me. He indicated I could stay in a room without paying. I was wary as a woman led the way, and shooed her away when she tried to stay in the room with me. Moments later, another woman appeared at my door, but I rejected her too. They got the message that I wasn't interested, and finally left me alone.

I was too frightened to fall asleep, though, fearing I might be robbed, or worse. I kept the light on and my clothes too. Struggling to stay awake for the next few hours, I tried to think of excuses for my disappearance. As soon as I heard early morning traffic, I left and caught a bus back to the commune.

The team in town had informed the leader when I didn't return to the inn, so he was relieved that I was safe. I hadn't thought of a credible excuse, so I told him the truth about what happened. He didn't discipline me. Instead, he left that up to Abby and Medad, who were responsible for the mission in Korea and, coincidentally, were arriving in a couple of days on a previously planned trip.

Perhaps my tale of transgression with US servicemen prompted some sympathy from those two military veterans, because when they questioned me about it they weren't as hard on me as I expected. This time, they were more like parents holding back a smile while chastising a child for something they've done themselves.

That wasn't the only accidental adventure I had during my stay in Seoul that summer. South Korea's military government was led by President Park Chung-hee, a former general who came to power in a 1961 military coup. More than once while out litnessing, I encountered student-led protests against his authoritarian government as they clashed with heavily equipped riot police and soldiers, and had to flee from the confusion and tear gas.

On August 15, 1974, I got caught up in a protest with a different purpose. I was in town litnessing when my partner and I began hearing reports that a foreigner had attempted to assassinate the president. We called the commune for instructions. The leader didn't know any more than we did, so he suggested we stay off the street for a while in case the assassin turned out to be a westerner. We bought some street food and went to a small, walled garden park to wait for more details. We still didn't know what was happening when a group of chanting protesters entered the park, followed closely by a squad of soldiers who locked the lone gate behind them.

Everyone in the park became virtual prisoners for a couple of hours, which was probably safer for us in that volatile situation. As soon as we were freed, we returned home and learned that the failed assassination attempt occurred during a speech the president was giving to celebrate Korea's independence from Japan, its former colonial ruler. The assassin, who was an ethnic Korean born in Japan and a North Korean sympathizer, did kill the president's wife and a bystander.

Another time, I was litnessing on a crowded street when someone deliberately bumped into me, pushed a piece of paper into my hand and hurried off in the opposite direction. It was like those cut-and-paste ransom notes you see in movies, but instead it warned about a secret tunnel used by infiltrators from North Korea.

The spectre of war with the North haunted the South. The oil crisis had severe economic effects, including rationing of the country's most important staple, rice. Martial law imposed ridiculous rules on citizens,[11] such as limits on the length of men's hair and women's miniskirts, and soldiers stationed everywhere guarded against the turmoil of protests by a society in transition. I was glad to return to the peace and stability of Japan, though the risk of war was just as real there because of the numerous US military bases around the country.

— — —

I celebrated my nineteenth birthday with sake and squid on the overnight ferry back to Japan. With a new visa, I was able to stay six more months. During the year I spent in Japan, I had several run-ins with police officers in various cities, always while I was litnessing. Usually, it was just a curious foot-patrol officer working out of a *kōban*, a small neighbourhood police office. Often, they didn't speak much English, so they would simply record my passport or alien registration information and tell me to leave the area. I was never formally arrested, although once I was taken into a main police station in Tokyo.

It was just my luck that one of the few times I forgot to bring my ID with me, a police officer stopped me. I was selling literature outside the Tokyo zoo, and he asked to see my passport. When I couldn't produce it or an alien registration card, he made a radio call. Within minutes a cop car came, and they ordered me into the back seat. A little boy of about five was there and started crying louder when I got in. They took us both to the station, where I nervously waited while they located an English-speaking officer.

When I was finally able to explain that I'd forgotten my passport at home, but that someone could bring it in for me, they let me make a phone call. About an hour later, Medad brought my ID and gave the officer some explanation that seemed to satisfy him. They let me go with a warning. I never thought much about that incident, or any of the other times I was stopped by police, until I was caught by an immigration officer who threatened to deport me for breaking the law.

After my trip to Korea, I returned to the Osaka commune and spent the next few months litnessing there and in other cities in the region. While on a road trip, my partner and I plastered posters depicting a map of Israel surrounded by the Antichrist's armies. It was also the cover of the doomsday Mo Letter "Israel Invaded" that we were selling.[12] It warned of America's imminent destruction and the invasion of Israel by Russian-led international forces that Berg claimed would result in the endtime battle of Armageddon.

My partner and I were selling the letter outside a train station, each at a different entrance. I was hopeful when a man appeared to reach for his wallet after I said, "*Sukoshi kifu kudasai*" ("Please donate a little"). Most people gave us coins, so if they pulled out a wallet, it usually meant a larger donation. But instead of handing me paper money, he asked for my papers and showed his ID. He was an immigration officer. When he told me my visitor visa didn't permit me to earn money, I knew I was in serious trouble. Police officers who previously stopped me for ID checks never brought that up.

I suspect someone who didn't like Berg's message, or foreign proselytizers, had complained to his department, so he'd set a trap to catch me in the act. I expected him to take me into custody, but instead, he simply confiscated my passport, gave me his business card and ordered me to report to his office the following day. After he left, I searched frantically for my partner, hoping to find him before he got caught too. We informed our leaders of the situation, but I really had no options. I had broken the law by violating my visitor visa conditions. I couldn't hide, at least not for long, and couldn't run without a passport, and so had to report as ordered.

I wasn't the only foreigner from a fringe religious sect being interrogated in the immigration office. Seated at the desk next to mine was a member of the Hare Krishna. I had encountered other foreign proselytizers around Japan, such as the Moonies and Mormons, but they didn't compete with us on the street like the Hare Krishna did. Selling literature was just as important to those Hindu evangelists as it was to the Children of God, and just like us, they probably ignored the law to do it.

It appeared the immigration officers were playing the same good cop/bad cop routine with both of us, so seating us beside each other was probably deliberate. First, they made me wait awhile before someone finally came and started berating me in broken English for breaking the law. After spending several minutes denouncing my delinquency, he pointed to the Hare Krishna member, said I would be deported like him, and then left me alone again to nervously await my punishment.

The next official who came was calmer and spoke better English. He was looking at a file that probably included documents related to my border crossings, visa renewals and alien registration application. Although electronic data and file sharing through computer communication had barely begun in those pre-Internet days, it's possible the file also contained reports from police in other cities who had stopped me.

He told me I could be deported, but I didn't know how the process worked, so I asked where they would send me. He said it would be up to me, which I assumed meant I could simply go to another nearby mission field. That wouldn't have been the worst outcome, since I was intending to do that soon anyway. Instead, he unexpectedly said I could stay if I made a written statement promising to obey the law and not earn money during the two months remaining on my visa. Relieved, I wrote and signed the statement. He gave my passport back, and I immediately returned to Tokyo.

Abby and Laadah were now living in a western-style house in a residential neighbourhood in Nerima, four subway stations from the Ikebukuro apartment building. They wanted to keep an eye on me until I left Japan, so I moved in with them and their staff. Since I couldn't go out litnessing, I mostly helped with shopping, cooking and household chores.

When I'd left Hawaii, I hadn't expected to remain in Japan for a year. My original destination was supposed to be Hong Kong. Now, leaders had a new plan for me. The recently established mission in the Philippines was beginning to expand. An American-Filipino member had set up a front group that enabled foreigners to get two-year missionary visas, which prevented the kind of immigration problems I had in Japan.

The Manila commune sent out a recruitment cassette tape of songs and messages inviting members to move there. Laadah encouraged me to go by telling me there were several single sisters there, thinking that might motivate me. She was right. One of them was a Filipina named Maria who enticed me with her siren songs.

Chapter 10
Welcome to the Jungle,
or The Guest Who Wouldn't Leave

In the spring of 1975, I left Japan for the Philippines, where I had a two-year missionary visa. Filipinos were very receptive to our gospel message, which wasn't surprising, considering that around ninety percent of the population is Christian and it has the world's third-largest Catholic population. This was advantageous, considering the affinity many Catholics had to our mission, and Berg's emphasis on evangelizing to them. Filipinos are also extremely hospitable, so road teams always had a free place to stay, usually with people we met while proselytizing. Sometimes priests offered us a room in their church, perhaps as a way to scrutinize the strangers evangelizing in their territory.

In smaller towns with fewer street crowds to sell to, we often went to high schools and asked for permission to pass out free pamphlets to the students. Principals of both Catholic and public schools permitted us to pray with the children and give them literature, either all at once in the morning assembly, or in their classrooms. With captive audiences of hundreds of students saying the salvation prayer and getting Mo Letters, we easily boosted our statistics.

When I wasn't on the road in the provinces, I lived in the crowded capital, litnessing to the millions in Metro Manila. The leaders of the mission, Zichri and Shalisha, lived in a three-bedroom bungalow in a walled complex of middle-class homes in Marikina, one of the sixteen cities composing the metropolis.[1] He was a Filipino-American who helped set up a front organization so that foreign members could get missionary visas. She was an American too. About half of the dozen or so members of the commune were foreigners. The other half were locals, including Maria, the Filipina whose seductive singing had lured me there.

Maria was a few years older than me. She had dropped out of the University of the Philippines to join the Children of God. I had a crush on her, so I tried to spend as much time with her as I could. That wasn't easy, since our lives were tightly scheduled and we had little time for ourselves. Sundays were our only days off from scheduled routines. It was a free day for rest and recreation, but we weren't really free to do whatever we wanted. We didn't have personal money, so our options were limited to what the leaders permitted and the commune could afford. That usually meant only inexpensive activities, like picnics at a popular swimming spot on the Marikina River.

Some Sundays, I was able to spend several hours alone with Maria. She played guitar, and I had learned basic chords after joining the Children of God, so we practised songs and recorded them on a cassette tape I sent to my family in Canada. Other times, we went for walks in some of her favourite spots, sometimes in the warm rain, which she loved to do. One time, I went with her to visit a relative. If we had some free time before lights out, I spent it with her.

One day, Shalisha assigned me to accompany Maria to a medical appointment. She was examined for excruciating menstrual pain she suffered every month. Afterwards, she told me the abnormal pain was caused by her tilted uterus, which would likely shift to a less painful position after pregnancy. It occurred to me that I could help with that and end her suffering, but we didn't have a sexual relationship, and I was too shy to suggest it. Although I was falling in love with Maria, I didn't know if she felt the same way. I found it difficult to discern the difference between gestures of sisterly love and romantic love.

The old marriage and dating rules still applied in the Philippines. No singles were sexually sharing, and I wasn't aware of anyone who was flirty fishing either. I think Shalisha recognized and subtly encouraged my crush on Maria, though. That may be why she sent me with her to the doctor, and it might've also been Shalisha's idea for Maria and I to be part of the team setting up a small outreach base in central Manila, as a satellite colony of the main commune.

Commuting by bus from Marikina to litnessing spots around Manila consumed valuable time. Teams regularly got trapped in one of the city's notorious traffic jams. A downtown base eliminated that commute. After John, a Filipino member, and I found a small apartment within walking distance of lucrative litnessing locations, Maria and Chronicles, a Canadian I knew from the Nanaimo commune, moved in with us. We spent our days on the streets, from mid-morning to early evening.

Early one evening, when John and I returned to the apartment, Maria wasn't there. Chronicles said she'd gone to her relative's place to see her parents, who were visiting from the island of Mindoro. I was suspicious, wondering if Maria knew beforehand of their visit, and if so, why she didn't tell me and went alone. Whether she knew or not, I feared her parents planned to persuade or coerce her not to return to us, especially when she didn't return that night, or call to say she was all right.

I remembered the address of Maria's relative, whom I had visited with her once. So, desperately hoping that's where she was, I went alone first thing the next morning without informing Zichri and Shalisha, or waiting for their instructions. When I got there, I was relieved to find a friendly reception. Her relative invited me in and introduced me to Maria's parents.

I asked to see her, but they said she was still sleeping, so I made small talk with them for a while. They were concerned about Maria's future and wanted her to return to school or come home with them. Unsure of how it would play out, I remained calm and friendly, and asked if I could at least speak to her before I left. She eventually came downstairs, appearing groggy. Suddenly, without saying anything, she ran out the door.

We all froze for a second, not sure what was happening. Then I jumped up and dashed out the door too, chasing Maria down the middle of the street. Without looking back to see if we were being followed, I caught up to her. She flagged down a taxi and we jumped in before it had fully stopped. She said they had given her medication, probably sleeping pills, and wanted her to leave the Children of God.

I didn't know what to think or do, so I just followed her lead. Her first thought was to go to the mountain city of Baguio, so we went to an inter-provincial bus depot. But she changed her mind once we got there, and decided to wait out the situation instead. Reluctant to return to our apartment or commune, she called a former classmate, who put us up in her Manila apartment for a few days.

We had disappeared from the group without permission and couldn't be traced by anyone. Our leaders would've certainly ordered us to return, so we didn't call them. If Maria was struggling with doubts and deliberately delaying a decision while she weighed her options, she didn't tell me. I was obliviously happy to be with her and didn't care if I got in trouble. I probably would've followed her anywhere in the heat of the moment, even if she decided to return to her real life.

For the next few days, lost in a fantasy romance, I ignored my mission. We roamed the city, ate her favourite foods from street vendors and market stalls, saw a Filipino movie I couldn't understand, walked hand in hand on the seawall along Manila Bay, and cuddled and kissed in the glow of a spectacular sunset. Alone in the apartment one night, we made out awhile, which led to heavy petting and an unsuccessful, awkward attempt at sexual intercourse, like that time with Keiko in Tokyo. But our short love story was about to come to an end. With little money left and no plan, we had to make a move, so Maria called Shalisha, who convinced her to return.

Fleeing and hiding from relatives was fairly common among members of the Children of God, so we didn't get in trouble for that. However, the leaders clearly didn't trust us to be left unsupervised in the downtown base, so others took our place there. We moved back to the commune. A few days after we returned, a brother asked me to take a walk with him around our gated community. It was Sunday, so this was not an unusual request, but I suspect I was intentionally manipulated into leaving the house for a while.

When we returned and neared the house, I saw Maria a block and a half up the street, carrying a suitcase, walking toward the exit gate. I called out to her several times, certain she could hear me, but she didn't turn around or respond. I stood stunned in the middle of the road, completely confused about what was happening. Zichri and Shalisha heard me shouting, came out of the house, and explained that Maria was backsliding, leaving the group and God's will. They said I needed to let her go, and recited Luke 9:62: "No man, having put his hand to the plough, and looking back, is fit for the kingdom of God."

My heart broke in that moment, torn between my hopeless love for Maria and my fearful love of God. If she had turned and called me to come with her, I might've left too, but she didn't, so I didn't. Instead, my indoctrination kicked in. I obeyed my leaders and remained a prisoner of God's will. They never shared with me Maria's reasons for leaving, no doubt to protect me from her doubts. I felt betrayed by how my leaders handled the situation, and let down by Maria, but I couldn't get her out of my mind. A few months later, I regretted not going with her when I had the chance.

Perhaps to help me get over Maria's defection from our endtime army, the leaders sent me north to Baguio. Daniel, an American, and his Filipina wife, Ruth, led the small commune there.[2] Soon after I arrived, Daniel told me that while he was praying the Lord revealed to him that I should change my Bible name, from Obil (the camel driver) to Michael (the archangel), so I did. Everyone had called me Obi for short. Now they called me Mike.

Baguio City, a mile high in the centre of the highland province of Benguet, had a population of about two hundred thousand. The relatively fresh air and cooler climate were a pleasant relief from Manila's pollution and the sweltering tropical heat of the lowlands. The subtropical highland climate is ideal for growing vegetables not suited to extreme heat, making the province the salad bowl of the Philippines, supplying about half of the country's fresh produce.

Once a week, we went around to every stall in the public market and begged for donations of food to support our missionary work. Generous vendors never failed to provide us with plenty of vegetables and fruit, and sometimes eggs, fish and meat, although I think most assumed we fed the poor with it, not ourselves.

Our house was within walking distance of the main parts of town where we litnessed, including the large park in the centre of the city, where we sang and danced to attract people. Some evenings, a few of us sang our gospel songs in coffee houses and bars that had open-mic nights. Road teams also regularly travelled to towns in the other northern provinces. I spent a few months there, and when I returned from one of those road trips, Daniel told me that I was being sent back to Manila.

— — —

I loved living in the cooler north under Daniel and Ruth's laid-back leadership, so I would've stayed if given a choice. There were now two communes in Manila, and new leadership. An American military veteran was now in charge of the Philippine mission. He was much stricter, and many of the new rules and policies he implemented seemed arbitrary and unnecessary to me.

I felt fairly free serving the Lord my first year in the country, but the new rigid regime made life less enjoyable than it had been under the previous leaders. Zichri and Shalisha were more easygoing, like the Filipino people, while the new leader at the top of the hierarchy was more like President Marcos, the dictator ruling the Philippines by martial law. I soon faced wrathful punishment from both.

One day, police arrested me for jaywalking across a major thoroughfare that circles Manila. Jaywalking was common on the crowded, traffic-jammed streets, so suddenly being arrested for what pedestrians did everywhere in the city confused me. In the police van, another arrestee explained that this was part of the military government's law-and-order campaign, cracking down on petty crime in Marcos's New Society.

At the police station, an officer fingerprinted me and ordered me to report to the headquarters of the Philippine police force the next weekend. Camp Crame was a major detention centre for anti-Marcos rebels, so that worried me, but he said I was being sent there only for a day of lessons on obeying the law.

About a hundred others who had also violated minor rules, like breaking curfew, were seated with me in a hall, separated by gender. The officer who lectured us for about an hour spoke mostly Filipino, with a few English words and phrases thrown in. At one point, he noticed I wasn't paying attention, so he shouted at me to stand up. He waved his pistol in my direction and criticized me for breaking the law as a guest in the country. He ordered me to sit with the women, probably trying to humiliate me. He must've made a joke or insulted me in Filipino, because everyone laughed.

After the lecture, we marched outside to a marshalling field and lined up in rows. I was shocked, scared and unsure when several military transport trucks drove onto the field and toward us. After loading us into the trucks, the convoy drove us to a construction site in the middle of Manila, where we spent the rest of the day digging a ditch in the intense tropical heat and humidity.

The new leader of the Philippine mission criticized me for having that avoidable run-in with the law, but he was more concerned about rule violations that threatened his authority. One of his new policies required us to address leaders as "sir" or "ma'am," as a way to improve compliance and conformity. I thought that formality was unnecessary and felt awkward saying it. I also resented the stricter discipline and harsh reprimands for what I considered trivial matters. It didn't take much to provoke an unreasonable rebuke or punishment.

One day, my litnessing partner and I were late getting back to the commune. Zichri and Shalisha would've just shrugged off our tardiness as an unavoidable fact of life in Manila, but the new leader furiously criticized us. When we argued over whose fault it was, that enraged him more, so he decided to make an example of us. In the early years of the group, David Berg had a policy of forcing people who had personality clashes to spend all their time together until they learned to get along.[3] So that's what the leader did with us: he sent us on the road together indefinitely and said not to return until we had changed our attitudes.

He also demoted us to "friends" status, which meant we couldn't take any members-only Mo Letters with us, only public letters to sell. Being demoted and kicked out like that for such a trivial matter shocked me. It was like pouring salt into the emotional wound I still had from Maria's mysterious departure. We left the next morning and headed to Olongapo, the site of an American naval base at Subic Bay.

Americans gave generously, so after a few hours of litnessing we had enough to rent a cheap room. Over the next days, I continued to bitterly dwell on our unreasonable punishment and resented the leader for it. I kept my increasingly negative thoughts to myself, though. We were well-indoctrinated not to voice doubts or do anything to cause others to stumble and lose faith. I also didn't want my partner to talk me out of an impulsive decision.

I waited until we were litnessing in different spots before breaking my invisible chains. When he was out of sight, I snuck back to our room to get my backpack. I took the cash we had stashed there, and the remaining supply of Mo Letters. With no plan other than to pray that God would direct my path, I headed for the highway and hitchhiked back to Manila. My second ride was with a retired teacher who offered me a room in his home for a few days while I decided on my next move.

I still believed in Berg's endtime prophecies, so I wasn't ready to return to my old life in Canada even if I could. The only money I had was from a week of litnessing. With one year left on my missionary visa, I decided to wait it out and stay in the Philippines as long as I could. I hoped some cataclysmic endtime event would occur before then that would determine my next steps. I intended to continue spreading the message and living by faith, begging for money, food, services and shelter, just like I had done on all my road trips. I would trust God to provide and guide my way.

There was a hitch in my independence plan, but I didn't let it stop me. My passport was still in the Manila commune. For safekeeping, the leaders kept the passports of members like me, who had alien registration ID cards. It was the only possession I still had there that was worth retrieving, but I knew they would try to persuade me to change my mind about leaving, so I didn't go back to get it.

I wanted to avoid encountering members, so I planned to get as far away as I could from all five communes, which were in the north and central Philippines. At Manila's port, I eventually found a sympathetic shipping agent who gave me free passage on a small cargo ship headed to Mindanao, the southernmost island in the Philippines. Both communist and Muslim rebels were actively fighting the Marcos regime there, and had kidnapped foreigners, so it seemed unlikely I would run into members there.

The island-hopping trip took a couple of days, so I slept out on the open deck alongside a few other third-class passengers, and ate the same simple but nutritious food the deckhands ate. Life in the Children of God had accustomed me to eating whatever was available or offered, regardless of circumstances or conditions, especially when travelling in remote locations with few options.

One of the other passengers spoke fairly good English. He was going to visit his mother during her village's annual fiesta and invited me to join him, which I took as a sign from God. When the ship arrived in Cagayan de Oro on the north coast of Mindinao, we went straight to the bus station. While my companion paid his fare at the ticket counter, I asked to speak with the manager and was directed to his office upstairs. Handing him a Mo Letter, I explained I was exploring the region for my missionary group and begged him for free fare.

My new friend looked puzzled when I got on the bus without a ticket, but I offered no explanation. We were on our way to Portulin, a small barrio of Medina, just over a hundred kilometres away. Today, the trip is only a two-hour drive on the highway, but that was still being constructed then, so it took our bus about eight hours to wind its way along the bumpy, dusty road hugging the coast, stopping at every town and village along the way.

It was twilight when my companion suddenly called out to the driver to stop. We seemed to be in the middle of a jungle. At first, I saw only palm trees and other tropical vegetation, but then I spotted a few bamboo houses on the ocean side of the road. The bus left us in a cloud of dust, and once that settled I saw a few more houses on the other side. One of them was his mother's humble hillside hut.

Strolling around the next morning, I realized the village was larger than it first appeared in the dark. Word had already spread that there was a foreign visitor. When I stopped to chat with a few people setting up a fiesta stage in the square, they seemed relieved when I told them how I met the guy I arrived with. They explained that his mother was one of the poorest villagers, so it would be more appropriate for me to stay in one of their homes instead. I later learned they were concerned because he had a bad reputation.

The barrio captain said I could stay in his home, proudly explaining that it was the only one with a refrigerator, but Ricky had invited me first. He was a security guard in Medina, and his wife, Gloria, was a teacher at Portulin Elementary School. They spoke better English and were closer to my age, so I preferred to stay with them in their bamboo-stilt house near the beach.

Ricky showed me around the community, pointing out the outhouse I should use and the communal well where I could take an outdoor bath. When he learned I played guitar, he encouraged me to join the performers onstage that evening. I borrowed a guitar and sang some Children of God songs and a few by Simon & Garfunkel, Cat Stevens and John Denver. When I sang Denver's "Country Roads," they enthusiastically sang along. The music helped me break the language barrier and befriend the entire village.

Afterwards, Ricky and Gloria led me in the dark to an extremely comfortable mosquito-netted bed. I was exhausted from three days of travel and a long day of festivities, so I collapsed before realizing it was the only one in the house. The next morning, I was embarrassed when I realized they had given me their bedroom and slept on the living-room floor. I apologized and insisted I would sleep on the floor the next night, taking for granted that I was welcome to stay longer.

I was accustomed to living off the generosity of others in the Children of God. We justified our begging for material support as giving donors an opportunity to gain spiritual rewards, for "it is more blessed to give than to receive." (Acts 20:35) So I simply saw their continuing hospitality as God's providence, without considering any negative impact it might have on them. It didn't occur to me I was overstaying my welcome even when, a week later, Ricky suggested I move to his parents' place.

His parents and two sisters lived in a larger, wooden house on the hillside. Beside it, they had a partially constructed concrete-block house that had a roof and walls, but not much else. His brother slept there, and they let me stay in one of the unfinished rooms. For the next few months, they housed and fed me without asking for anything in return. I took advantage of their hospitality and became the guest who wouldn't leave.

A couple weeks after arriving in Portulin, I sent a letter to my family describing my latest journey and included a hand-drawn map to give them an idea of where I was. I didn't tell them I'd left the Children of God, though. A few weeks later, I got a reply from my mum with twenty dollars for my birthday; later, she sent more for Christmas.

I still had most of the money I'd left Manila with too. I had only spent a bit for food on my trip, and had few expenses while living off the charity of others in Portulin. I wasn't completely oblivious to the fact my hosts bore additional costs to feed me. Although they grew much of their food or harvested it from the jungle, they still needed to purchase things like oil, rice, sugar and spices, so I gave them a bit of money for some of those staples. They were grateful, even though it probably didn't completely compensate them.

I tried to help out in other ways too. One time, I joined them and their pack pony high up a jungle path to harvest avocados on their relative's property, which they sold in the Medina public market. Another time, I helped them make smoke-dried *copra* from the kernels of mature coconuts. They sold sacks of that to a coconut-oil producer. A few times, I visited Gloria's elementary classes to talk to the students about Canada.

Some days, I would go into Medina to explore the town, or wander far along the beach at Portulin. One day, I came across a few men sitting around a table outside a bamboo beach hut. They invited me to join them for a glass of palm wine called *tuba*, from the sap of palm trees that immediately begins to ferment when exposed to air. After finishing a gallon of the mildly alcoholic, naturally carbonated, delicious drink, they took me out in their outrigger canoe to check on their fish trap. Back onshore, they divided the catch, and one of their wives prepared a bowl of *kinilaw*—cubes of raw fish mixed with tuba vinegar, spices and juice from a lime-like citrus fruit called *calamansi*, ubiquitous in Philippine cuisine.

Everywhere I travelled in the Philippines, I experienced hospitality like that, only now I was fully dependent on it. When I first deserted the Lord's army, my intention was to continue evangelizing, supporting myself by litnessing and begging. But on my own, with no peer pressure, it didn't take long for me to lose my missionary zeal. I no longer proselytized, talked about my life with the Children of God, or distributed Mo Letters, unless it was to beg for a meal or a place to stay.

I still believed in Berg's endtime message, though, so I continued to bide my time, anxiously waiting for America's destruction, the collapse of the world's political and economic systems, and the rise of the Antichrist, who had to be alive if Christ was returning in 1993, as Berg predicted. I searched for signs in English newspapers in the Medina library whenever I went to town, hoping that some significant endtime event would soon end my predicament.

I had been in Portulin for several months with no obvious means of support. I often disappeared for days to visit other towns in the region, so it's not surprising that people grew suspicious and began gossiping about me. One laughable rumour I heard was that I might be some kind of foreign agent. My hosts never questioned me, though, and if they gave hints I should leave, I missed them. But I knew I had long overstayed my welcome and needed to move on.

With less than six months before my missionary visa expired, my time in the country was running out. The easiest way to renew that visa would've been to return to the Children of God. I wasn't ready to do that. So, in order to stay, I had to find a way to get a different visa. I decided to move to Cagayan de Oro, where I first landed. I had more possibilities of finding an opportunity to remain in the country in that large city. Its population of several hundred thousand was also large enough to produce income from litnessing if I changed my mind and returned to evangelizing for the Children of God.

Joe, one of the people in Portulin I often had long conversations with, told me his best friend, Jun, managed a motel in Cagayan. Joe said he was certain Jun would help me out and gave me an introduction letter for him. I took it as a sign I was making the right move. The referral letter from his close friend in Portulin helped me gain Jun's confidence.

I told Jun I was on a scouting mission for the Children of God, and gave him a couple Mo Letters. After learning I was from Canada, he offered me a shot of Canadian Club whisky and we chatted awhile. He was interested in talking about spiritual matters, and told me he recently met other missionaries who were members of Ananda Marga, a controversial tantra-yoga sect. They were as evangelical as the Hare Krishna and Children of God, and had a commune in Cagayan de Oro.

Jun gave me a free room and we had regular conversations during the week or so that I stayed there. He was a very kind man who probably would've helped me even without a referral from his friend. When the motel became fully booked, he extended his hospitality, inviting me to stay with him and his wife, Amy, and their three children, Whilcey, Sandy and Maris.

They lived nearby on a street bearing their family name, in a modern three-bedroom house behind a high brick wall topped by broken glass and razor wire. The only condition was that I would have to share a room with Whilcey, who was an autistic teen. Jun was very pleased to see Whilcey and me hit it off. Though he was mostly non-verbal, we connected on some level, probably because I talked to him no differently than I did to anyone else. He shadowed me whenever I was in the house.

Initially, I considered looking for a job, assuming that would allow me to get a work visa. I spoke with a lawyer who explained that I was only eligible for a work visa if I was indispensable to a potential employer because no Philippine citizen was suitable, able or willing to do the job. But I was a twenty-one-year-old high school dropout with no skills or work experience. It was highly unlikely I could find a job that fulfilled the visa requirements for foreign workers.

Other visa categories also allowed extended stays in the country, if I had a substantial amount of money. The only other way was to marry a Filipina citizen, but in my desperate situation, finding someone for a legitimate marriage, or even a marriage of convenience, seemed just as impossible as finding an eligible job. I was also reluctant to return to either the Children of God or Canada.

The only other way I could stay in the country was if Berg's predictions came true before I had to leave, and I became a refugee. So I continued to rely on Jun and Amy's hospitality, while waiting for America's destruction. I stayed with them for a couple of months, usually going out for the day and returning for dinner. Instead of making practical plans, I continued to delusionally delay the inevitable, until my hosts gave me a much-needed wake-up call.

At Christmas that year, 1976, they included me in celebrations with their extended family. At times over the evening, I sensed some conflict between a few relatives when they spoke Filipino, which I didn't understand. Everyone was very friendly with me, though, so I assumed either I misinterpreted the tone of their conversation or it was merely minor family tensions that typically arise on such occasions. It didn't occur to me that they might have been talking about the guest who wouldn't leave.

My hosts eventually had enough of my freeloading, but like those in Portulin, they didn't directly confront me and ask me to leave. Instead, I came back early one evening to find my backpack outside their front door. They had buzzed me through the security gate so I could get it, but wouldn't open the door when I knocked. I deserved to be evicted, so I didn't blame them, but I was shocked and not sure where to go.

Fortunately, I had befriended some of their neighbours, a small community of tinsmiths and labourers who were squatting on a block of land just down the street. Their weathered wooden houses and tinsmith workshop lined most of that block. I walked by every day, and often stopped to chat, so when one of them saw me with my backpack at the *sari-sari* convenience store on the corner, he spread the word that I needed a place to stay.

Although everyone's home was overcrowded, I soon had two invitations and ended up staying with a three-generation family in their two-storey house. They gave me a closet-sized room to sleep in. None of the houses had plumbing. On the opposite side of the property, there were four crude, seatless outhouses. There was a well in the courtyard, but the water wasn't potable, and so was used only for laundry and bathing. They got their cooking and drinking water from a water tap outside the sari-sari store.

I made quite a spectacle at the well each morning. Little kids gathered around and stared, while women washing clothes giggled at the sight of a skinny white guy in shorts taking an open-air bath. They teasingly told me the "white lady," a female ghost who lived in the well, would be attracted to me and probably pay me a visit at night. They might have been only half-joking.

Belief in the supernatural is widespread in the Philippines, so when I got extremely sick with a fever my new hosts called for a shaman, who performed an Indigenous healing ritual that included elements of Christianity. Chanting or praying in his native tongue, he first anointed me with oil, making the sign of the cross on my forehead. Then he moved his hands an inch over my entire body as if massaging me. At each joint he made a sweeping motion away from my body while forcefully blowing air in the same direction, perhaps to push maleficent spirits out. He ended by giving me a herbal concoction to drink.

The squatters treated me as one of their own. I often socialized with some of the tinsmiths, drinking tuba at the sari-sari store in the evening or hanging out with them on their day off. They took me to an illegal, clandestine cockfight, and another time, emboldened by alcohol, we helped one of them serenade a girl he had a crush on. One of them even asked me to be one of his compadres, a co-godfather to his newborn son.

I also spent a lot of time with Sammy, Sec and Third, a trio I met at a bar where I sometimes sang on open-mic nights. I often tagged along to their gigs around town, including nightly performances in a production of *Jesus Christ Superstar* during the 1977 Easter Holy Week. Through them I met a student at Xavier University who was the son of a government official in the South Pacific island of Vanuatu. He smoked cannabis, which I hadn't encountered before in the Philippines. It was a serious crime under martial law, and so was risky.

I hadn't smoked cannabis since joining the Children of God, so I got quite high and slightly paranoid when we smoked a couple of joints before going to a movie. The drug intensified my fearful reaction to *The Omen*, which was about the Antichrist as a child. It was a jolting reminder that the Antichrist was alive, according to Berg, and would soon instigate the final endtime events leading to Christ's return.

— — —

I was doing nothing but killing time, which was almost up. I had also used up most of my money. Shortly after Christmas, I received a card from my mum with a bit more, but I had been living for almost an entire year with-out any source of income and couldn't survive much longer. So, in my reply to her, I finally explained my desperate situation. Stranded with no money and needing to leave the country soon, I asked if she could arrange a flight back to Canada for me.

Although I accepted the inevitable, one last possibility remained that might've allowed me to stay in the country. One of the squatters frequently flirted with me. Nida, a single mother of a toddler, lived with her mother in one of the shoddier shacks in the back. Like many unwed mothers in the Philippines, she was stigmatized and shunned by some, but that didn't stop me from being friendly with her. We often sat and talked on her tiny porch.

When I explained my limited visa options to Nida and told her I had to leave the country soon, she quite boldly declared we could get married so I wouldn't have to leave. I'm sure she saw that possibility as mutually benefi-cial. I seriously considered Nida's proposal, so when she suggested I talk to her uncle about it, I went to see him. I thought he might encourage our rela-tionship as a way for Nida to escape her social circumstances. Instead, he discouraged marriage by reminding me of practical considerations. I was only twenty-one, with no money, job or reasonable prospects, living off the generosity of others. How would I support a wife and child when I couldn't even support myself?

That conversation was my final wake-up-to-reality call. My only option now was to return to Canada. My parents borrowed money from my mater-nal grandmother to pay for my airfare. They mailed me instructions on where to pick up my ticket, and included a bit of cash for travel expenses. I also sold a good-quality watch the leaders in Tokyo bought me when I was living with them.

Before leaving Cagayan de Oro, I threw a farewell party for my hosts to thank them for their hospitality. It was the least I could do, as it hardly made up for their generosity. They appreciated the gesture, though, and told me to invite my friends in the squatter settlement, so I bought enough food and beer for everyone. On departure day, a few of them came to the dock to see me off, including Nida, who was heartbroken, tears flowing down her face as I boarded the passenger ship to Manila.

When the ship docked a couple of hours on the island of Cebu, I rushed to the travel agent who was holding my airplane ticket. Back on board, I encountered two Children of God from the local commune, passing out Mo Letters to passengers before the ship sailed. I had lived with one of them in Manila, so we talked for a bit. It sounded like things hadn't changed much, and he didn't try to persuade me to return. It seemed that he agreed with some of my criticisms.

When I got to Manila, I booked a cheap room in a sleazy hotel, and immediately went to the Marikina commune to get my passport. Everyone was standoffish when they learned I wasn't returning to the fold. The leader informed me that because of my temporary-resident visa, I needed to apply for an exit permit in order to leave the country. If I had gone straight to the airport, immigration officials would've stopped me from boarding. That would've been disastrous, as I had no contingency plan and little money left.

The next morning at the main immigration office, I spent several hours standing in lineups and filling out forms. I panicked when one bureaucrat asked me for a letter from the police in the last city I'd resided in that confirmed I had no outstanding criminal charges. My flight was the next day, so there was no time to get that. My only alternative was to get an affidavit from the Canadian embassy attesting that I committed no crime while in the Philippines. I only had a few hours to get it before the immigration office closed.

I got a taxi and promised the driver double fare to drive as fast as he could to the embassy. It was like an action film as he raced at high speed, crossing lines, weaving through traffic, barely beating red lights. The consular officer was sympathetic to my plight, but it took a couple of hours before he had an official declaration from the deputy ambassador for me to co-sign. I rushed back to the immigration office with just enough time to finish the process and get my exit permit. The next day, I was in the air, backsliding to the doomed system, and returning to the family I'd left almost exactly five years earlier, in 1972.

Chapter 11
The Prodigal Child Returns

In the summer of 1977, a year after I left the Children of God, I returned to Canada. After three and a half years in Asia, and five years since I dropped out of the system to follow the endtime prophet, reverse culture shock hit me doubly hard. I felt like a foreigner in my own country, an outsider who didn't fit in. I was nearly twenty-two years old, a high school dropout with no work history, money, possessions or plans. Fortunately, I had a family to return to, which made my readjustment to life back in Port Alberni easier than if I'd had no one to depend on for help.

My parents' new house had one less bedroom. My sister Brenda had since moved out, and my nearly twelve-year-old sister, Crystal, had her own room, but my ten-year-old brother, Jay, had to share his with me. He was only five when I left, and didn't really know me, so I wasn't upset when he called me Meathead, after the counterculture character on the sitcom *All in the Family*, Michael—ironically, my religious alias.

I suspected Jay's sarcastic attitude toward me came from our dad, who had never accepted my decision to join a group of Jesus-freak fanatics. But it was more than that. Jay told me years later that he felt abandoned by his big brother when I disappeared from his life. He was right, of course. I had abandoned him, my sisters and my parents for what I thought was God's will.

Now, five years later, I was no longer certain what God's will was for me. I still believed in the Bible and Berg's endtime prophecies, but my indoctrination marred my mind, making it more difficult to reintegrate into society. My abnormal transition from adolescent to adult while socially isolated in the Children of God left me unprepared to live in the real world. I believed the world would soon end anyway, so it seemed pointless to plan my future. I just needed to get by until the Antichrist appeared, signalling the final few years before Christ's return in 1993. I kept my beliefs to myself, though, and never talked about my Jesus-freak life to anyone.

I applied for welfare benefits and gave my mum enough to cover my share of food and utilities. I also gave my grandmother $100 a month until I repaid the $800 she loaned my parents for the airfare. Receiving social assistance required taking workshops on resumé writing, job interviews and other topics designed to help young people enter the workforce. I accounted for the past five years by characterizing my overseas experiences as independent Christian missionary work. Without a list of employers or jobs, it was a very thin resumé, so fortunately I didn't need one for my first few jobs.

Nepotism helped me get my first jobs, at the pulp and paper mill where my dad worked, and then at the sawmill where my uncle and cousin worked. Although a life working in a mill was one of the things I was running from when I joined the Children of God, I thought I might be able to do it short-term. However, I quit the pulp mill after just one graveyard shift. I didn't even last a full shift on the green chain at the sawmill. Those union jobs paid well, the most I could expect given my lack of education and experience, but after my life in the COG I found it difficult to be a cog in the system's machine.

I wasn't well-suited for the physicality and monotony of manual labour. I was more of a people person. After a brief seasonal job at a herring process-ing plant, I was hired at a workshop for adults with various developmental disabilities, where my personality was more pertinent than my experience. Part of my interview included meeting and chatting with the clients. The job required a special Class 4 driver's licence for transporting clients in their passenger van. I only had a regular licence, which I got shortly after return-ing to Canada, but the manager was pleased with my amiable interactions with the clients, so he offered me the job on the spot. He gave me lessons in their van before I took the road test for that specialized licence.

That job was only subsidized for six months, but the experience enabled me to get other jobs that required a Class 4 licence. My next one was driv-ing a passenger van for the city's parks and recreation summer program for children. After that, I drove cabs for the two taxi companies in town. For the two and a half years I remained in Port Alberni, I was just spinning my wheels, going nowhere fast, waiting for the world to end. Although I anxiously scanned the news for signs of the expected global conflict that would lead to America's destruction and the rise of the Antichrist, I made no effort to prepare for those events. Instead, I drowned my worries in drinks and drugs.

After I had moved back in with my family, the monthly welfare I received wasn't sufficient to get my own place, but even after I started working, I wasn't in a rush to move out. Though now twenty-two, I still felt unable to stand on my own, having never lived alone. I was focused on adjusting to my new situation, trying to fit in, while feeling like an outsider hiding a secret past. If my parents and siblings were struggling with their own issues, I was too preoccupied with mine to notice.

It wasn't until my first Christmas back that I realized how rocky my parents' relationship was. My maternal grandmother and her partner were visiting on Christmas Day when my parents had an argument before dinner. My dad retreated to their bedroom, where he spent the rest of the evening sulking. It was awkward for everyone.

My relationship with my dad was very strained too. Still estranged, we barely spoke. When we did, it didn't help that he often ridiculed me with stinging sarcasm or snide put-downs, and called me "brainwashed" whenever I said something he disagreed with. He clearly still resented me for joining the Children of God. I wondered if he blamed me for their failing marriage. Another incident seemed to indicate that he did.

Walking home from the bus stop one day, I could hear, from the street, loud yelling inside the house as I approached. Not wanting to interfere, I hesitated at the entrance to the driveway. Suddenly, I heard the back door slam and saw my dad jump in his truck. He revved the engine and in a fit of rage raced directly at me. Swerving at the last moment, he barely missed me as I stepped out of the way. Shocked, I could hardly believe that happened.[1] Did he really want to harm me by running me down, or was it just an uncontrollable outburst of his pent-up anger toward me? Either way, he crossed a line, so I moved out soon after.

— — —

I don't know what was more shocking and confusing: my dad driving his truck straight at me as if to run me down, or meeting his mother, who I had always assumed was dead. He had never spoken one word to me about his parents. I did know he had an older brother, uncles, aunts and cousins in other parts of the province. We visited some of them a few times on summer holidays, but I never heard any stories about my paternal grandparents. I knew nothing about them, unlike my maternal grandparents, who lived in Port Alberni.

Growing up, I was intrigued by a framed photograph on my parents' bedroom dresser. It was of a woman wearing a long Edwardian-era dress, from what I called the "olden days." It fascinated me because I could see a strong resemblance to my dad in her facial features. All my mum told me was that it was Gramma Bulwer, my dad's grandmother. He never talked about her either, so I never learned anything else about her.

One other bit of information I learned as a child from my mum, after questioning her about my name, was that my dad named me Perry after his best childhood friend, and gave me the middle name Arthur after his father. That was the only thing I knew about my paternal grandfather. I learned young that questions about my dad's parents would be deflected or ignored, so I soon stopped asking. Perhaps they were just protecting me from details they thought I was too young to understand.

I did know that my dad and his brother lived part of their childhood with their aunt and uncle on a farm in the Okanagan Valley, in the Southern Interior of British Columbia. I have a few memories of visiting their farm on summer holidays. What I didn't know was why the boys had lived there, or what had happened to their parents. I don't recall any discussions they had about my dad's father or mother during those visits.

One time, I eavesdropped on a conversation and heard my dad talking about living on the farm and helping with the harvest, and about the time his brother got tied to the bed to stop him from sneaking food from the kitchen at night. He also described a memory of his mother boarding a train, leaving him and his brother behind. I gleaned from that bit of information that they weren't orphaned babies when they moved to the farm. That's the only time I heard him talk about his mother, though, and he never mentioned his father, so I could only speculate on the circumstances that brought the boys to the farm without their parents.

My dad honoured his father by giving me his name, which indicated that it was more likely he died than abandoned his family. But if his mother was a widow incapable of caring for her children on her own, why didn't she move to the farm with them instead of disappearing from their lives? Why didn't he ever talk about her to me, and why wasn't she involved in our lives now? Maybe she was dead too.

It wasn't until I began digging into my family history for this memoir that I finally learned some facts about my father's story. His first cousin Hamish created a genealogy going back to my great-grandparents, Benjamin and Laura, Gramma Bulwer in the photograph. My dad was named after her maiden name, Rodwell. They emigrated from England around the turn of the twentieth century. Their first of ten children, Mary, was born in England. She was the aunt who took in my dad and his brother. After the family moved to Canada, their second child, Arthur, was born in Vernon, British Columbia, which is where he married Ruby Sparks and their boys were born.

Hamish told me that Arthur died of tuberculosis when my dad was seven years old. For a couple years before that, Arthur was isolated in the Tranquille Sanatorium tuberculosis hospital in nearby Kamloops. Because of that quarantine, my dad had been unable to visit him during those years, so any memories he retained of his father were from when he was four or five years old. Perhaps those memories were too vague, and the death of his father too painful, to tell his son about his grandfather.

Hamish said that while Arthur was in the sanatorium, Ruby started running around with men, leaving her young boys alone at night, or bringing partiers back to her place. As her behaviour worsened, several neighbours became concerned enough about the boys that they called the police. After Arthur died, there was a family-court custody hearing concerning the children, who were then ordered removed from their mother's care and placed in separate foster homes. Their aunt Mary was eventually granted custody of the brothers.

If I had known my dad's story, I might have at least partly understood why he never talked to me about his parents or his childhood. But not knowing those facts, I always assumed both his parents died while he was very young, and that he had few memories of them to talk about. That's why I was so shocked when, out of the blue, my dad introduced me to his mother and half-brother.

It happened after I had moved out of my parent's house. When my mum called me one day to come meet some relatives, the last thing I expected was to be introduced to my grandmother, who I thought was dead, and an uncle I didn't know existed. Dumbstruck and confused, my head was spinning, trying make sense of this revelation. We made small talk, but our conversations stayed superficial, and I didn't ask her or my dad the questions I had. Had he always known she was alive and where she was? If so, why did he keep her a secret from us until now?

Perhaps I was hoping they would provide the answer to those and other questions in the various conversations going on, but that didn't happen. By the time she left a few days later, all my unasked questions remained unanswered. I still knew next to nothing about her or her relationship with my dad. I don't know if they stayed in contact with each other after that, but I never saw or heard of her again.

— — —

During the two and a half years I remained in Port Alberni, most of the socializing I did involved lots of alcohol. I also smoked cannabis regularly, which was almost as prevalent and easy to obtain, despite prohibition. Perhaps I was self-medicating to relieve the stress of my existential anxieties. I remained chained to dogmatic Christian indoctrination, and had difficulty conforming to a world I believed would soon collapse into chaos and end in 1993, when Jesus returned. My dead-end jobs were just means to an end while I waited for doomsday. Getting drunk and stoned helped me endure the wait.

Readjusting to the real world was difficult. Revealing my radical religious beliefs would've made it even harder, so I never discussed them with anyone. I kept my past a secret and friendships superficial, staying emotionally aloof, never letting anyone get close enough to know the real me. How could I? I was a stranger even to myself, living an unexamined life. I had platonic female friends, but I was unwilling to get intimately involved with a woman who didn't share my beliefs, which impeded any possibility of a romantic relationship. I was a lonely twenty-four-year-old virgin.

By the summer of 1979, it had been three years since I left the Children of God. The last time I had spoken with any member was two years earlier, in Manila. Then, one day in July, I encountered two members litnessing in the parking lot of a liquor store. I was sitting in my car, waiting for a friend who was buying booze, when one of them approached and offered me a Mo Letter. She got excited when I told her I was a former member.

She opened a notebook with a list of friendly contacts that included my parents, with my name next to theirs, and asked if that was me. I had mixed feelings about this encounter, but sympathetically offered them a place to stay overnight. I was now boarding with an uncle and aunt. They were out of town on a summer holiday, so I had the place to myself.

Initially, I intended to avoid any serious discussion with them, so I brought them to the house, set them up, then went to a party with my friend. I planned to stay out late, until I was certain they would be sleeping, but after a couple of drinks my curiosity got the better of me. Eager to know about Berg's latest endtime revelations and predictions, I left the party early and spent a few hours talking with my guests about some of the developments in the past three years.

The most significant information they shared was not related to Berg's endtime timeline, which was still on track, but rather to the fact that the Children of God had recently gone through major organizational changes that were particularly relevant to the reasons I left. They also had a new name, the Family of Love. Before leaving the next morning, the two disciples gave me the contact information for two Family homes, one in Courtenay, about an hour and half drive from Port Alberni, and the other in Vancouver.

— — —

The first thing that struck me when I visited both Family homes in the fall of 1979 was that they were single families, which was a significant change from the group's previously mandatory communal lifestyle. Both were preparing for the coming chaos of war. The couple in Courtenay was planning to live in their travel trailer with their three kids and drive down to Central America. I knew the couple in Vancouver from years earlier, when we'd lived in the Victoria commune. They now had four children and were about to move to a rural refuge outside of Salmon Arm, a small town in British Columbia's Southern Interior.

During my overnight visits with those families, I was able to read a few Mo Letters explaining recent organizational changes. The most significant change had come in 1978 with the Reorganization Nationalization Revolution (RNR). Berg demoted three hundred top leaders he said were abusing their power and authority over regular members, or disobeying him in some way.

Berg created a new centralized leadership structure and reporting system that gave him direct, dictatorial power over his followers, while seemingly giving them more democratic decision-making control of their day-to-day lives. He declared: "The king is taking back the reins of government and we're going back to a direct dictatorship! It's going to be a very benign, liberal and loving dictatorship."[2]

One of the many Mo Letters related to the RNR, "Dear Friend or Foe,"[3] was addressed to former members like me, encouraging us to return to the fold and promising that we would have a greater say in how things were done at the local level. That letter seemed to validate my reasons for leaving the group in the Philippines, so I foolishly fell for the apology it contained and was persuaded by Berg's sales pitch that things had really changed for the better.

In November 1978, while Berg was implementing the RNR, Jim Jones was murdering over nine hundred members of his Peoples Temple cult in Jonestown, Guyana. The Children of God had faced negative publicity since its inception, but Jonestown raised the level of public concern over alternative religious groups living outside society's norms. Berg tried a few tactics to counter the intensified scrutiny of the group, including changing its name to the Family of Love.[4]

Berg also ordered larger communes to split into smaller ones, limited the number of Americans in each non–US commune, and encouraged those affected by the changes to pioneer in new places or even return to their home countries. They were mostly superficial changes intended to deceive the public that the Children of God had disbanded and no longer existed. It was a lie, of course. A cult is the same by any other name. In May 1979, Berg wrote "To the Media — From a Guru — About the Sects":

> They call us a "cult" or a "sect," which…today means any crazy bunch of religious fanatics that just doesn't happen to belong to one of your major faiths, or anyone who differs or disagrees with you!…You're going to have to outlaw all of the major religions, because all of them began as sects and cults!… Personally, I'm sick of hearing about the cults and the sects and how dangerous they are!…The established systems are far more dangerous!…Don't worry: we won't hurt you!…We've already disbanded!…So now what are you going to do about us?[5]

The number of Family homes doubled during this period as communes split up and members dispersed. While many still lived in smaller communes, changes established by the RNR, which included different levels of membership, meant that individual families could live on their own and still receive the group's publications.

Each Family home, whether communal or individual, now mailed their monthly activity reports and tithes (ten percent or more of their income) directly to World Services (WS), the group's clandestine administrative and financial operation firmly under Berg's control.[6] In return, each home received the latest Mo Letters, books, magazines and audio cassette tapes of Family music and Berg's sermons. To strengthen their direct connection to Berg, whom most members, including me, had never met or seen, even in photographs, they were now encouraged to write to him directly if they had any concerns or complaints.

After the Jonestown massacre made headlines around the world, Berg instructed his followers to keep a low profile, limit litnessing, blend in more with the system, and even get jobs if necessary. But that was temporary. In the summer of 1979, Berg began remobilizing members with a ten-part series of instructional letters titled "Have Faith, Will Camp"[7] and a twenty-five-part series titled "Have Trailer—Will Travel."[8] He encouraged them to return to evangelizing while living in campers, trailers or motorhomes, like they had in the group's formative years. Mobile living made it easier to flee from communities or authorities opposed to their presence, which the Family always considered to be persecution for preaching the gospel.[9]

That summer, Berg also began pushing members back onto the streets to sell Mo Letters. Disruptions caused by the RNR restructuring and Jonestown publicity caused a drastic drop in literature sales and, consequently, in tithes to WS. That prompted Berg to write a letter demanding disciples step up their sales of Family publications, or else they would lose access to the latest Mo Letters.[10] It was an effective threat, since Berg's followers were indoctrinated to equate his words to God's Word.

— — —

Meeting those two Family members who were on a road trip in the summer of 1979 stirred many memories of my former life. Just a few weeks later, while still in that reflective, emotional state of mind, I had two experiences with pop culture that I believed were divine signs related to that encounter. It was after those experiences that I visited the two Family homes to learn more about how the group had changed.

First, I saw the coming-of-age movie *Breaking Away* about competitive bicycle racing. In the movie's inspirational climax, the injured protagonist gets back on his bike after falling and, cheered on by the crowd, wins the race. I felt a surge of spiritual emotions as I recalled a Bible verse I'd memorized years earlier: "Wherefore seeing we also are compassed about with so great a cloud of witnesses, let us lay aside every weight, and the sin which doth so easily beset us, and let us run with patience the race that is set before us." (Hebrews 12:1) I saw the movie as a metaphor. I had stumbled and was out of the spiritual race for a while. Now God was telling me to get back into the race, while angels and departed believers cheered me on from the spirit world.

Shortly after that, I heard the song "Gotta Serve Somebody" from Bob Dylan's new gospel album, *Slow Train Coming*. I interpreted it as an even more direct message from God. When I first heard it on the car radio, I immediately parked so I could listen to the lyrics. It was astonishing to hear Dylan paraphrasing the same scripture that Children of God recruiters first impressed on me seven years earlier, when they encouraged me to drop out and serve Jesus: "No man can serve two masters: for either he will hate the one, and love the other; or else he will hold to the one, and despise the other. Ye cannot serve God and mammon." (Matthew 6:24) The song evoked a strong emotional reaction. My indoctrination had been reactivated.

While I was considering the changes in the Children of God, and contemplating the divine signs calling me to return to the Family, I suddenly became homeless. When my uncle verbally abused me in a drunken rage, I packed my bags and moved out the next morning. For the next few weeks, I slept on couches, first with a friend and then with my cousin, until I finally found my own furnished apartment. It was the first time in my twenty-four-year-old life that I lived alone, but it didn't last long.

A couple weeks after I moved in, my landlady gave me an eviction notice without any warning. She lived directly below me and claimed I was making unreasonable noise. I was shocked by her unreasonableness, but I was too inexperienced to know I could've fought the eviction and probably won. That was the last straw. I gave up trying to conform to worldly expectations.

In some ways, life with the Children of God had infantilized me. My abnormal adolescent transition to adulthood within the strictures of a secretive, socially isolated sect had not properly prepared me to handle the responsibilities, difficulties and uncertainties of living independently in the real world. I saw my inability to stand on my own and secure stable housing as another sign directing me back to my spiritual life as an itinerant evangelist.

For quite a while, I had been feeling unfulfilled, frustrated and lonely, living a mundane life while waiting for doomsday. Serving God with like-minded disciples in the Children of God had given my life meaning and purpose, and provided many exotic adventures. Now, with no anchors keeping me grounded in reality, nothing was stopping me from returning to them. So, before my eviction took effect and I had to find a new place, I decided to drop out a second time and rejoin what I was convinced was the new and improved Children of God, rebranded as the Family of Love.

One of the road-team members I put up that summer was a Chinese-Canadian woman, Fai Lok, an alias meaning "happy." She had kept in touch by letter, and her latest one had come a month or so earlier. She had moved to Halifax on Canada's East Coast, joining a Family commune consisting of a married couple with five children, a single mother with two children, and a single brother. She invited me to join them, and included a phone number, so I called her and told her to expect me there in a couple of weeks.

My mum choked up when I told her my plan over the phone, just as she had the first time I told her I was leaving home. At that time, she didn't know anything about the Children of God, so didn't know how to dissuade me. Realizing she couldn't stop me this time either, she wanted to know one thing: if I had children, would the leaders take them away from me? I was taken aback by her question. I hadn't talked with her about my time in the group, but she was obviously aware of some the criticisms and allegations made against it.

I was still conditioned to respond to all allegations of abuse as lies concocted by enemies persecuting God's people, so I downplayed my mum's concerns and assured her that it wasn't true. I explained that there were child-care helpers who cared for and taught the children during the day, but over the four years I was in the group I wasn't aware of any situation where children were taken away from their parents. That was true, at least in my limited experience. However, Berg's writings certainly made that practice possible, particularly as the second generation grew older. It took me far too long, but I would eventually realize that my mother was right to be concerned for the welfare of children in the Family.

Chapter 12
On the Road Again

In early December 1979, I separated from the system a second time and left Port Alberni to rejoin the Children of God, now known as the Family of Love, or just the Family. I had accepted Fai Lok's invitation to join her in a small commune in Nova Scotia, on the opposite side of the country. I spent the entire six-day, six-thousand-kilometre train trip from Vancouver to Halifax in a coach car. I was on the road again. My indoctrinated mindset and missionary zeal were re-emerging as I returned to the Family and a life of constant change. In just a couple of months, I would be headed back west, but not alone.

Although it was Fai Lok who enticed me to come to Halifax, it was Rachelle, a single mother of two, whom I soon hooked up with. Aaron, Angie, their five children, and a single brother, Nicholas, also lived in the row house, which they rented using welfare benefits. I'd met Aaron years earlier in Vancouver, and again in Hong Kong when I'd passed through on my way to the Philippines.

It took me a while to learn about all the new Family policies and practices. There were over three hundred Mo Letters published during my absence, and with new letters arriving every week, it was difficult to catch up on all the old ones. They fit into a few general categories: 1) random letters describing Berg's various dreams, visions, spirit trips, prophecies and predictions, and relevant world events; 2) lengthy Bible lessons and sermons; 3) two long series promoting the mobile ministry and providing practical advice for camping and living in travel trailers; 4) a long series of letters revealing previously unknown details of Berg and Zerby's flirty-fishing sexcapades in England and Tenerife; and 5) numerous letters detailing administrative changes related to the RNR.

Some changes in Family culture were immediately obvious to me. The power dynamic in communes was certainly different. Previously, I had no control over what home I lived in or what country I went to. I did what leaders told me to do and went where they told me to go. Now members had more freedom to make those kinds of decisions for themselves.

Also, members dissatisfied with the leader of a Family home could now vote to replace them, join a different home or set up their own. Aaron and Angie were reporting as a Family home before the others moved in with them, so they were the leaders by default, but they didn't have absolute control over the rest us.

Another obvious change was the sexual ethos of Family culture. When I left the group, flirty fishing and sexual sharing between members were not yet practised in the places where I lived. I had read the earliest Mo Letters introducing those new doctrines and practices while I was in Japan and the Philippines, but wasn't aware of any members in the homes I lived in who were FFing, or any singles having sex with each other. Both were happening in the Halifax home.

We mainly evangelized on the streets or door-to-door, but Fai Lok and Rachelle also went FFing together, sometimes in a club. From their conversations afterwards, it seemed to me similar to the way we had witnessed in bars, restaurants and other social venues in the early years of the Children of God, except for the sexual flirtation. I also realized they were both having sex with Nicholas when I overheard them scornfully ridiculing him behind his back over his persistent neediness. It sounded like they reluctantly took turns satisfying his sexual needs, not out of desire, but as an obligation.

Having not read all the Mo Letters on the subject yet, I didn't know if there was a casual-sex protocol for singles to follow. I was too shy to ask, and certainly wasn't interested in begging the women for pity sex like Nicholas was apparently doing. Maybe I just had a low libido or needed to feel some romantic attraction or emotional connection before pursuing a sexual encounter. Whatever the reason, having never asked a woman out on a date or had sexual intercourse, I didn't have the self-confidence to make the first move.

A couple weeks after I moved in, Rachelle approached me in the bathroom while I was brushing my teeth before bed and boldly blurted out a sexual invitation, asking me if I wanted to "share." I didn't know if she felt obligated to ask or was genuinely attracted to me, but I instantly said yes. If it had been Fai Lok who asked me first, I probably would've said yes too, and my life may have taken a very different turn.

Rachelle prepared bedding on the living-room floor, put on music and lit candles. With her long, lustrous, wavy brown hair, Rachelle was vivaciously attractive, and I was aroused by her playful flirtation, but my sexual inexperience made me anxious, and when I get nervous I talk, so we talked almost till dawn. We cuddled and occasionally kissed, but didn't copulate. She was probably waiting for me to initiate that.

We did consummate our sexual relationship the next night. It was my first time to go all the way. We started sleeping together every night after that. She was thirty-three, nine years older than me, with two children and two ex-partners, so was far more experienced. She often teased me over my sexual naiveté. It was more than just casual sex; we were becoming closer emotionally. I didn't have sex with the other two women in the home, and as far as I knew Rachelle stopped sharing with Nicholas, but I suspected that occasionally she still had sex with her children's father, who was not in the Family.

Rachelle's kids, Karen and Peter, were twelve and nine. She had recently joined the Family with them, recruited by her sister-in-law, Bobbie. Rachelle was in the process of divorcing Bobbie's brother, Steve, who was neither a Family member nor the children's biological father. That was a married man Rachelle had a long-term affair with before she married Steve. He was a businessman in Halifax, and both kids had his last name. Because their affair was illegitimate, Rachelle didn't tell her devoutly Catholic parents about Karen until a year after she was born.

Sometimes the kids' father would give money to Rachelle for them. She would meet with him and spend the night. I was certain they had sex, since there was no other reason for her to stay over, but we didn't talk about it. I don't know if it was her free choice, or if he demanded sex in exchange for money, and she felt obligated because the home was struggling financially. She may have considered sex with her ex as a form of FFing for financial support.

Less than two months after I arrived in Halifax, Rachelle got a phone call from Bobbie and her husband, Norm, inviting her and the kids to join them in Calgary. Bobbie had recently received a small inheritance and had used it to buy a school bus that had been converted into a motorhome. They were following Berg's latest instructions to hit the road with mobile ministries. Their initial plan was to travel around Alberta and British Columbia, visiting Family homes and evangelizing along the way. When Rachelle told them about me, I was invited too.

The Halifax home was not functioning well. We had already discussed shutting it down and going our separate ways, so the invitation was a timely opportunity. Rachelle and I both liked the idea of living on the road. I had fond memories of my road trips around Japan and the Philippines. Rachelle hadn't travelled nearly as much, but she was no stranger to alternative lifestyles. When she was married to Steve, they lived for a while in a teepee in Alberta, and then in a cabin in a hippie community on a small island near Nanaimo.

With few other options, and bearing in mind Berg's endtime predictions, we accepted their invitation. Living on the road would give us the ability to quickly head for the hills and avoid the chaos that would follow America's imminent destruction. Bobbie warned Rachelle there was limited storage space in the bus. I was used to living out of one suitcase and a carry-on bag, which was convenient for constant moving and quick escapes. But Rachelle hadn't yet experienced the luggage limit imposed by Berg in the early years.[1]

Rachelle and her kids had not yet been forced to forsake most of their belongings. It was particularly hard for the children to give up their things. They were not in the Family by their own free choice, but dragged into it by their mother. Karen, who was entering her teen years, especially resented having her freedom restricted and being forced to give up worldly activities, friends, classmates and most of her possessions. She just wanted a normal teen life, but life for Family children was far from normal.

Rachelle's parents purchased sleeping berths for our five-day train trip to Calgary. For the next nine months, we travelled around Alberta and British Columbia, visiting Family homes and going door-to-door in the towns we passed through, selling literature and yellow plastic buttons with slogans like "God's Only Law Is Love." Bobbie was also very skilled at convincing businesses to donate goods and services to us, including restaurant meals, groceries and gas. Having her niece and nephew with her helped when making appeals in person, as people were more likely to give when children were present.

Karen and Peter were still attending public school in Halifax before we left, but they had no formal education while we lived in the bus. Instead, they participated in all our evangelical activities. According to Berg, they didn't need schooling beyond the elementary level. He opposed secular education, insisting that studying the Bible and the Mo Letters was the best education for children being raised as endtime Christian soldiers. Most Family children were home-schooled, not only to shield them from worldly influences, but to hide deficiencies in their education from secular authorities.[2]

In May 1980, we visited the family I'd stayed with overnight in Vancouver several months earlier. They had since moved to a rural area in the Southern Interior of British Columbia and were stockpiling supplies to survive the coming war. While we were there, Mount St. Helens erupted in Washington state. The destructive volcanic explosion spat out a gigantic ash cloud that spread over a dozen US states and into southern BC. We were astonished to see the sky ashened from that explosion eight hundred kilometres away.

That made us realize there was a much greater threat from Washington. The US Navy base on the Kitsap Peninsula, just 160 kilometres from the Canadian border, had recently armed its nuclear submarines with new Trident intercontinental ballistic missiles, so it would likely be a target when the Cold War turned into a hot one. If dust from the eruption could reach southern BC, then so could radioactive fallout from a nuclear attack on that base. A safer refuge would need to be farther north, or much farther south.

That same month, Berg published "The End Is Here". In the late 1970s and into the early '80s, much of the developed world suffered a severe economic recession. It was also a period of military buildup and heightened tension between the US and the Soviet Union. Berg believed those developments were signs confirming his prophecies of impending system collapse and nuclear war.

> I do not see how this coming war can possibly be anything but the last one before Christ's coming for us....The end is coming, & it's getting mighty close!...Flee the country in this case, maybe even flee the continent....This should shake a few more of you guys up & get you out of North America! The end is here![3]

In July, just a year after Berg encouraged members still in the US and Europe to live on the road, he changed his mind about the mobile ministry. In the letter "Keep Your Caravans at Home!" he renewed his calls to abandon America, and Europe too, instructing members to sell their trailers and motorhomes rather than shipping them overseas.[4] He made an exception for those in the US and Canada headed to Central America.

We received Berg's latest warnings and advice when we got to Vancouver. We decided to seek a safe haven in the south rather than farther north. Considering the volatile political situation in parts of Central America, we set our sights on the relatively safe, peaceful countries of Belize and Costa Rica. We began making preparations, including getting yellow-fever vaccinations. But before heading south, we returned to Alberta so Bobbie could help her disabled mother move into a senior's care home. While there, we watched TV coverage of Ronald Reagan's landslide victory in the November 1980 US election. He was our enemy, so that worried us.

— — —

Ronald Reagan was governor of California in the late 1960s and early '70s, when Berg formed the Children of God in Huntington Beach. After the group was accused of brainwashing its members, Reagan's special assistant for community affairs, the well-known African-American community activist Ted Patrick, became personally involved in helping parents rescue their children from the Children of God.[5]

In 1971, acting on a mother's complaint that the police would not search for her missing nineteen-year-old son, Patrick discovered that he had joined the Children of God. He then learned that the group had tried to recruit his own son. Patrick began an investigation, which included briefly joining the group under false pretenses. It was from his experiences with the Children of God that Patrick developed his controversial theory on how to extricate people from cults, and became known as Black Lightening, the father of deprogramming.[6] A 1974 report described his deprogramming process:

> Enter Ted Patrick, kidnapper of kids, deprogrammer of Jesus freaks. Black Lightening, as he likes to be called. His technique sounded a little heavy: getting parents to abduct their kid from a colony, locking the kid in a motel room for three days, berating the kid to "think for himself" until—sometimes—"the fever broke." The kids Patrick worked on often went through "relapses" and escaped back to the Children of God.[7]

Patrick started working closely with concerned parents and helped form the Parents Committee to Free Our Children from the Children of God (FreeCOG).[8] He and his accomplices began kidnapping and deprogramming Children of God members, with varying success.[9] Berg described Patrick as "a Satanist...who believes in voodoo and demonology...a Black devil!"[10]

That danger put the group on high alert, leading to the kind of serious security measures I was part of as a night watchman in the Burlington, Washington, compound. Securing our safety became a central feature of life in the Family, which included using aliases, fronts, secret cells, encrypted communications, nightly security checks and even home-invasion escape drills in the event of raids by authorities or enemies. We lived in a heightened state of fear, always ready to run at a moment's notice with packed "flee bags" prepared for any emergency.

Watching the results of the 1980 election, we considered Reagan's landslide victory over President Carter an ominous sign pointing not only to imminent war, but to increased anti-cult persecution, as Berg confirmed in a letter he wrote the day after that November vote:

> This vote was literally a vote for war, a possible war, & rearmament for it!…So [Reagan] became our bitter enemy, obviously, through being misinformed or informed by our enemies & tolerating their persecution & inquisition & deprogramming & all the rest. So I doubt if he's changed on that a bit. If anything, the Evangelicals who helped elect him will encourage him in it, to crush the sects & crush the cults & to persecute & deprogram. I'm sure he's thoroughly behind it.[11]

Reagan's election made us even more anxious to head south to safer foreign fields. However, our plan abruptly ended when the bus broke down on the highway between Edmonton and Calgary. Norm had it towed to his parents' empty farmhouse about an hour away, but after Berg's recent recommendation to abandon the mobile ministry, they weren't sure they would keep the bus after it was repaired. They intended to stay there until then, but the house was too small for all of us.

We were homeless now. With few options and almost no money, Rachelle and I decided going to Port Alberni was our best move until we could figure out a new plan. We were able to get travel assistance from the government welfare office, which paid for our bus, train and meals for the overnight trip. When I'd left Port Alberni almost exactly a year earlier, I was single and had one suitcase. I returned with a wife, two kids and about a dozen bags. We crowded into my parents' house and spent the Christmas holidays there, while we considered our next move.

After we moved into a three-bedroom apartment, we received a new Mo Letter that narrowed our options. Berg instructed members to give up the idea of surviving the coming war in a refuge of some sort. Previously, setting up survival refuges as a specific endtime ministry was always an option for members.[12] Now, in 1981, Berg changed his mind about setting up safe havens to survive the coming chaos of the Great Confusion. He wrote:

> Forget your God-damned refuge farms! The Lord is our refuge!
> Forget your damned survival supplies, you don't have to
> survive! Die for Jesus!...I don't want to hear any more about
> refuge farms & survival! Even in the hottest war zone in the
> world, which is going to be the U.S., I think you're wasting your
> time there in the first place! You ought to get out of the country
> & go to the mission field![13]

Berg's war-cloud warnings never stopped. As the doomsday clock ticked
down on his predicted timeline of endtime events, he grew ever more
convinced that nuclear war was just around the corner. He continued to
push members in North America and Europe to flee, suggesting half should
end up in South America and the other half in Southeast Asia and the South
Pacific.[14] If Berg was right, and endtime events were about to unfold as he
predicted, then a great war involving the US was necessary by 1985 at the
very latest. In November 1982 Berg wrote:

> For the Antichrist to begin ruling for seven years in 1986 & for
> the Tribulation to begin in 1990 & for the Lord to come in 1993,
> then the nuclear or great war has got to occur before 1986, with
> the Great Confusion following before the Antichrist arises! So
> the war has got to occur within the next three years —1983,
> 1984 or 1985![15]

I always hoped to return to Asia one day, so was excited by that possibility. Although Rachelle was a bit apprehensive, a new Family magazine
regularly featured testimonies from members around the world about the
success they were having in serving the Lord in foreign fields, which helped
convince her we could do it too. The magazine had frequent help-wanted
appeals for people to join established missions in various countries, so we
kept an eye out for a suitable opportunity.

We began saving sufficient funds for airfare and living expenses for the
first few months after arriving in whatever country we eventually decided
on. Because of a severe recession and high unemployment, I couldn't find a
job, but Rachelle had experience working for an insurance company, so she
was hired by the government office that processed employment insurance
benefit claims from laid-off workers.

Rachelle earned much more than I could've, and her office was so busy
that she frequently worked overtime, which allowed us to save quicker.
While she made the money we needed, I was a househusband doing most

of the chores, shopping, cooking and tutoring Karen and Peter at home. We had neglected their education while living on the road. Constantly moving made it easier to avoid the legal requirement that children attend school, but now, to avoid any trouble, we applied for an exemption to home-school them.

Rachelle and I met with the school district superintendent and explained that we were planning to move overseas as missionaries and would home-school Karen and Peter there, so wanted to start that transition now. He expressed some concern for their social life without other kids their age to interact with, but he granted us the exemption anyway. We were required to teach the official curriculum using the school system's correspondence courses. We also had to mail in their school work and tests for a certified teacher to check. So they got about two more years of formal education.

In the summer of 1982, we went to a weekend fellowship with about twenty Family members and their children from around British Columbia. We gathered at the homes of two families who lived on the same block of a quiet street in White Rock, a small city near Vancouver. Bobbie and Norm were there with their infant daughter; it was the first time we had seen them since parting ways a year and a half earlier.

They had sold their bus after replacing the engine and were soon leaving for Fiji in the South Pacific. They told us they believed the reason God allowed the bus to break down was that they hadn't been totally committed to Berg's sexual revolution during the year we lived with them. They apologized for not having shared sexually with us, which I found odd because I never considered it as necessary.

I interpreted Berg's sexual teachings from an altruistic perspective. In my mind, the sexual freedoms he promoted were intended for the purpose of sacrificially saving souls, and unselfishly satisfying the sexual needs of single members. Neither condition applied to our relationship with Bobbie and Norm, so I saw no need for us to share with them then, or now, but they wanted to make things right with God before they left for the mission field.

I feared appearing spiritually weak and unrevolutionary, so didn't object. Neither did Rachelle, but I don't know if she also felt obligated like me, or if she really did want to swap partners. That evening, we found two separate spots where we had about an hour of privacy. I spent most of it talking with Bobbie. The sex was very awkward and didn't seem spiritually revolutionary at all. Rachelle and I didn't talk about it afterwards.

In the middle of the second night, we experienced direct persecution for the first time. The couple whose house we were staying in had recently tried to recruit a woman and had received verbal threats from her relatives. Karen was sleeping on their living-room couch when someone shot a gun through the window. One of the bullets embedded in the wall had passed right above Karen. If she had been sitting up, it could have hit her. When the police came, they discovered an unexploded pipe bomb under the couple's van.

Months later, in February 1983, more persecution shook us up when we saw a TV news report about government officials removing thirteen children from a Family home in Richmond, another city near Vancouver.[16] One of the children was at the centre of a bitter custody dispute between two estranged parents. The father alleged in court documents that his three-year-old son had been sexually molested and physically abused, and that his common-law wife was planning to take the boy to India. Child protection authorities took the boy into custody and attempted to corroborate the father's claim, but concluded it was unfounded. Although there was insufficient evidence to lay criminal charges, the investigation continued, and three days later, the other twelve children were seized by child protection officials accompanied by a police officer. Two infants were returned to their parents shortly after, but the rest were placed in foster care. The government later announced it intended to seek custody of ten of the children for one year, on the grounds they needed protection from their parents, who were involved with the Family.[17]

Rachelle and I didn't believe the TV report we saw alleging sexual and physical child abuse. We later learned a few of the details from some of the parents involved. The father who had made those claims in his custody dispute admitted in court documents that he drank, smoked marijuana and was violent with his wife, so we saw this case as a Family mother protecting her child by seeking full custody, and the father retaliating with lies.

Although the Family had always faced negative publicity, media reports now often focused on the welfare of minors. Around that time, members in other countries also lost custody of children to relatives or governments out of concern for their well-being.[18] What we saw as persecution was hitting closer to home and seemed as real a threat for us to escape as the coming nuclear war. We had already moved to Asia in the summer of '83 by the time Berg wrote "Guard Your Children" at the end of that year.

> Quite a few of our parents have lost their children to Systemite mates, grandparents & relatives or even governments....All the latest articles have [claimed] we are the lowest, vilest, filthiest, nastiest people on Earth who abuse our own children & encour-

age sex & child pornography & blah blah blah!—And any court of law or smart lawyer could probably take some things we've said & twist'm & make'm sound like that....So in this new propaganda wave in this new form of attack...what advice would you give the Family? (Peter: I suggest that they go to the mission fields for a starter, because when you're not in your home country they've got less of a chance of doing something to you.) Right![19]

Karen made it clear she had no interest in moving to Asia with us, so we suggested she go to Puerto Rico, where a new Family commune was being set up for teens. We thought being around Family children her age would be more inspiring for her, but she refused that too.

She didn't say so, but Karen's reluctance was certainly related to the Family's beliefs and restrictive lifestyle, which she had not chosen for herself. She didn't have a normal teen life of going to school, socializing with classmates, having fun with friends and fads, and learning to find her own way in the world. She was dragged into the Family at the age of twelve by her mother, and now wanted her own life, which didn't include being a Jesus-freak missionary.

Now fifteen years old, Karen knew there was no way we could force her onto a plane. Our plan to leave Canada was her chance to break out of the box we tried to keep her in. It was easier to keep Peter in that box, shielded from worldly influences. He was too young to go anywhere alone. It was harder to keep Karen cooped up, so we gave her a bit of freedom and let her socialize with my sister, Crystal, who is about the same age. On weekends they often went to the roller-skating rink, which is where Karen met Monty and found her escape route.

She probably kept their budding romance a secret from us for a while, but eventually introduced Monty as her boyfriend. It wasn't long before she told us she was pregnant and that they wanted to get their own place together. It's possible Karen deliberately tried to get pregnant as part of her emancipation plan, although I doubt she would've been using birth control in the first place. I don't know how much sex education Karen got from her mother, but after joining the Family, whatever Rachelle taught her certainly came from Berg's writings. Everything he wrote on the subject instructed women not to use birth control of any kind, because it was "almost as bad as abortion, which is just plain infanticide, or child murder."[20] Karen may not have wanted to serve God with us, but she was still a Christian.

Having as many children as possible was God's will, according to the divine commandment in Genesis to "be fruitful and multiply." It was such a strong moral imperative for members, most of whom had multiple children, that Rachelle felt guilty about having had a tubectomy. She told me her ex-husband, Steve, had pushed her to do it, and now she wanted to undo it so she could have babies with me. Though the procedure is considered a permanent form of birth control, she said it was possible to reverse it.

I was actually relieved when Rachelle told me in Halifax that she couldn't have more children. I never had a desire to have kids, and the thought of bringing a baby into our unstable life terrified me, especially since I had been barely able to take care of myself. I didn't think now was an ideal time to have a baby, as we prepared to move to an uncertain situation overseas, and endtime events were about to explode. I wanted Rachelle to leave things as they were, but I didn't tell her how I felt for fear of offending her and revealing my lack of faith.

I agreed to go with her to a naturopathic doctor, who said her fallopian tubes could be reattached, but she would have a low possibility of pregnancy, especially since she was in her mid-thirties. I concealed my relief and used that information to convince her that the high cost of the low-chance surgery was money better spent on our missionary move overseas. Why bring a baby into a world that was about to collapse into chaos, I reasoned, when the millennial heaven on earth was just a few years away and we could have all the children we wanted then?

A few months after Karen turned sixteen, she moved into an apartment with Monty. She left the Family at the same age I had joined it. In hindsight, hers was obviously a much wiser decision than mine. Karen wanted to marry Monty, but minors under nineteen needed parental permission. We thought it was a bad idea that she might regret one day, so Rachelle refused to give her consent. We needed a court order to make my mum Karen's guardian, so instead we got a notarized affidavit stating Rachelle was giving my mum permission to make decisions on Karen's behalf, if necessary.

Our initial plan was to go to India, based on Berg's recommendation for Commonwealth citizens. We kept our options open, though, by answering a few appeals for help in the Family magazine. One was from a family in Macau, a Portuguese colony on China's southern border. The other was from a couple with two children in Malaysia. We didn't hear from the Macau family, so we accepted the invitation from the other couple to join them on the tropical island of Penang. We left Canada in the summer of 1983.

Chapter 13
Pearls of the Orient

In mid-1983, Rachelle, Peter and I arrived in Penang, the Pearl of the Orient. That Malaysian tropical island shares the title with a few other places, including Hong Kong and Shanghai. We would soon live in the former and I would visit the latter, but Penang was the perfect place to start our foreign adventure, especially for Rachelle and Peter. Our life there was fairly laid-back, so they were able to slowly adapt to the culture shock of living outside Canada for the first time.

Malaysian Esther and her Maltese husband, Ben, lived alone with their toddler and infant. Their home served as a guest house for foreign Family members living in Thailand who came to renew their visas for that country. Most of their monthly expenses were covered by donations from Family visitors and a subsidy from the regional office, which reduced the pressure of needing to raise funds.

Shortly after we arrived, we used some of the money we brought with us to help them move to a larger house. The new place was in a quiet residential neighbourhood just half a block from a small, semi-secluded sandy beach on the northern coast of the island. Another family living nearby had a couple of children around Peter's age, so he mostly stayed with them.

We limited our socializing with other members and were cautious when we congregated, because the law at the time criminalized meetings, assemblies and public gatherings of five or more people without a permit. Although that law was primarily for preventing serious public disorder, we didn't want to give anyone a reason to report us. We also had to limit our evangelism.

Islam is the state religion of Malaysia, and all Malay citizens must be Muslim. They are prohibited from renouncing Islam and converting to another religion, and it is illegal to proselytize Muslims. However, Malaysia is a multicultural society with large ethnic populations who are free to practise and propagate different religious beliefs. They can also be proselytized, so we distributed literature with the disclaimer "For non-Muslims only."

During the four months we lived in Malaysia, Rachelle and I didn't sexually share with Ben and Esther. There was no physical need to, and none of us suggested it. Although the spiritual motive for free sex among members was, according to Berg, to unite the Family as "one wife," the bride of Christ, we didn't think that step was necessary in our situation. I wasn't aware of any sexual sharing between members in other homes either, or of anyone who was flirty fishing. It was easy to ignore the new sexual freedoms now part of Family life, until a German family living in Thailand visited.

The three adults were in a polygamous relationship and had clearly embraced Berg's libertine sex advice more lasciviously than any members I had met so far. I was shocked by the lustful greeting I got from one of the women, unlike any holy kiss on the cheek I'd ever experienced in the Family.

I was sitting on a sofa reading when they walked into the house. Without getting up, I twisted my head back to say hello. Suddenly, the woman leaned over, grabbed my head and aggressively thrust her tongue into my mouth before I could react and pull away. I was so disturbed by her forcefulness that it triggered a traumatic flashback to when I was assaulted in a similar way by three men in Port Alberni after I returned from the Philippines.

A woman I met in a bar had taken me to her friend's house party. At one point, I was alone in the living room with three guys I didn't know. Suddenly, two of them tackled me to the floor and held me down while the third one tried to force his tongue into my mouth. I struggled helplessly, terrified they were going to rape me. Instead, they let me go and began laughing as I fearfully ran out the door. Humiliated by the violation, I was too embarrassed to ever tell anyone, and never thought about it again until that day in Penang.

The German threesome had three children who were in the first, most contagious stage of whooping cough. They probably mistook the early symptoms for a common cold, and so didn't warn us before they came. Ben and Esther's children, as well as Rachelle, got violently sick with the dangerous disease. Clearly, none of the children had been vaccinated, and if Rachelle had been as a child, it had worn off by then.

Berg didn't absolutely prohibit vaccinations, but he distrusted and discouraged them. His claims about vaccines in 1994 were echoed by other evangelical conspiracy theorists almost thirty years later, during the COVID-19 pandemic. The Antichrist, he wrote, is going to control people with the computer chip in their forehead or their right hand!—The Mark of the Beast, which is designed to control everybody, except we who refuse to take it. Now they're even able to sneak it in by vaccinations, so if you take vaccinations you're not apt to know whether you've got a chip or not! Scientists are making the chips small enough to insert with a hypodermic needle, & at the same time they're urging everybody to get inoculations!...Vaccinations have been a threat for years! When Mother Eve & I were living mobile in the trailer, rather than have our kids vaccinated we'd move to some other school where they didn't require it.[1]

Berg's scientific ignorance, conspiracy theories and spiritual peer pressure undoubtedly led to many unvaccinated Family children and the spread of contagious childhood diseases within homes, and from home to home.

— — —

After nearly four months in Malaysia, we received a message from the top leader of the Asia-Pacific region. Keda had read our letter replying to the help-wanted ad by the couple in Macau. She instructed us to go there as soon as possible to help them, so they could work full-time translating Berg's writings into Chinese.

All Family members knew Keda[2] from two stories about her published in June 1978. One was her testimony[3] of how she lived openly as a lesbian before meeting the Children of God in the US in 1972, but hid her sexuality from members after she joined. She describes her joy of coming out after reading Berg's "Revolutionary Sex" in 1973, where he claims that the Bible doesn't mention lesbianism and equates it to masturbation and sexual massage.[4]

Although Berg appeared to approve of lesbianism in that letter, he actually thought it was a perversion if the women weren't bisexual. Less than a year later, at the end of 1973, he wrote "Women in Love" and referred to Keda without naming her: "She's always been a lesbian, and to me that sounds like a form of perversion. When a girl has never had any normal desire for a man, I begin to wonder if it's a spiritual thing. It is certainly not normal or natural as God intended, therefore such Lesbianism is a perversion."[5]

The other publication that came out in 1978, at the same time as Keda's story, was a letter Berg wrote about her. After joining the group, she returned to her native Australia, where she became a top leader, eventually overseeing the entire region. Berg had assigned a woman, Toni, to be Keda's assistant and travel companion as she supervised Family homes around East Asia. However, Toni refused to have sex with her boss, and after a few months together they each wrote a letter to Berg explaining the situation.

Keda complained that she needed a sexual companion, but couldn't persuade Toni to have sex with her, and Toni asked for a transfer to a different job. In his scathing response, Berg bitterly denounced Toni for her lack of faith, selfishness and disobedience to him. "[She] reminds me of some of our selfish sisters in the Family who have gone all these years without helping one single brother, not giving one of them a tumble, not once! How selfish can they get?"[6]

Berg's thinly veiled threats condemning Toni for disobeying his and God's will were a clear warning to all Family members who were not submissive enough to willingly participate in his sexual revolution, or obey other dictates. Berg was spiritually coercing not only reluctant women to submit to sexual requests, but all members to yield to those with authority over them. The letter's title, "The Girl Who Wouldn't," became an epithet to spiritually shame those who didn't. That letter was on our mind when we got Keda's order to go to Macau.

Within days we were on the train to Bangkok, where we could get cheaper flights. The twenty-six-hour trip through the tropical countryside of Malaysia and Thailand reminded me of my train trips in the Philippines. Bangkok was much like Manila, too, with crowded streets and chaotic traffic jams. We stayed in a Family commune for a couple of days, waiting for our flight. The German threesome were among the dozen or so adults living there. It soon became clear that their overt lasciviousness was the norm, not the exception.

The night before our flight, the home held what I expected would be a typical inspirational gathering where we sang songs, circle danced and praised God, like the old days. Instead, it was more like a secular party with people dancing as couples. I hadn't seen that in any other Family home before.

The dance was in full swing when I returned late from a last-minute errand in town. I noticed people were leaving the living room in pairs, and realized this was a swingers' party. Apparently, I'd arrived in time to stop Rachelle from participating. She was slow dancing in a tight embrace with the German polygamist. I had never even danced with her like that. It was obvious he was lustfully seducing her, and she didn't seem to be resisting. I was instantly jealous and upset.

According to my understanding of Berg's Law of Love, sexual sharing was done out of love, not lust, and required necessity, transparency and the consent of all parties, which didn't apply to this situation.[7] But like lust, jealousy is one of the seven deadly sins, and demonic according to Berg, so I tried to suppress mine.[8] I managed to pull Rachelle away by telling her we needed to prepare for our flight the next day. The green-eyed monster hiding under my bed followed me from then on, and I eventually paid the price for harbouring it.

— — —

We arrived in Macau near the end of 1983. Situated on the west side of the Pearl River estuary, across from Hong Kong, it was still a Portuguese colony at the time. Macau was the first European colony in sixteenth-century China, and the last one remaining when China resumed sovereignty over the territory in 1999. Parts of the city are frozen in time. Centuries-old forts, churches, temples and neoclassical buildings stand in sharp contrast to the gaudy bright lights of modern casinos.

American Danny and Taiwanese Becky lived with their three young boys in a three-bedroom apartment near Senado Square, the historic centre of Macau. We arrived in the middle of a meeting they were having with other Chinese translators based in Hong Kong. We were surprised to see Keda there too, who was overseeing their work. She explained she had recruited us because, unlike most Family couples, we had only one older child, so we were well-suited for this situation. Taking care of Danny and Becky's children and running the home would enable them to focus full-time on translating Berg's letters.

Keda and some of the other visitors stayed overnight. That evening, I saw her play the "girl who wouldn't" card by pressuring the wife of a Chinese couple to have sex with her. The husband looked as disturbed as I'd felt the night before in Bangkok, suppressing my jealousy. Seeing Keda's carnal compulsion in person was unsettling, but the sexual scene in Thailand now made sense. She supervised the work there too, so on her visits she would've modelled practices she saw in Berg's household. After-dinner dances, like the one I saw in Bangkok, originated in Berg's home.

Top leaders like Keda sometimes visited Berg's highly secret home. He referred to them as bellwethers who led his flock, showing them how to obey his teachings and follow his example. Very few ever knew which country Berg and Zerby were living in at any given time. After fleeing the US in 1972, they had lived in various European countries until 1981, when they moved to South Africa for about a year. They were living in the Philippines when Keda visited in early 1984, shortly after we met her in Macau. Berg wrote six letters about her during that visit, known as the "Keda Series."[9]

Berg was such a narcissistic, capricious leader that he used an innocent comment Keda made to denounce her in an extremely disparaging diatribe filled with derogatory, demeaning language. He clearly felt his authority was threatened by her, so he attacked her sexuality. Declaring his disgust for lesbianism, he regretted approving it and now considered it as demonic as male homosexuality. He claimed it was the source of Keda's self-righteous pride and anti-male, anti-authoritarian, rebellious spirit from which she needed deliverance through an exorcism. Berg forbade her from further same-sex relationships, teamed her with a male partner, and renamed her Magdalene. We called her Maggie from then on.

Though Keda's behaviour in Macau made me uncomfortable, I felt honoured she had recruited us to help with Danny and Becky's important work. After being closed to the outside world for over twenty-five years, communist China was just beginning to open up, so I was excited to be part of that mission. Although we weren't personally evangelizing, the literature Danny and Becky were translating would reach far more people than we ever could ourselves. By serving them, we served God.

Rachelle cared for their five-year-old twins and toddler, while I did the shopping and most of the cooking, and helped wherever needed. Sometimes I went on outings with Rachelle and the kids, or took the youngest for a walk on the nearby seawall. Three times a week, I worked a few hours as an English teacher. Part-time teaching jobs provided many members with visas and financial support, and cover for their missionary work, especially in countries where proselytizing was restricted, or where selling Family products didn't provide sufficient funds.

There were a couple of other small Family homes in the city centre. On the outer island of Coloane, there was a larger commune where Berg's son, Jonathan,[10] lived with his two wives, Esther and Ruthie,[11] their six children, and a few other families. Known as Hosea, or Ho, he had been a top leader in the formative years of the Children of God. Although Ho was no longer part of the Family's leadership hierarchy, he was still respected as part of Berg's "royal family" and supported financially by his dad, or more accurately, by the money Family members tithed to Berg through World Services, the group's secretive financial operation.[12]

Ho's compound contained a few hundred-year-old conjoined Chinese cottages and a couple of small houses, in a rural village next to Hac Sa Beach, on Coloane's eastern shore. There was a bit of farmland and a small corral and stable that housed three retired horses from the Macau Jockey Club. They also had a donkey and a dog. Although the commune could accommodate about seventy people, there were about twenty living there at the time. We called it "the farm."

Ho had four sons around Peter's age, and the Hong Kong leader's son was also living there. Ho invited Peter to join them so he would have other teens to socialize with. There was one condition. We had to surrender our parental authority to Ho and consent to his disciplining Peter with physical force in the form of beatings with a wooden paddle if he considered it necessary. Ho was a stern disciplinarian who, like most Family parents, followed his father's biblical commandment to use harsh corporal punishment on children of all ages, from toddlers to teens.[13]

Without children of my own, I hadn't given much thought to corporal punishment. I had been spanked only twice in my life, once by my Grade 2 teacher with a wooden pointer, when that was still allowed in public schools, and once by my dad with a belt, when I was ten and got in trouble with the police. I had never spanked a child myself.

In Halifax, I'd known that Aaron harshly spanked his toddler son and older stepchildren behind closed doors, but I'd never seen Rachelle hit Karen or Peter. Later, in the bus and on our own, we never considered corporal punishment, even when Karen became rebellious, which is when she most needed to be beaten, according to Berg's dogma on discipline. That wouldn't have changed her mind, though; it would've just made her more determined to live her own life.

I couldn't imagine spanking Karen then, when she was fifteen, and I felt the same about Peter now that he was twelve years old. I didn't think Ho would ever have any reason to beat him. We discussed it with Peter, so he knew that corporal punishment was a possibility, but he was still excited to join other kids his age on a farm with horses that was right next to a beach. We didn't see Peter much after he moved to Ho's place. Some weekends, we visited him for recreational outings and Sunday fellowship with everyone. Peter rarely lived with us again after that, though we always travelled together on visa renewal trips or when moving to new countries.

At the beginning of 1984, shortly after moving to Macau, we received the Mo Letter "Guard Your Children," Berg's response to reports of Family children being seized by child protection authorities in various countries, including Canada, just before we left. He advised couples with children to get legally married as one way to avoid child custody problems.[14]

Though legally divorced, Rachelle still had her second husband's name, and Peter had his biological father's name. A few times when crossing borders, immigration officials asked why the three of us each had a different last name in our passports. To avoid that extra scrutiny and questioning, we took Berg's advice and got married at Hong Kong City Hall on May 4, 1984. Rachelle then got a new passport with my last name, which made our situation less suspicious and easier to explain.

That summer, Peter and I crossed the border into China to deliver new publications and other items to two families living there undercover as English teachers. In 1978, after twenty-five years of China closing its doors to the rest of the world, Deng Xiaoping, the new leader after Mao Zedong's death, declared an open-door policy. To boost the economy through international investments, Deng designated special economic zones to attract foreign companies. One of those zones was the city of Zhuhai, bordering Macau. Restrictions on the tourism industry were slowly ending too.

Initially, tourists could go only to select areas of the country as part of an official tour group. That restriction no longer applied when Peter and I went. The policy was fairly new, though, so the government agency that issued our visas insisted we hire a car and driver from them. They said it was for our own safety. It was really just a money grab, but it made our crossing easier. We felt like VIPs as we arrived at the border in a Mercedes-Benz and quickly passed through, while nearby a tour bus unloaded its passengers for individual inspection.

In September 1984, there was a fellowship conference for all members in Hong Kong and Macau, except for those living incognito in secret World Services units. About a hundred of us gathered for four days at a YMCA campground in rural Hong Kong that had cabins, a communal kitchen and a conference hall. On the last day, Mark, the leader in charge of all the regular homes, pulled Rachelle and I aside and recruited us for his office home in Hong Kong.

A suggestion or request from a leader was essentially an order. We were expected to respond with, "Thy wish is my command!"[15] Peter also moved to Hong Kong but stayed in a regular outreach home in Kowloon.

— — —

Mark's office home was in Sai Kung, on the east coast of the New Territories, about a thirty-minute drive from downtown Kowloon. The large, two-storey hillside house on the outskirts of town offered a spectacular view of sunsets over the sparkling harbour. It was the fanciest Family home I'd lived in so far, and seemed excessive for low-level local leaders like Mark and his wife, Amana, and their small staff.

Considering the privacy that its isolated location provided, surrounded by seashore on one side and hilly park reserves on the other, and with no nearby neighbours, I suspected that World Services staff or leaders higher up the hierarchy, who lived relatively luxurious lifestyles compared with regular members, might have previously lived there and turned it over to Mark and Amana. Twenty or more Family members could've squeezed into a house that large, like they did in most communes, but there were only nine of us, six adults and three children.

As in Macau, Rachelle helped care for the kids, while I cooked, did chores and ran errands. I also got to take another courier trip to China, this time alone by train, taking publications and products to Family missionaries disguised as English teachers in the southern cities of Guangzhou (formerly Canton), Hangzhou, and Shanghai.

I was extremely excited to once again participate directly in our undercover mission to the communist country, one of the last we still had to reach with our endtime gospel message before Jesus returned. I was also a bit nervous smuggling sensitive Family material, which I buried at the bottoms of my backpack and large suitcase, under a pile of products I was bringing that weren't yet available in those early years of China's modernization. Almost everyone in the customs line had similarly overloaded baggage, so, fortunately, the agent did only a superficial inspection before waving me through.

Shanghai was the most modern of the three cities I visited, but it was still the old China. The disparity between the austere communist mainland that was just beginning to modernize and the gaudy, bright-light commercialism of Hong Kong was obvious on every step of my journey across southern China. The difference was even more stark when I arrived back in the British colony at night during capitalism's favourite season, Christmas, with colourful holiday lights blazing brightly from many buildings.

That Christmas of 1984, Karen came to visit and introduce Rachelle to her baby granddaughter, Amanda. Because we were living in a leader's home, they weren't allowed to stay with us, even though we had the space. Instead, Mark arranged for us to stay with them in a regular Family home in Kowloon. Peter joined us there too.

Karen had never been outside Canada before, so the culture shock hit her hard as soon as she left the airport. When we took her out the next day to do some shopping, she was overwhelmed by the crowds. It was almost more than she could handle, so we found refuge in a McDonald's, where at least the food was familiar to her.

I understood from my own travels how disoriented she was by the sensory overload from sudden exposure to strange sights, sounds, smells and massive crowds of people who didn't look or talk like her. Revisiting the Family's communal culture and zealous religiosity likely contributed to her anxiety. On the verge of panic attacks, Karen wanted to leave almost as soon as she arrived. We tried persuading her to stay longer, as planned, but she returned to Canada after just a few days.

— — —

While staying in that Kowloon home, I got a glimpse of how flirty fishing was now being practised in the Family.[16] Initially, members copied Berg and Zerby's FFing method in Tenerife's bars and nightclubs, where Berg would pay for everyone's drinks, including the men they were flirting with. Of course, he had the benefit of receiving that money from members around the world. But that tactic was unaffordable for most homes. So, four years after it began, Berg dropped the pretense that FFing was simply a radical new method of evangelizing and saving souls. He revealed it for what it was: religious prostitution.

In the Mo Letter "Make It Pay," Berg suggested that soliciting money while FFing, whether or not sexual intercourse was involved, was no different than asking for donations when distributing literature or other Family products. Berg made it clear that FFing was also a commercial transaction, writing: "If you're to be God's whore you can't have much pride! If you don't know how to let these guys know that you need money you ought to get out of the FFing business! It's nice to win souls, but it's got to pay for itself."[17]

For many members, the main motive for flirty fishing soon degenerated from a spiritual ministry to merely a method of gaining material support. It's not surprising that Berg's instructions to "make it pay" soon led women to work with escort agencies or as freelance escorts. It was a primary source of income for many Family homes, while it lasted. Some became so financially dependent on it that they stopped witnessing to their clients so as not to jeopardize their jobs with the agencies.

A how-to guide on FFing through escorting helped spread the practice around the world. It was in the fourth volume of a series titled *Heavenly Helpers*, which contained instructions and testimonies from members describing various ministries that could provide financial support.[18] While visiting with Karen in the Kowloon home, I got a clearer idea of what escorting involved when I overheard a couple of women discuss details of their escort "dates" with high rollers.[19] I was surprised by how materialistic they seemed and realized it must have been extremely lucrative.[20]

In James Chancellor's 2000 book *Life in the Family*, he includes his interview of a current Family member about the FFing and escorting ("ESing") she did when she lived in Hong Kong in the 1980s. She told him:

> At first, I was not into FFing very much. Then we moved to Hong Kong. Like the other sisters, I started to work for an escort service to meet men. It was quicker and safer than the bars....ESing brought in very good support for the home. We became used to the big money. That is when things really started to go negative....I, and many others, even began to hold back our witness. We did not want to lose our jobs with the escort service. We had to keep the money coming in. Our home came to depend on it. It was not all negative. But mostly it was pretty difficult for me. The ESing was to produce money to support the home. It was that simple — everybody understood. Then, I got pregnant. And it got real tough. ESing was all over the East. It was very, very common in Hong Kong, Japan, Singapore, Thailand, all over. A lot of homes became very dependent on it. [Chancellor: I don't mean to be judgmental, but this sounds like prostitution.] It was prostitution. That was what we were doing, lots of us....There was a lot of fighting over money and possessions. We really lost the Spirit. It all blew up there in Hong Kong. Persecutions came and we all had to flee."[21]

The Family officially stopped flirty fishing in 1987 and reinstated the original prohibition against sex with outsiders.[22] But Berg had not changed his mind about the biblical basis for FFing. Instead, the ban was due to concerns over the global HIV/AIDS crisis and increasingly negative media reports surrounding the Family's sexual doctrines. In some places, those reports prompted closer scrutiny by authorities, which led to the evacuation of members from various countries throughout the 1980s, including the Philippines, Malaysia and Hong Kong.

In early 1985, Mark informed Rachelle and me that his office, along with all regular outreach homes in Hong Kong, were closing down. I suspected this was partly to protect the secret World Services units based there. Most members were moving to Japan. I had always hoped to return there one day, and this was the perfect opportunity.

Chapter 14
I Shook Hands with the Butcher of Beijing

Rachelle, Peter and I were in the last group of escapees fleeing the persecution that forced regular Family homes in Hong Kong to close down. Dozens had already fled to Japan or other countries. In early 1985, our small group arrived in Osaka at night, still on edge from the flight. Our van driver was extra cautious and took a circuitous route back to the commune to ensure he wasn't being followed, which added to our anxiety. Still, I was thrilled to return to Japan eleven years after I'd first gone there.

Berg's daughter Faithy was in charge of the Osaka combo, which is what we called large, multi-purpose communes of forty or more people.[1] The former inn was large enough to accommodate perhaps over twice that many, but the influx of refugees passing through from Hong Kong temporarily overcrowded it until new situations could be found for everyone.

While us newcomers waited for leaders to direct our next move, we were added to the daily work schedule. Rachelle helped with child care and I assisted the kitchen staff, or went with a partner and a child or two to sell a new, lucrative evangelical tool door-to-door: cassette tapes of original Family music.

A few weeks after we arrived, Faithy unexpectedly gave Rachelle and me our marching orders by punishing us in a way similar to how leaders had treated me in the early years, before the RNR. Members were now required to write daily reports of their activities, and disclose their inner thoughts and feelings, which leaders used to monitor and control them. The Open Heart Reports were meant to be confessional, but some used them to snitch on others.[2]

Faithy learned from some reports that Rachelle and I had openly complained about a couple of minor things. Complaining, or "murmuring," which is what we called any expression of unhappiness or discontent, was a serious sin. A malcontent murmurer was ungodly, according to the Bible.[3] Negative attitudes were a spiritual contagion disrupting the unity necessary for communal living. Most leaders considered complaints as challenges to their authority.

One evening, Faithy called an unscheduled meeting, and it quickly became clear she didn't think our complaints were trivial. Without warning, Rachelle and I, and two others from Hong Kong, were called on the carpet. We sat on the floor in the centre of the large living room, surrounded by most of the others, while Faithy angrily lectured and lambasted us for selfishly complaining and being ungrateful for the emergency help our brethren in Japan were providing us.

Faithy ended her severe scolding by expelling us from the home. Public humiliation was hurtful enough, but being kicked out of a Family home, even if we weren't meant to stay there, seemed unnecessarily harsh for such minor sins. The next morning, Peter joined us for the six-hour drive to Tokyo. It all happened so fast I wondered if it had been the plan all along, and Faithy had simply taken the opportunity to make a dramatic example of us to warn those remaining under her leadership.

The home we were sent to in Shibuya was apparently part of our punishment too. In just a few weeks we had gone from living in a leader's luxury home in rural Hong Kong, with all our expenses covered, to an old, well-worn wooden house in the middle of Tokyo, living with a dozen other demoted, despondent disciples in financial difficulty.

Compared with our previous homes in Malaysia, Macau and Hong Kong, which were partially or fully subsidized by World Services, it seemed like we were now relegated to the Family's fringe, thrown into a sink-or-swim situation with other castaways to see who would survive. Like us, a few of the others were there for bad attitudes or breaking rules. Most were single parents, not by choice, but because they had been sadly separated from their spouses, who were assigned to special projects.

We didn't report to World Services as a separate home. Instead, it was a satellite unit for misfit members under the leadership of Hezekiah and Mary, who lived in another outreach home nearby. Peter lived there during our time in Tokyo. Perhaps because Rachelle and I were the only couple, we were given the responsibility of scheduling everyone's daily housework and witnessing teams, but otherwise had no authority over them.

Our immediate priority was improving the home's income, so each of us went out five or six days a week to sell literature and music cassettes, even moms with toddlers and babies in buggies. Kids attracted attention, which helped increase sales. In "The Advantages of Having Children," Berg wrote:

> Every child should be a litnesser or a litnessing asset....Take the children litnessing and provisioning and use the children!... Children are one of the biggest assets you've got! My children practically put me in business, and yours can do the same for you if you train them right and if you get them out witnessing and litnessing. My kids finally were supporting me![4]

Within a couple of months, the home's finances dramatically improved. Apparently, leaders took notice, and Rachelle and I were out of the doghouse now, because I was given a special assignment: to help find and set up a rental house as a base for witnessing at the world's fair, Expo '85, being held that summer in Tsukuba, about an hour by train from Tokyo. I hit the road with a Japanese partner, Seiko, while Rachelle remained in Tokyo during the two months I was away.

After we found a two-storey house not far from the fair site, a couple of others came to help us set it up. One had been unwillingly separated from her husband and children in the Osaka home. She confessed that she was the one who reported Rachelle's complaints to Faithy. She sadly regretted that after experiencing Faithy's unreasonable punishment herself.

A few others joined us and we began spending our days at the fair, covertly evangelizing. We couldn't openly distribute literature or sell music tapes, so we returned to our origins, personally witnessing one-to-one, like in the early years of the Children of God. I was especially intrigued by the Russian and Iranian pavilions, two countries that featured prominently in Berg's endtime predictions. I spent a lot of time talking to staff about their lives back home under the constraints of a godless and religious dictatorship, respectively. One day, I got a rude reminder that my life was also restricted by dictatorial religious rulers.

Faithy suddenly showed up and took over the home. Her new assignment was to take her flock of flirty fishers she arrived with to the fair every day. I'd met one of them in the Hong Kong home, the one who wrote part of the guide on escorting. I had to surrender the upstairs bedroom I was using to Faithy and her companion for the Expo mission, Ezra, one of the top leaders in Japan. I joined the others on futons crammed side by side on the floors of the two remaining bedrooms and the living room.

Too excited to sleep that first night, everyone kept asking me questions about the fair, but apparently my voice was the only one Faithy heard. She sent Ezra downstairs to chastise me for talking too loud and keeping her awake. That was similar to the complaint I'd made in Osaka that she'd kicked me out for, but I doubt she was aware of her double standard. Faithy wanted me out, and so ordered me to return to Tokyo first thing in the morning. She seemed to still have a hate-on for me. The driver who took me to the train station told me he thought Faithy was unfairly harsh and that I didn't deserve to be treated that way.

Back in Tokyo, reunited with Rachelle, I heard about a meeting on evangelizing China that occurred while I was away. It had been led by Maggie (formerly Keda), who was now a co-leader of the Asia-Pacific region with Chris,[5] Ezra and his wife Ginny. The meeting provided practical information for anyone interested in teaching English there.

Inspired by my two courier trips, I was intrigued by the idea of living in China as an undercover missionary. Though I was a high school dropout, I thought being a native English speaker would be sufficient qualification, as it was for my teaching job in Macau. I didn't want to miss this opportunity, and so, after discussing it with Rachelle, I wrote to Maggie, expressing our desire to go to China.

My letter arrived at an opportune time. Maggie had just ordered a couple, Sam and Angel, to remain in Japan, where they were visiting during the summer break from his teaching job in Beijing. Thinking I might be able to step into Sam's job at the start of the fall semester, which was just a couple of months away, she approved our request. She told me to meet with Tommy, who would help me forge a university degree, a required credential for getting a work visa in China.

Like many members, I had committed immigration fraud by illegally working as a missionary, but I had never used fake documents before.[6] Tommy had all the necessary materials, and I copied the design layout from his fake degree. I then made photocopies to conceal the crude counterfeit. If anyone asked to see the original, I would tell them I left it with my parents in Canada.

In September 1985, Rachelle, Peter and I were on the move again, flying to China on a wing and a prayer. From Hong Kong we took a ferry up the Pearl River to Guangzhou, where flights to Beijing were cheaper. There were three other families in the capital, each living in a separate unit of the Friendship Hotel's apartment complex, which was reserved for foreigners. We couldn't get an apartment without a work visa, so while I searched for a job we stayed with one of them.

The first thing I did was personally deliver a letter from Sam to his former employer explaining why he couldn't return to his job and recommending me as his replacement. The university administrator who met with me read Sam's letter and my padded resumé. After a brief interview, I could tell he was skeptical about this unusual situation. He didn't get back to me.

Next, I sent my resumé to all sorts of schools, hoping someone still had a vacant position so close to the start of the semester. I should've had someone proofread my cover letter first, though, because I spelled a word wrong. All I could do was hope no one noticed it. The fact that I was already in the city, and so was immediately available, turned out to be an advantage for both me and the only school that replied, the Central Institute of Finance and Banking.

Renamed the Central University of Finance and Economics, it is now China's top economics university. It was shut down during the Cultural Revolution in the 1960s and early '70s, along with all other educational institutions, and some of its buildings were taken over by a tobacco factory. It had reclaimed most of them since then, but when I went for the interview, I could tell from the aroma wafting through the campus that the factory was still operating in at least one building.

My interviewer told me that a teacher they'd been expecting to come from the US had backed out, so he was relieved to receive my letter. After a brief interview, he was doubly pleased to hire me on the spot. The students were expecting a native English speaker, so they wouldn't be disappointed, and I was a cheaper alternative to the American because the school didn't have to pay my airfare and I agreed to be paid entirely in renminbi (RMB), China's currency.

Foreign teachers, classified as "foreign experts," were usually paid in both US dollars and foreign exchange certificates (FECs), which could only be used in designated businesses. However, there was a new black market for exchanging dollars and FECs for RMB, so foreigners were now using the local currency to shop in regular stores and markets.[7] I didn't negotiate my salary. My main priority was securing a work visa, which the school would arrange.

The salary was sufficient for our basic monthly expenses, since we were also provided a rent-free apartment in the state-owned Friendship Hotel complex. No apartments were available until the end of the fall semester, though, so in the meantime we were given a single room in the main hotel building, where Rachelle and I lived for the next three months. Peter stayed with one of the other families until the school updated our visas. He then went to help a family living alone in Chongqing, about sixteen hundred kilometres away, where he remained until we left China the next summer.

At the end of 1985, we moved into an apartment. Although Peter was now living in a different city, he was still registered as living with us, so we were given a two-bedroom unit. The free apartment also included house-cleaning, but the other members there advised us to decline that service, saying it was simply a way for staff to spy on us. They also warned me that I would be closely monitored in my classroom. We had to assume suspicious government spooks or neighbourhood snoops were always watching.

— — —

I taught twelve hours of classes a week to first-year students. One intro-duced himself as the spokesperson for the others and said he was a member of the Communist Youth League, a branch of the Communist Party. I assumed he was assigned to monitor the content of my classes in case I strayed into forbidden topics. His English was better than the other students', and a few times he pointed out a grammar mistake I'd made, a subject he might've had more formal training in than I did as a high school dropout.

Although I had no professional training in how to prepare appropriate lesson plans, I had various teaching materials left by Sam that were useful for reading and writing exercises. I also taught one class a week in a new language lab, giving my students aural exercises, such as transcribing the lyrics of an English song. But both my students and I preferred conversa-tional lessons. For those, I had everyone sit in a circle so they could more easily participate in discussions.

My democratic approach was probably unusual in that authoritarian education system, where teachers feed facts to passive students for the purpose of passing exams. Some students were uncomfortable with my teaching style at first, but I invited them to ask me personal questions about life in Canada, or to talk about any topic they wanted, which helped draw in those who didn't see the value of unstructured learning.

There were few opportunities outside of class for students to hear native English speakers, so showing them a movie was another tool I used to help them improve their aural comprehension. I had a videocas-sette recorder that Sam and Angel left behind, and about fifty films to choose from. Movies were the only form of outside entertainment Family members were permitted. We couldn't watch any movie, though, only ones that were approved by leaders based on Berg's spiritual criteria. They couldn't contradict his teachings in any way and had to have positive, inspiring messages with "happy endings."[8]

The Family's spiritual censorship was similar to China's censorship of "spiritual pollution" from western culture that was proliferating after the "open door" economic reforms. At the beginning of 1986, the government issued strict censorship guidelines for foreign films: no sex, violence, decadence, superstition, distorted history or science, or anything that could harm diplomatic relationships.

I wasn't aware of those new guidelines yet, but knew I had to carefully consider the government's political sensitivities when choosing a movie to show my students. The first one I chose was the 1977 film *Close Encounters of the Third Kind*. I thought its happy ending, with its positive message of learning to communicate with aliens, was a good metaphor for students studying a foreign language with one. It was a rare chance for them to see a foreign film that wouldn't be released in China until 1990.

One morning, I arrived at class to find my students very excited by a rare, light snowfall. They convinced me to take them on a field trip, explaining that this was an extraordinary opportunity to see the ancient Summer Palace buildings and gardens scintillating under a thin blanket of snow. My job enabled me to see a few other historical sites, but Berg condemned sightseeing as the prideful worship of man and his creations, a policy that kept me from going to the Great Wall.[9]

University administrators took us foreign teachers to the Tanzhe Temple, an ancient Buddhist complex outside of Beijing. In my spare time I also visited the Forbidden City, entering the five-hundred-year-old former imperial palace complex through the enormous Gate of Heavenly Peace that features the famous portrait of Mao Zedong overlooking Tiananmen Square.

My school also gave me a ticket to the opening ceremony of a special Communist Party national conference of party delegates held in the Great Hall of the People, on the west side of Tiananmen Square, where I joined other foreign experts, dignitaries and diplomats invited to witness that public part of China's political process.

Among the politicians seated onstage were the paramount leader, Deng Xiaoping, the general secretary of the party, Hu Yaobang, and Premier Zhao Ziyang. Hu was a reformist whose death in 1989 prompted pro-democracy protests. Zhao was the principal architect of the open-door policy established by Deng. He was later denounced and purged for supporting the protesters in Tiananmen Square.

I had a kind of *Forrest Gump* moment at another official event I attended, a banquet for foreign experts to thank us for contributing to China's modernization. Among the uniformed officials at the banquet's head table was the vice premier at the time, Li Peng. After speeches and dinner, Li strolled the room, speaking with some of the guests. When he got to my table, he addressed me through his interpreter. After a brief conversation, he shook my hand and moved on.

I didn't know it then, but I had just shaken hands with the Butcher of Beijing.[10] That's the epithet given to Li by those holding him responsible for the Tiananmen massacre three years later. By that time, he was the premier, the person who declared martial law and sent troops and tanks to violently end the student-led democracy protests. Thousands were injured or killed. I was living in Hong Kong then and watched news reports of the protest and slaughter, wondering if any of my former students were in the crowd.

— — —

Clandestine Christian evangelism in a communist country required extra precautions. Many citizens still considered foreigners suspicious by default, so we assumed that eyes were always on us, everywhere. We certainly couldn't appear to be missionaries, so we restricted our Christian witness to individual conversations. It was an impossible mission to reach one billion people that way before Jesus came back in 1993, but if that occurred to me at the time, I brushed it off. As long as I was part of the Family, I believed I was doing God's will.

While Rachelle spent most of her days helping with the children of the other couples, I taught only twelve hours a week, so I had plenty of free time. I often rode my bike, exploring back lanes that form the traditional residential neighbourhoods of old Beijing, known as *hutongs*. The Friendship Hotel complex is in the university district, so I also rode around the campuses of Peking University and Renmin University, looking for people to talk to.

Another nearby place convenient for meeting people was Purple Bamboo Park. Locals gathered in a garden grove informally called English Corner to improve their oral skills by conversing with one another.[11] Foreigners infrequently participated, so when I showed up I was immediately surrounded by a crowd eager to practise with a native speaker. It wasn't wise to proselytize in that situation, so I tried to single out those who might be receptive to my message and arrange to meet them later.

Although speaking English had been a punishable offence during the Cultural Revolution, Deng Xiaoping's economic reforms created a need for English speakers. China's first English Corner started in Shanghai's People's Park in 1978. Others sprang up around the country soon after, including Beijing's first one in Purple Bamboo Park. The government tolerated the informal gatherings, but undercover security officials certainly monitored them. After the 1989 democracy protests, most of the high-profile English Corners were shut down for a while by officials fearful of free speech fomenting further unrest.[12] Later, student activists in Beijing relocated the one in the park to the campus of Renmin University.

Family members had converted a Beijing couple who then defied the government's one-child policy. The mother avoided forced sterilization after her first child, and had a second one. Consequently, the father lost his government job and benefits, and they suffered other financial penalties. We helped them as much as possible, but it was too risky for them to visit us because locals had to sign in at the hotel's front gate. Instead, we took turns going to their apartment, but only at night while wearing hats and scarves to conceal ourselves from nosy neighbours.

We used a similar disguise on a student we smuggled into the apartment complex in a taxi. She attended university in Shanghai and associated with Family members there. During the winter break, she came to Beijing to visit her family. She wanted to visit some of us before going back to school. The couple in charge of the Family members in Beijing, Austrian Alex and his Taiwanese wife, Mercy, told us to put her up for a few days since we had an extra bedroom. Mercy went out to pick her up and they returned in a taxi, which the guard waved through when he recognized Mercy. Mercy came over every day to study the Bible and read Mo Letters with her.

Although I invited my students, including one who had happily accepted a Chinese New Testament from me, none were willing to visit me in our apartment. They were probably afraid of being asked why they were visiting foreigners, and having their name recorded in the visitor's log. The only other local visitor we had was a judge. He came for a secret rendezvous with an American Family member, Rose, a flirty fisher he'd had sex with at a legal conference in Manila. She had brought Family publications, videos and other items for all of us and stayed in our spare bedroom a few days.

One of the purposes of flirty fishing was to win the favour of influential or politically powerful people who might come to our aid or defence in times of trouble, so Rose had maintained communication with the judge. She let him know she was in Beijing, and they arranged to meet in our apartment.

When he arrived, Rachelle and I made small talk before making an excuse and leaving for a couple of hours. Rose gave us explicit details of their sexual encounter when we returned. It wasn't clear to me, though, how FFing this judge could possibly benefit the Family in any way. It was unreasonable to expect him to defend us, and I doubt he could've helped us just a few months later, when government persecution forced us to flee China.

Near the end of the 1986 spring semester, Alex received an urgent message from Maggie's office in Japan. Government authorities had raided two Family homes in Guangzhou, arrested the foreign members, and confiscated personal documents and Family publications. We had to assume it was only a matter of time before an investigation spread to other cities and investigators connected them to us in Beijing.

Alex told Rachelle and me that we had to leave the country as soon as possible and return to Japan. He contacted the home where Peter was, and while we waited for him to return to Beijing I helped Alex get rid of Family materials he and others had accumulated over a few years. There were several boxes of Mo Letters, pamphlets, books, video and audio cassettes, Chinese Bibles and other incriminating evidence of illegal evangelism we had to purge in some way.

Over the next few nights, I rode my bike down dark alleys with a couple of bags hanging on the handlebars, looking for places to discard them where they might not be found. I threw most of the bags into different dumpsters, hoping they would disappear under garbage, but on my final trip I saw someone eyeing me suspiciously before I could dump the last ones. I didn't want to be caught with the stuff, so I raced away in a panic. As I crossed a small bridge, I threw the bags over the side and into a shallow gully.

There were still a few weeks of classes left and I hadn't examined or graded my students yet. Alex insisted it was too dangerous to remain in the country much longer and told me not to return to the school. I felt guilty about abandoning my students, leaving them without final grades and suddenly disappearing without saying goodbye, but with the looming threat of arrest, I obeyed him.

We didn't have much time before my next scheduled class. Failing to show up without notice would surely arouse suspicion, so the morning after Peter arrived, we went to the airport and bought full-price tickets directly from the airline, which we had never done before. We then rented a room in a small inn nearby, where we waited for our flight later that day.

Unsure if authorities were on the lookout for us, we were highly anxious as we passed through immigration and customs inspection. We momentarily froze in fear when the suitcase scanner alarm sounded and agents conducted a search. Fortunately, it was only because of a six-inch jackknife Rachelle had been travelling with since leaving Canada, which they confiscated.

Relieved, we finally relaxed on board, a moment made easier after an attendant upgraded us to business class just before the flight took off, though I had mixed feelings about leaving China and returning to Japan. My daily life in that restrictive communist country had been relatively free from direct supervision by Family leaders, compared with the more controlled, communal life we were returning to.

Chapter 15
Mr. Big in Japan

Not long after Rachelle, Peter and I returned to Tokyo, I heard that Alex had been arrested in connection to the government raids in Guangzhou. When I met him several months later, he told me he spent a few weeks in jail before embassy officials from his home country, Austria, helped get him out. He explained that if we had not fled China when we did, Rachelle and I would likely have been arrested too. The authorities questioned him about us because he had used our apartment address on an official document related to his young daughter, Esther.

About a month after we arrived in Tokyo, Maggie recruited Rachelle and me as house servants for the Pacific Area Central Reporting Office she co-managed with Chris, Ezra and Ginny.[1] Their secretary was Sweetie, whom I knew as Mercy when I was in Japan in 1974. Her US military father was stationed there when she joined the Children of God at the age of fifteen. She was now married to Pete, Japanese member.

The luxurious house, with a mix of Japanese and western-style rooms, was in an upscale residential neighbourhood in Kamakura, a municipality south of Yokohama. As well as being a secret office for managing the affairs of members, it was the place where the Japanese Mo Letters were printed for a while, on an offset printing press in the detached garage.

There were ten adults and five children in the home at the time. Rachelle helped take care of the kids, while I took care of the kitchen, made most of the meals, and was always on standby to run errands. Sometimes I helped with parts of the printing process, or accompanied a driver delivering items to and from another office home about twenty minutes away, where a team translated all the Family's publications into Japanese.

Peter didn't move with us to the office, so we didn't see him again until December, when our six-month visitor visas expired and we had to leave the country in order to get new ones. Instead of going the usual route by ferry to South Korea, as most foreign members did, we were sent by Maggie to the Philippines. The office was fully funded by World Services, so the cost of airfare wasn't an issue, as it was for regular homes.

Although I didn't meet anyone on that trip I knew from my previous time in the Philippines, there was someone from my past living in the home we stayed in. Joanna, the daughter of Caleb and Lydia, who led the Burlington commune in 1973, was one of the children who had lived in the child-care house where I had often helped out. She was about the same age as Peter, so they hung out while we were in Manila, and quickly formed a bond. They would get married two years later in a collective wedding with other teen couples in Japan.

After we returned to Japan, a Family VIP visited the office. Mordecai Printer, or Inky, as Berg called him in various letters, helped establish the Family's publishing operations around the world. As an important Family dignitary, members owed him the same deference they gave leaders. So when Maggie told Rachelle that Mordecai wanted to "share" with her, even though there were two single women in the home, we had to unquestioningly accept it as God's will.

Whether or not Rachelle was willing, she had to submit or risk being labelled a disobedient "girl who wouldn't," like Maggie's reluctant former assistant. We were under extreme peer pressure to conform and spiritually coerced to obey leaders in that totalitarian environment. Considering the power imbalance, Rachelle couldn't have freely given her consent, and I certainly felt forced to accept their liaison even though I thought it was unnecessary.

Living closely with those top leaders, I was beginning to clearly recognize their double standards. They had more luxuries and freedoms, lived by their own rules, and did things regular members would be reprimanded for. I had to accept that and keep my mouth shut, but it wasn't easy to suppress my doubts and jealousy when I had to sleep under the dining-room table like an obedient dog, while Mordecai was having sex with my wife in our bed.

I was tormented further when Mordecai and Ezra later came into the kitchen and began a long, loud conversation, thoughtlessly uncaring that they were disturbing my sleep. Ezra had helped Faithy kick me out of the Expo home for exactly the same reason. I was furious at his cruel hypocrisy. My blood boiled as I barely contained my anger, but I didn't dare criticize him.

At least I was aware of that situation. I became even more agitated when I learned that Rachelle was having an affair with Pete without my knowledge or consent. Sweetie shocked me one day when she asked me if I was aware that her husband had been having sex with Rachelle. Apparently, I was the only one who didn't know about their affair. I was deeply disturbed by their deception, especially when I realized how manipulative their most recent tryst had been.

The evening before, Pete told me he wasn't feeling well and asked me to take his place on the courier trip to the translation home. When I returned a couple of hours later, I had sex with Rachelle, completely oblivious that she had just had sex with Pete behind my back. When Sweetie revealed the affair to me, I realized Pete had manipulated me. He wasn't ill, he was lustfully lovesick for Rachelle. Learning he'd lied to me and she'd betrayed me made me sick at heart.

Later that day, I pulled Rachelle aside to the nook under the staircase and confronted her over their deliberate deceptions. Though I didn't shout or strike her, I could barely contain my anger. I was deeply hurt and heartbroken, so I pushed her away in a reflexive gesture of rejection when she tried to tearfully hug me. I don't know if others heard me angrily vent my jealousy, or if Rachelle told Sweetie about my reaction.

All four leaders were away at the time, but they sent me a message accusing me of being "out of the spirit" and distracting them from their important work. They said Rachelle and I needed to be separated. They considered her more yielded and useful to them, so deemed me the guilty party and ordered me to move to a regular home. Afterwards, in a small storage room, I broke down and sobbed. It's the only time I've cried aloud as an adult.

Although I had sinfully yielded to jealousy and anger, I thought the leaders had unjustly singled me out for condemnation and punishment when Rachelle and Pete were also guilty. I believed Rachelle and Pete had violated Berg's initial rules governing sexual relationships, and that the leaders' response to the situation was contrary to the guidelines first set down in the letter "The Law of Love." Distressed by their cruel double standard, I decided to write a complaint letter to Karen Zerby (Maria), Berg's co-leader.

Berg's initial explanation of that foundational doctrine had included conditions attached to the new sexual freedoms. Their affair wasn't unselfish or sacrificial love, so in my opinion the leaders also broke that law by excusing the lustful couple while condemning my reaction. I said so in my letter to Zerby, which included the following quotations from "The Law of Love" to support my complaint:

Any variation from the norm of personal relationships, any substantial change in marital relationships, any projected sexual associations should have the willing consent of all parties concerned or affected, including the approval of leadership and permission of the Body. If this is lacking in any quarter and anyone is going to be harmed or unduly offended, then your action is not in love nor according to God's law of love!… Are you doing it because you want to unselfishly and sacrificially help someone else who really needs it, and by which you can show them God's Love, or are you doing it selfishly and unlawfully, not in love for others and God, but merely "to consume it upon your own lusts"?[2]

Criticizing leaders was taboo, and I had been punished for far less, so writing the letter was risky, but Zerby never responded directly to it. I spent the next couple of months in a commune in Kawasaki, a city in the Greater Tokyo Area. They needed a second driver, and since I still had a valid Canadian licence, I was able to get a Japanese one without taking a driver's test. Driving became one of my main jobs from then on.

From there, I was sent to help the staff of a new training and media production centre, where they needed my ability to drive and cook. Although it was officially named the 21st Century International School, we called it the Heavenly City School (HCS).[3] The recently built, two-storey main building was provided to the Family by a wealthy Tokyo nightclub owner and his wife, Masataro and Tsutako Narita.[4] It was in a mostly empty rural subdivision on the outskirts of Tateyama, a small town at the tip of the Bōsō Peninsula on the eastern edge of Tokyo Bay.

When I first moved to the HCS in the fall of 1987, it had primarily been used for a six-week teen training camp a year earlier.[5] Similar ones were held around the world in an attempt to keep Family teens indoctrinated and inspired to serve God.[6] Now a small crew was preparing for a series of leadership meetings, after which the place would become a boarding school and the Family's main music and video production centre. Carpenters were building more dining tables and dozens of bunk beds to accommodate large numbers of people.

I lived at the HCS on and off over the next few years. During that time, the main building underwent various renovations, and rooms were rearranged or repurposed. Other buildings were added to the complex, including a large production studio for filming music videos, and a two-storey dormitory, which increased the compound's capacity to accommodate two hundred or more.

Family members also occupied the Naritas' two-storey, western-style house directly across the street from the entrance to the main building. We called it the "white house." The Naritas had a luxurious house in Tokyo where Masataro spent most of his time, while Tsutako lived in their large, traditional Japanese house three blocks from the HCS. She used only the first floor, so after our numbers increased, she let some of us move into her four bedrooms upstairs. I lived in one for a while.

The Naritas spent hundreds of thousands of dollars financing daily operations at the HCS and other Family projects around Japan. They weren't just financial supporters of our Christian evangelism, though; they were true believers in Berg's endtime prophecies and apocalyptic predictions. Their personal experiences in World War II made them susceptible to Berg's doomsday warnings, so it's not surprising they built an underground bomb shelter below the left wing of the main HCS building.

There were two levels below the ground floor. A disguised door opened to stairs down to the first level, which was adapted for various purposes. At one point, it had a room for post-production video editing, and several small rooms for sex dates. The bottom level was a concrete bunker accessed through a hatch on the floor of the first level. A ladder led down to an empty room only large enough to provide temporary safety for perhaps a dozen people. It wasn't set up for long-term survival.

Those secret underground floors were where the leaders and other VIPs hid in the event of a raid by authorities. We held occasional emergency drills to prepare for that possibility. Security staff played a certain song over the compound's speaker system, which was the signal for leaders and foreigners with visitor visas to immediately flee to their designated hiding spots.

During my first drill, a large group of us, which included over a dozen children, went into the nearby woods at the edge of the subdivision and waited for an all-clear signal. In a real raid, there would be no way to hide for very long from determined immigration officials or police doing a thorough investigation. There were no other escape plans. Only a few leaders hiding in the secret bomb shelter might have been safe.

Not long after I moved to the HCS, Maggie and her three co-leaders came to conduct a series of retraining seminars for leaders of regular homes around Japan. They had also led the earlier teen training camp sessions there. One day, Ginny took me aside and apologized for the way they handled my reaction to Rachelle and Pete's secret affair. I got the impression she was doing so on Zerby's instructions. The apology felt forced and insincere, so I wondered if there was some manipulative purpose for it.

Then, one evening, I almost died. While cleaning the kitchen on my own, I carried a large garbage bag down the long flight of stairs to the dumpster outside. I was wearing short pants and the heavy bag brushed against my bare leg as I swung it into the can, but otherwise I felt nothing unusual. I returned to the kitchen and continued cleaning for a couple of minutes when suddenly I heard someone yelling, "Mike, you've cut your leg!" Ezra was running toward me in a panic.

I had severed an artery and blood was spurting out of my right calf and all over the floor behind me. Ezra grabbed a towel and began compressing the wound to stop the bleeding. Security staff down the hall heard his shouts for help, and he told them to call Mrs. Narita, who called her doctor. She came with us to his closed clinic in town, about fifteen minutes away. Blood spattered all over his white coat while he was closing my wound with two layers of stitches.

An injury like mine was considered a sign of sin and a security breach. If I had died, it could've jeopardized the mission at the HCS. If someone had sinned, though, I didn't think it was me. I knew that if anyone was responsible for my injury, it was the person who improperly disposed of a broken dinner plate that was so sharp it sliced open my bare leg like a razor blade, which is probably why I didn't feel it at first.

Someone ignorant of the long-standing safety rule in Family kitchens on how to safely dispose of sharp objects had placed it in the garbage bag without properly wrapping it. I thought the culprit was most likely one of the leaders, who outnumbered the small staff at that particular time. Most were probably unaware of basic kitchen rules, because leaders didn't do such menial work. My prime suspect was Ezra, since he was first on the scene, and having lived with him before, I had seen his privileged double standard when it came to rules.

No one else was nearby when it happened, so if Ezra hadn't appeared when he did, I could have gone into shock, fainted before I realized what had happened, and easily bled out. He undoubtedly saved my life, but he also might have caused my injury. So I had mixed feelings about him, especially since, three times previously, he'd played a role in arbitrarily kicking me out of a home.

According to Berg, God had removed his protection from me and allowed my injury for a reason.[7] But if my injury was a sign of sin in my life, then the person who caused it and refused to confess was also sinning. However, instead of trying to identify the careless culprit who caused my life-threatening injury by investigating and questioning everyone until someone confessed, which was often done for far less serious matters, the leaders simply blamed and punished me. That confirmed my suspicion that I was a convenient scapegoat for a leader who was covering up their own guilt.

I have a seven-centimetre scar from that injury and a six-centimetre one from the appendix surgery I had when I first lived in Japan over a decade earlier. Those two incidents also left psychological scars from the related spiritual abuse. Both times, my life was physically endangered through no fault of my own, yet leaders blamed and punished me for being out of God's will.

— — —

After Berg and Zerby fled to England in the early 1970s, they stayed hidden from their followers. Most members didn't know what they looked like, even after they appeared in public while flirty fishing in Tenerife. They then disappeared again and continued to conceal their appearances from their followers. They frequently moved from country to country, finally settling in the Philippines in 1982, where they lived incognito for the next five years, until the government ordered all Family members to leave the country.

The number of members living at or passing through the HCS steadily increased after I first moved there in 1987. Many musicians, performers and technicians came to participate in some aspect of music video production. Numerous refugees from the Philippines also arrived. Only Maggie and her co-leaders knew that Berg, Zerby and their staff had also come to Japan from the Philippines. I learned years later that they went to Tokyo in November 1987, a month or two after I was first sent to the HCS. Then, one day in February 1988, I saw the endtime prophet in person.

At mid-morning that day, everyone in the compound was called to gather in the dining hall, which was unusual. Curiously, all the curtains were closed, so clearly something important was up. A stranger with an air of authority came into the hall and started speaking about the importance of staying security-conscious. He told us we would start to see numerous unfamiliar faces around the compound and warned us not to speculate or gossip among ourselves, or talk to anyone we didn't know unless they talked to us first.

I was sitting beside one of the windows and noticed the silhouettes of two people in the parking lot. Curious, I peeked through a crack in the curtains and saw the profile of a bearded man wearing a cloak and walking arm in arm with a woman. They were headed up the hill behind the compound to a small pyramid-shaped structure Mrs. Narita built as a prayer room after reading Berg's letter about the supposed supernatural powers of pyramids.[8] I suddenly realized that the mysterious couple was Berg and Zerby, and that the stranger speaking was their right-hand man, Steven Kelly, known to us as Peter Amsterdam.[9]

This was both a thrilling and a terrifying turn of events. Although it was exciting to be at the centre of the action, I was spiritually intimidated by the prophet's presence. Berg's endtime predictions motivated me, but his dictatorial, capricious nature frightened me. His letters contained many examples of how, in a fit of self-righteous indignation, he lashed out at those around him with wrathful verbal abuse and punishments for minor matters.[10] He published those accounts as warnings to toe the line or else, so I was treading carefully after Peter's lecture.

A few days later, as I was about to enter the front door of the main building, I heard someone call out "Good morning, son" from the window on the upper floor of the white house directly across the street. Immediately recognizing Berg's voice from audio recordings, I froze, afraid to turn and face him. Was he talking to me, or to Silas, who was doing some landscaping nearby? Relieved when I heard Silas answer him, I entered the building without turning around and replying to Berg.

Considering how things turned out, Berg may have seen my failure to face him and respond as a disrespectful insult, and formed a low opinion of me from that first impression. If Berg did feel slighted by that, I'm sure he would've held a grudge against me, even more so if he learned I was the one who had challenged authority by criticizing Maggie and her co-leaders in my complaint letter to Zerby about the Law of Love.

Berg, Zerby, Kelly and their household moved into a rented house just up the road from the HCS complex. Although they remained there for about eight months, those three leaders didn't hold any public meetings with regular members. I only saw them once more, as fleetingly and obscurely as the first time. I was in the parking lot when an unfamiliar car with tinted windows drove past. Someone in the back seat waved at me, but the car passed before I could wave back. I realized too late that it had been Berg and Zerby, so immediately worried I had unintentionally offended Berg again.

I was one of the main drivers, so a few times I drove Zerby's son, Ricky, and his minder to town. Known to members as Davidito, Ricky was the love child of one of Zerby's first flirty-fishing affairs in Tenerife, a "Jesus baby," as the Family referred to children fathered through FFing.[11] Raised in isolation from society and Family members, Ricky was groomed to be the Family's future leader. I was told not to talk to him during our trips to town. He probably had similar instructions. Outwardly, he seemed like any other shy thirteen-year-old. I didn't know he was harbouring dark secrets about life in Berg's home.

— — —

Shortly after Berg and his entourage arrived, Rachelle and I were reunited when she came to live at the HCS too. There was a growing number of children and teens living there. Many had come without their parents to perform in or assist with music-video productions, so the HCS was now also operating as a boarding school, although one that indoctrinated more than educated.

Zerby allowed Ricky, his nine-year-old half-sister, Techi, and Davida, the daughter of Zerby's personal child-care assistant, Sara Kelley, to participate in some school activities with other Family children for the first time.[12] Rachelle had been caring for the children of Maggie's leadership team, so they likely recommended her as someone trustworthy to assist with Techi and Davida when they were at the HCS.

I was glad to be back together, but when Rachelle told me she was working with Techi, I realized that was probably the real reason she came to the HCS, not because the leaders wanted us to renew our relationship. It was hard to trust Rachelle after she lied to me, so I was wary of confiding in her, unsure if it would stay between us. That made it difficult to restore our emotional connection. When she was given the sensitive responsibility of helping to organize a sexual sharing schedule, I realized she even had a higher status than me now. The dynamic of our relationship had changed, and we were becoming estranged.

When I first joined the HCS staff, before Berg came, we were temporarily prohibited from sexual sharing while leaders from around the country were there for retraining. In 1983, Berg banned all sexual contact between members who lived in different homes, to prevent the spread of sexually transmitted diseases.[13] Within homes, members were divided into those with and without herpes, and could only sexually share with others in their group.

Since separating from Rachelle, I'd had only one sexual encounter. I didn't mind being celibate, but when the visiting leaders left, sexual abstinence ended for the HCS staff who were either single or separated from their spouses, which was most of us. We were free to share, though it wasn't a free-for-all. Instead, our sexual partners were arranged by a leader. I had two more one-night stands before Rachelle and I reunited.

The HCS population had boomed to about a hundred adults by then. The leaders imposed a sharing schedule that was implicitly mandatory for everyone, to ensure the sexual needs of all the single or separated adults were met. At least, that's how I interpreted this more methodical application of the Law of Love, that it was meant to be altruistic, not egoistic. But it was also an effective way for leaders to monitor, manage and manipulate everyone's sexual relationships.

Now that I was back with Rachelle, it would've been fine with me if we didn't participate, but I couldn't opt out without appearing unrevolutionary and rebellious. Although she had broken basic sexual sharing rules requiring transparency and mutual consent, in the Family's sexually permissive ethos her impropriety was preferable to my prudish jealousy. So it shouldn't have surprised me when Rachelle was put in charge of organizing the sharing schedule. It also agitated me that my wife would decide who I had sex with, but that I had no say in her choice of sexual partners.

Like everyone else, I had to give Rachelle the names of three people I preferred as my sharing partners. If mutual preferences couldn't be matched up, we had to share with whoever was chosen for us. I had no close connections with anyone, so I didn't have much to base my list on, other than superficial factors like physical attraction. There were probably others like me with low libidos or no emotional desire for those on their list, who felt the process led to lustful or perfunctory, shallow sex, but I'm sure no one wanted to be condemned as "the girl who wouldn't."

Sometimes, factors besides personal preferences informed the matchmaking. For example, Rachelle asked me to share with someone not on my list. Beth was a new disciple from Sweden. She arrived with Arthur, who had recently recruited her.[14] He was a sort of Family celebrity, Zerby's first flirty-fishing lover in England. His seduction and recruitment was documented in great detail in a series of Mo Letters titled "King Arthur's Nights."[15]

Rachelle told me the leaders who gave final approval of the sharing pairings asked her to match Beth with an appropriate partner to introduce her to that practice. I think she suggested me because I wasn't sexually needy or demanding, but was tender and talkative, so it wouldn't be a "Wham, bam, thank you, ma'am" experience. I craved an emotional connection with any sexual partner, so I usually engaged in prolonged foretalk before foreplay.

Arthur wasn't the only "celebrity" at the HCS. Many of the Family's best musicians came to work on music video productions, including Jeremy Spencer, who would've been a real-world celebrity if he had remained with Fleetwood Mac instead of dropping out in 1971 to join the Children of God.[16] From the very beginning, music played an important part in the Family's evangelism. At first, it involved simply witnessing in-person by singing and dancing in public places. Later, Spencer and other Family musicians recorded several albums, which were sold in record stores.[17]

From the mid-'70s to the mid-'80s, many of those musicians played on the Family's radio show, *Music with Meaning*, produced in Greece and later Sri Lanka.[18] It aired around the world, with versions in Spanish, French, Italian and Portuguese. Members also began to sell cassettes of those radio programs and other original Family gospel music. Now, many of those musicians had come to the HCS to produce a new proselytizing tool and source of income: thirty-minute VHS music video cassettes.[19]

Children and teens featured prominently in most of the music videos, as either singers or actors, and some helped with other aspects of their production. Rachelle's son, Peter, was among them. Now sixteen, he came to the HCS around the same time as his mum to participate in the teen training program. It was the first time in four years we'd all lived together. In the summer of 1988, the three of us took our last visa trip together, this time by air to Seoul.

Later that year, Rachelle got a letter from her daughter, Karen, saying she wanted to visit us again that Christmas. Leaders gave their approval, but as in Hong Kong, she wasn't allowed to stay with us, though she could visit the HCS under controlled conditions. So she stayed at a nearby *ryokan*, a traditional inn, and her mum and brother joined her for the week she was there. I visited her a few times, and on several occasions brought them all back to the HCS so Karen could participate in some Christmas activities.

Certain security protocols were in place whenever outsiders were on the premises, and a troupe of kids and teens trained to entertain and witness to visitors was always on call, ready to perform. Each time Karen visited, they would love-bomb her, a recruiting tactic where a potential new member is lavished with affection to create a social connection in an attempt to reel them into the group.[20]

We tried to convince Karen to return to the fold instead of returning to Canada, but although she missed her mum and brother, she missed her two kids more. They were staying with their father, whom she was now separated from. She was anxious to get back to them and her new boyfriend, who had paid for her trip. I'm sure she also preferred her freedom to our controlled lives.

An incredible coincidence happened the day I accompanied Karen on the train to the airport for her flight back to Canada. Soon after leaving the station, the train suddenly stopped in its tracks. Japanese trains are very punctual and delays are rare. This was a long delay, and I was unable to understand the message playing over the train's speakers. But whatever the cause, I believed there was a supernatural explanation.

I told Karen it must be a sign from God that he didn't want her to leave. I opened my Bible and showed her the passage where God supposedly stopped the sun for a day.[21] If God could stop the sun, I reasoned, he certainly could stop a train. After about thirty minutes, she started to worry she might miss her flight, so I don't think I convinced her it was God's plan. When the train suddenly jerked into reverse motion and headed back to Tateyama, I was as surprised as Karen was concerned. The few times I'd been on a train that stopped in the middle of the tracks, it had always continued its journey.

I showed Karen another biblical passage, where the shadow of a sundial supposedly moved backwards ten degrees.[22] Those two biblical events, time stopping and reversing, reinforced my belief that God was speaking to Karen by stopping the train and turning it back. I explained there wasn't enough time now to drive her to the airport. She was silent on the short trip back. It seemed her mind was racing to make sense of it.

Back at Tateyama station, I called the HCS to have someone pick us up. When we arrived at the compound, a crowd gathered to love-bomb Karen. Everyone was welcoming her back with hugs and hallelujahs, praising God for the miracle, proclaiming it was God's will for her to stay with us. I doubt she was susceptible to that spiritual and emotional manipulation, or ever considered not returning to her children.

Aware of our security concerns, Karen knew exactly how to make us back off from trying to emotionally and spiritually coerce her. After she called her boyfriend to tell him she missed her flight, she told us he threatened to come to Japan and bring her back himself if she didn't rebook. She left a couple of days later. That Christmas was the last time all four of us were together. In early 1989, what remained of our little family unit broke apart for good—for the good of the Family, according to Berg's One Wife doctrine.

Returning from town one evening, I saw Rachelle with a top leader I knew as Gary, strolling on the street between the main building and the white house.[23] I had never spoken to him, but knew he was in Berg and Zerby's trusted inner circle, so I immediately suspected something significant was up. They both looked at me as I drove past to the parking lot. The timing and location could've been coincidental, or perhaps Gary intentionally planned it so I would see them.

After a while, Rachelle came to our bedroom and told me she'd been asked to serve on Berg's support staff. Her voice quivered as she explained we would have to get a legal divorce before they allowed her to join them. That was an emotional gut punch, and felt like another betrayal approved by leaders. I didn't dare express my resentment as I had when I learned of her secret affair. I suppressed my feelings and accepted the inevitable.

It shouldn't have surprised me that they only recruited Rachelle. She was more obedient and servile, while my disposition made me a less desirable servant. I was more likely to occasionally question, criticize and express minor disagreements instead of keeping my thoughts to myself. After Berg arrived at the HCS, top leaders reprimanded me more than once for trivial things, including expressing my opinion, which they considered talking back and challenging authority.

I shouldn't have been surprised about a forced divorce, either. Most top leaders, and staff members in Berg's inner circle, were purposely separated from their spouses, ensuring they had no divided loyalties. We didn't really have freedom of choice about it. We risked the wrath of God if we refused a request from his prophet. There was no point objecting, so I made it easy for her and bluntly said I agreed to the divorce. Broken-hearted, my emotional connection to her finally broke in that moment.

The leaders wasted no time in getting me out of the picture. It would take a few months to get the divorce, so to avoid any awkward tension or disharmony between Rachelle and me while we waited, they sent me away a couple of days later. I moved to an office home in the residential neighbourhood of Shin-Urayasu, near Tokyo Disneyland. James, formerly Mark, and Sweetie were in charge. Both were also separated from their spouses and children. He was the leader in Hong Kong who had recruited Rachelle and me, and she was formerly Maggie's secretary, who had informed me of her husband's affair with Rachelle.

In our divorce application, we claimed irreconcilable differences. We told the Japanese family-court mediator that Rachelle wanted to return to Canada. I had no idea how close to the truth that was. Many years later, I learned that Berg and his staff had moved from the HCS to Canada, where they lived until 1993 in a rural area near Vancouver, British Columbia. I realized then that one reason Berg's team recruited Rachelle was her Canadian citizenship.

I didn't see Rachelle again until 1993, the year Jesus failed to come back. I didn't see Peter again until then either, although he did send me photos of his marriage to Joanna, and of their first child. Their wedding was part of a group ceremony with several other teen couples at the HCS in November 1989. I had left the HCS earlier that year, but would return about a year and a half later.

Chapter 16
The Exorcism of Merry

Soon after my divorce from Rachelle was finalized in May 1989, James and Sweetie relayed an order for me to move to a secret World Services unit in Hong Kong. The WS office was in a high-end four-bedroom, two-bathroom apartment on the west side of Hong Kong Island with a spectacular view of the busy entrance to Victoria Harbour. There were seven adults and three young children living there.

For the first few months, I slept in the small servant's bedroom just off the kitchen. Isaac, or Ike, as we called him, supervised the unit and used that room when he visited.[1] He was a top leader, helped manage the group's global finances, and was the Family's spokesperson on the US television show *Larry King Live* in 1993.[2] I saw him around the HCS when Berg was there.

My main job was to cook, clean and do trivial tasks, apparently so the others could do more important work. I was always on standby, ready to accompany someone into town or run an errand on my own. There was still one regular home in Hong Kong, and members from Macau and other countries frequently came there, so to avoid them I needed to be inCOG-nito when I went out. The leader's wife took me to town to help me buy a custom-tailored suit and shirts, several silk ties, leather shoes, a gold-plated watch and prescription sunglasses, to disguise me from other members, as well as to blend in with the HK business crowd.

They also gave me an emergency fund of $1,000 Hong Kong dollars, worth about $250 US dollars at the time, an ounce of gold then worth just over $400 US dollars, and a one-way airplane ticket to Manila in case I had to suddenly flee Hong Kong.

No one spoke to me about the work they were doing. I wasn't trusted enough to be involved directly, although they did have me make frequent phone calls to WS headquarters in Switzerland. The office had the latest computer technology, so I used a portable acoustic-coupler modem to send encrypted digital data from different telephone booths for each call.

Everything I did could easily have been done by one of the others, which made me wonder why I was really there. Manipulative secrecy, information provided only on a need-to-know basis, and the ask-no-questions mindset made it impossible for me to know the real reason. In hindsight, I suspect it may have been to maintain complete control over me, at least temporarily, after Berg's team had recruited Rachelle. I had less freedom there than when I lived in communist China. As Berg bluntly put it, WS members were virtual prisoners under house arrest:

> Some people can't stand the confinement of a Selah Colony [secret home]....Like somebody said, it's like living in prison or under house arrest. That's true. You don't have very much liberty here at all. Nobody's allowed to go anywhere but people who have business outside & have to go....Look, we have everything, everything a heart could desire! — but freedom.[3]

That's how it was. We lived in a constant state of high security bordering on paranoia. I may have been able to go out on my own to do errands occasionally, but I still felt like a spiritual slave bound by invisible chains, with every aspect of my extremely restricted life dictated by those in control of it.[4] Berg was only partly right. I didn't have freedom, but it wasn't true that I had "everything a heart could desire."

Working for World Services was supposedly a higher calling, yet I felt unfulfilled, sad and lonely. I was probably depressed. Whenever I went out alone, I quickly chugged two cans of beer from a corner store and then sucked on breath mints before returning, hoping no one would smell the alcohol. That didn't make me feel much better, though. The only thing that kept me going was my belief that in just a few years, Jesus was coming back in the clouds like a flash of lightning, with trumpeting angels gathering the true believers already in heaven and those still on earth. Given new, immortal physical bodies, we would then rule heaven on earth for the next one thousand years.

When Ike arrived a few months after I did, I had to vacate his room and sleep on the living-room floor, fitting for my servant status.[5] He came with a guy I knew at the HCS as Barry.[6] What I didn't know was that Barry was a long-time WS member in close contact with Berg and Zerby, and that he had been convicted of passport fraud in Australia several years earlier in a parental abduction case.[7] He had forged signatures and made false statements so that he could unlawfully take his son to Japan without his wife's knowledge. She eventually discovered his location in Tokyo and regained custody. Barry was deported to Australia, but sometime after his conviction he returned to Japan and lived at the HCS.

Ike and Barry had come to oversee the office's relocation to Switzerland. It was a major move, so I suspect the plan was probably already in place long before I arrived. I'm sure some of the encrypted messages I sent were about the move, and that I was the last one to learn about it. Both Ike and Barry treated me with contempt, often berating me over minor things. So, although I felt manipulated and deceived, I was also relieved to learn I would not be moving to Europe too, but would be remaining in Hong Kong.

I wasn't the only one staying behind; so was Pauly, a British single brother in that WS unit who mostly did menial tasks, like me. We moved to the last Hong Kong home, in Sai Kung, the New Territories town where Rachelle and I lived a few years earlier. Two couples, Mark and Deborah, and John and Joany, lived in a small house near a beach. Their sole purpose was to solicit free food and other products for Jonathan "Ho" Berg's commune in Macau. Mark and John were British citizens, Deborah was from Singapore, and Joany from Hong Kong.

Deborah and Joany did most of the solicitation by telephone. I took turns with Mark and John driving the van into Kowloon to pick up the donated items. Two of us guys usually went, although one of the women accompanied the driver when we went to public markets to beg in person for produce. We kept a portion of the food for ourselves, then piled the rest on pallets and shipped it by barge to Macau once a week.

Occasionally, we brought donated items to some of the refugee camps where fifty thousand "boat people" who had fled Vietnam after the US war were kept in prison-like fenced enclosures. Delivering food, clothing and other items to the compounds provided excellent public-relations photo opportunities, which were used to generate more donations. However, we kept most of what we received for our own needs, passing little on to the truly needy. When it came to giving to the poor, charity always began at home in the Family.

Pauly remained in Hong Kong because he had a special assignment. Once a week he made a business trip to the city. I always accompanied him, which gave me insight into some of the WS unit's operations. Dressed in our suits, we first went to post offices in Kowloon and Hong Kong Island. After Pauly collected mail from postal boxes, we went to a restaurant for lunch, where he would open his briefcase on his lap and process the mail. The lid partially blocked my view, but I could tell he was opening envelopes and removing their contents.

We then went to a couple of banks, and sometimes a gold bullion dealer. Pauly spent a few minutes with a teller before going to the vault where the safety deposit boxes were. I didn't ask and he didn't tell, but I assumed he was depositing cheques into accounts, transferring funds and putting cash and gold in a safety box. I had no role in that business, so I wasn't sure why I accompanied Pauly. Perhaps it was to protectively watch his back, or to keep on eye on him in case he strayed. I learned many years later that he was probably handling large sums of gold and cash. [8]

After nearly a year in Hong Kong, I moved to Macau in 1990. It had been five years since I'd lived in the translation home there. Ho's compound on the outer island of Coloane now had around seventy people. About half were children and teens, many without their parents. My ability to drive and run a kitchen was needed there more than in Hong Kong, but I continued to accompany Pauly on his weekly business trips. On those days, I took the one-hour high-speed ferry to Hong Kong in the morning, and returned in the evening.

I frequently drove people to and from the ferry terminal, did shopping and other errands, and picked up the weekly shipment of donated food from Hong Kong. One day, I was in town doing business, so I had my briefcase with me. I briefly set it down by my leg while purchasing a newspaper from a street stand. Seconds later, it was gone. I hadn't noticed a thing. My passport and the emergency cash, gold and airplane ticket to Manila I had from the WS unit were in the briefcase.

I would soon come to regret losing the ticket, cash and gold. At least my passport was replaceable, but I had to go to Hong Kong to get a new one. When I arrived there with a special permit to exit Macau, an immigration agent escorted me to the Canadian consulate. I received a temporary passport on June 6, 1990, valid for six months to match the expiry date on my stolen one.

My new passport had no previous visa stamps showing my travels to China. It had been four years since I fled Beijing, so the leaders thought this was a good opportunity to see if I could still enter China. At the border I applied for a visitor visa, and after a long wait a stern immigration officer emerged from a back room, shaking his head. He returned my passport without a visa stamp. When I asked him why, he only spoke Chinese, so another traveller translated for me. He told me the official simply said that I knew the reason why.

When I wasn't on other assignments, I usually worked in the kitchen with an older American teen, Sarah, teaching her things I learned while cooking for large numbers of people at the HCS. A few other teens took turns helping us. I soon realized that some of the teens were segregated from the others. They were under a separate, restricted regime and didn't participate in activities with others in the commune. The overseers of those teens, Michael and Crystal, lived in a cottage at the edge of the compound with some of the girls they supervised.[9]

I first saw those segregated teens as a group when Sarah and I were preparing breakfast. They looked joyless as they sullenly marched single file, like prisoners on a chain gang, down the lane outside the kitchen, with Michael leading from behind. Sarah told me they did stable chores for the horses and donkey every morning, went to a nearby field to cut hay, and did other menial jobs around the compound. At first, it seemed to me that they were just doing the kind of work that any teen growing up on a hobby farm would do, and that they probably didn't enjoy the early morning routine.

Then one day that work gang came to the kitchen to give it and the produce pantry a deep cleaning, scrubbing ingrained grime from top to bottom. Seeing up-close how closely controlled they were under Michael's harsh command, I realized they were being punished with hard labour. Eventually, after chatting with my teen helpers, and overhearing conversations, I learned disturbing details of other ways those teens were being mistreated. Their physical and psychological punishments included being confined in closets or attics, forced fasting, speech restriction, spiritual threats and brutal beatings with a wooden paddle.

Although I knew that Family children and teens were subjected to harsh spankings, usually with an instrument of some sort, I had never witnessed such beatings, and wasn't aware of those other forms of cruel corporal and emotional punishment. I didn't doubt they were happening, though, especially after I saw two teen girls subjected to forced silence and public shaming by wearing signs around their necks instructing people not speak to them because they were forbidden to talk.

One of those girls was Amber, an exuberant redhead I knew from a couple of years earlier, when I lived with her and her parents, Ezra and Ginny, in the Tokyo office. The other teen was Berg's granddaughter, Merry Jolene Berg,[10] known in the Family as Mene. She was the daughter of Berg's oldest son, Paul, whom everyone knew as Aaron.[11]

— — —

189

In 1973, when Merry was one year old, her father Aaron committed suicide by jumping off a cliff in the French Alps. At the time of his death Family members were told it was ruled an accident, but many years later Merry's mother, Aaron's second wife, revealed on an Internet forum for ex-members that after Aaron died she read his suicide note and sent it to Berg.[12] In her early years, Merry was shuffled between her mother and her grandmother, Jane Berg, before becoming a child performer with the Music with Meaning radio troupe.[13] She moved to her grandfather's home when she was eleven.

A few years after that, in a fit of rage directed at fourteen-year-old Merry, Berg told her: "Your father Aaron was insane! If it hadn't been for the Lord, he would have jumped off the cliff a long time before that." His acknowledgement of his son's suicide appeared in a Mo Letter entitled "The Last State — The Dangers of Demonism," which describes a violent exorcism Merry endured at the hands of her grandfather.[14] The title refers to a passage in Luke chapter 11 where Jesus is depicted casting out devils from people, and warns them not to allow the evil spirit to return, or they will end up in a worse state than before.

The letter's cover illustration shows a young girl using a broom to chase off a flying demon, and several shadowy demons surrounding her as she sleeps. The introduction explains that Merry's minders had previously subjected her to five exorcisms in the span of two months, attempting to expel the evil spirits they said she had sinfully succumbed to. When that didn't have the desired effect on her behaviour, Berg stepped in to conduct another exorcism himself. His co-leaders Zerby and Kelly participated, as did Sara and Alfred, long-time members of Berg's staff who supervised Merry and the other children.[15]

Most of the letter is a transcript of the exorcism. It started the moment Merry came into the room where the adults were gathered. Berg hugged and kissed her, asked her how she was, then suddenly started speaking in tongues, grabbed her head with both hands and violently shook her. As Berg described it, he "yanked it around and back and forth and side ways to side ways by my hands until I was afraid I was going to yank her head off or break her neck! God was so angry.... And then I hauled off and slapped her I don't know how many times tonight, hard, right?"[16]

After violently shaking her for a full minute, he told her to look at him, slapped her face and began rebuking the Devil. Merry repeated each line of his prayer commanding Satan to leave her. He then slapped her again, pushed her into a chair and began a fierce rant interspersed with repeated prayers and threats. Berg berated and spiritually condemned Merry for a couple of hours, and threatened to physically beat the demons out of her. He showed her a wooden rod, told her to feel how heavy it was, then made her bend over and whacked her with it, warning that next time it would be much harder, but on her bare buttocks.

The vicious verbal violence and spiritual threats Berg spat at Merry were fairly typical of his rants when he was speaking about his perceived enemies, but it was shocking to read such vitriolic language directed at his fourteen-year-old granddaughter, on top of the physical violence he inflicted on her. That's why Berg published the letter with those details. He intended it as a dreadful warning, especially to teens, not to doubt, disobey, disrespect, question or criticize their parents or leaders, which apparently were Merry's sins. The first paragraph of the letter states:

> Because [Merry's] spiritual problems and very sad present state have stemmed from what many might have considered "typical teenage characteristics" of resentfulness, pride and self-righteousness, a critical spirit and serious daydreaming, we are sharing this story with you, Family teens and adults, to clearly prove that anyone who yields to the Devil's devices and doesn't strive to win victories over these weaknesses and sins through desperate prayer and constant bathing of the Word, as well as very close shepherding and disciplinary measures, could end up in the very same dangerous situation as she. So beware![17]

Throughout his tyrannical tirade, Berg demonized Merry by claiming she was involved with witchcraft and Satanism, and possessed by devils that she deviously let back in after each exorcism. He repeatedly equated demon possession to mental illness, warning her that she would go insane and end up in a mental hospital if she didn't repent and change. Berg told Merry not only that her father was insane, but that other close relatives were too, including her mother, her grandmother Jane, and her aunt Deborah, Berg's first child.[18]

It's not surprising that Berg claimed those people were mentally ill. Each of them had intimate knowledge of his immoral personal life, and had criticized or disobeyed him. Labelling them and others as insane and possessed was a tactic to discredit them, which was why Merry was facing the same accusations.[19] She had honestly disclosed her true feelings and thoughts, including criticisms of her grandfather, in daily reports the children were required to write.[20] The adults who read her diary probably considered her honest criticisms of Berg's behaviour her worst sin of all.

In a note at the end of that letter, Sara, who also wrote the introduction, explains how they came to discover Merry's sins after considering her a "nearly perfect child" when she first came to live with Berg. She wrote:

> Usually, when having to use such severe disciplinary measures as mentioned in the above letter, you're dealing with some incorrigible, defiant and rebellious teen terror or criminal, but this is not so in [Merry's] case. She was always known and considered to be a very sweet and good girl.
>
> There was no outward indication whatsoever of her being the slightest bit yielded to the Enemy or even susceptible to such serious spiritual problems. The only slight indication of any "potential problem" area in her was her self-centredness, self-righteousness and being seemingly "too good"....
>
> It wasn't until we began to require a written Daily Report from the teens that we noted in [Merry's] "Lessons and Trials" section that she repeatedly, over several days' time, wrote, "I need more love so I won't criticise others," or "I'm praying for more respect for my leadership." By then probing into this more, asking her all about it and digging deeper and deeper (since we'd definitely detected a more defiant and self-righteous attitude in her by this time), we then worked at opening "Pandora's Box", so to speak, to find that she had really given place to the Enemy and had an almost uncontrollable habit of doing so by that time....
>
> Therefore, it is very important for all our parents to realise that not every "sweet little darling" may be all that good after all! Mama [Zerby] has often said that it's not the people with problems and weaknesses and battles that you have to watch out for. But the most serious type problems to watch out for are in people who think they're so good and never seem to have problems....like Dad [Berg] says, self-righteousness is one of the worst sins there is and it can be really demonic! So be aware of it![21]

In August 1987, several months after the events in that letter, Berg banished his granddaughter to her uncle Ho's commune in Macau. A year or so after Merry's arrival, Berg instructed his son and the top leaders of the region to set up a separate juvenile detention program in his compound. Known as the Teen Detention Home, it was the model for what became

Victor Programs in other parts of the world.[22] Teens deemed delinquent or rebellious, often over trivial matters, were subjected to punishments, confinement, hard labour and reindoctrination through constant study of scriptures and Mo Letters, all intended to break their will and force them to submit.

Among the first so-called delinquent teens sent to Macau was James, the son of Isaac, the leader who supervised the WS unit in Hong Kong. With Sara, Isaac co-wrote an article describing at length James's alleged rebelliousness and troublemaking, most of which would seem like normal teen behaviour to outsiders.[23] They also detailed their disciplinary dealings with him, which included Isaac beating James with a big plastic cane. The article includes a note Berg wrote to Isaac, telling him to threaten James that he would be sent to a mental institution if he didn't straighten out.[24]

— — —

After reading about Merry's horrific exorcism and the cruel physical and psychological torture that Berg had subjected his granddaughter to, I was so disturbed that I repressed the account in my mind. Merry had been at the Macau compound for almost three years when I moved there. I hadn't thought of her since reading about her exorcism, but when I saw her on the workgang the first time and realized who she was, my memory of that atrocity she suffered swiftly surfaced. The helpless girl I saw that morning, and later with the humiliating silence sign around her neck, was a disheartened, depressed, abused teen, not the devilishly dangerous one Berg maliciously claimed she was.

A few months later, I got an even closer look at how Merry was still being abused, which shook me to the core. Early one evening, one of the leaders sent me over to Michael and Crystal's cottage for a couple of hours to guard the girls living with them. Apparently, they needed a break from their 24/7 supervision of the "delinquent" teens and were being rewarded with a meal out at Fernando's, a popular Portuguese restaurant just a few minutes away, near the beach.

Considering what I saw when I arrived at the cottage, perhaps I was entrusted with that assignment because I was still doing secret work for WS. Crystal told me the girls would remain in their rooms for the evening, so all I had to do was sit in the living room and keep an eye out. One of those rooms was an attic reached by ladder, with a padlock on the outside of the ceiling door. Amber was one of the girls who slept there. Crystal had special instructions concerning Merry, and brought me to the door of her room, where she stayed alone. I wasn't prepared for what I saw next.

Merry was lying on her bed half-naked, her hands tied to the bed frame on either side. There was a crumpled top sheet on the bed, but Crystal said she kept kicking it off. She told me that Merry had recently become uncontrollable, refused to keep her clothes on, and was incontinent and self-harming, so for her own safety and the safety of others she had to be tied up at night. Crystal said she took Merry to the bathroom before tying her up, and told me not to go into her room for any reason, but to call one of the leaders if necessary.

I could barely hear what Crystal was saying. I was stunned by the shock of seeing Merry chained like a wild-child. There was a smell of body odour and urine in the room. She had tangled hair and a blank stare, seemingly unaware of our presence as she mumbled to herself. After Michael and Crystal left, I stood stupefied at Merry's door awhile, trying to comprehend what I was witnessing. She gave no indication that she knew I was there, and I didn't speak to her.

She continued talking to herself, which sounded at first like incoherent babbling until I realized that she seemed to be conversing with some of the fictional characters that appear in Berg's writings, which he claimed were his spirit helpers.[25] She mentioned the Pied Piper and Merlin the wizard, like a little child talking to imaginary friends. That freaked me out. I wondered if she really had gone insane, as Berg warned would happen.

I had no knowledge of, or experience with, mental illness. My only frame of reference was Berg's teachings that equated it to demonic oppression or possession, but deep inside I knew this situation wasn't right. Over the years, when my conscience conflicted with my indoctrination, I subconsciously compartmentalized Berg's more bizarre beliefs and dubious doctrines, and the extremely hateful aspects of his teachings. But seeing personally, up-close, the horrific consequences of his beliefs play out in the real world shattered me.

The image of that shocking sight was permanently impressed on my memory. I couldn't unsee it or put it in a box in the back of my mind. My emotionally agitated thoughts replayed the scene over and over again as I struggled to make sense of what I saw. I couldn't. I was confused and wasn't sure of what to think or do, but it seemed to me that if they had to resort to tying Merry up because she had lost her mind, then she was in desperate need of professional help. I felt helpless to help her, though.

I didn't know what to do. I wasn't close enough to anyone to confide my doubts about Merry's mistreatment, and I was too intimidated to express my concerns to the leaders responsible for what was happening. A rational person would've intervened and reported the situation to authorities, but I was indoctrinated to distrust government officials.

I also knew that Ho and his two wives had befriended many influential people, including several high-level dignitaries and the chief of police, which added to my wariness.[26] Uncertain who I could trust, I was trapped, wrapped in spiritual chains that made it difficult to escape my indoctrination and kept me from doing the right thing. So I kept what I saw to myself, even as it ate at my conscience.

Although I still believed in Berg's prediction that Jesus would return in 1993, time was quickly running out on it. Certain political events needed to occur soon, such as America's downfall and the rise of a global leader who would unite the world with an international covenant, but they seemed increasingly unlikely. Seeing the effect Berg's extreme abuse had on Merry made me question some of his other doctrines too. Seeds of doubt were growing, but it took a bit more time for them to crowd out my deeply rooted beliefs.

Although I didn't have physical restraints or constraints like the ones on Merry and the other abused teens, it wasn't really feasible to leave the Family at that time. If my emergency money and ticket to Manila hadn't been stolen, I could've have gone to the Philippines and perhaps survived awhile until I figured things out. But leaving while I was in Macau or Hong Kong, with no money and no one to turn to for help, would've been much more difficult. I was totally dependent on the group.

A few days after that shocking evening, I heard they had finally taken Merry to the local hospital. Knowing she was getting medically competent care helped to relieve some of my inner turmoil. I later learned that when Merry was released from the hospital, her uncle Ho took her to the United States to live with her grandmother, Jane Berg, who was no longer in the Family, but was still friendly. That was the last I heard of Merry for the next fifteen years, until I was under psychiatric care myself and spoke about that horrific experience for the first time.

The temporary passport that replaced my stolen one was about to expire. I had to get a new one in Hong Kong. So, in November 1990, a few weeks after Merry was sent to the hospital, I moved back to the Sai Kung home for a few months. In March 1991, I was ordered to return to the Heavenly City School in Japan.

Chapter 17
Heavenly Lunacy

When I returned to Japan, Berg and his entourage, including my now ex-wife Rachelle, were long gone from the Heavenly City School. I resumed my previous work there—cooking, driving, shopping and helping to cultivate good relations with our neighbours and local suppliers. There were probably around 150 people there now. The music and video studios were in full operation, producing audio cassettes and VHS tapes, which were a profitable source of income for Family members around the world.

When not working on the music productions or doing some other job under the supervision of an adult, the teens were grouped together and closely shepherded by Ricky and Elaine, who were part of the HCS leadership team. Indoctrination programs designed to turn children and teens into dedicated disciples and endtime evangelists had started to really ramp up. Just before I left Macau, Zerby published a letter regarding the dogmatic training of Family children. The acronym *JETT* refers to "Junior End Time Teens."[1]

> We recently sent a series of detailed questions to the Shepherds of our JETT/Teen Victor Program at the Heavenly City School. Their response was not only the reactions & information we requested regarding their program, & how they felt about this new "Techi Series,"[2] but they gave us something that was far more important & far more urgent as well!
>
> They vividly portrayed to us the very serious & urgent JETT problem that the Family is now facing. I expected that their answers would help show the Family how to set up Victor Programs for JETTs with special needs, & this they did beau-

tifully, but the Lord also used their answers to confirm something that He had already been showing us: That if we're going to save our kids, we've got to institute a new kind of intensified JETT Training Program not in every major Area, but in each individual Home throughout the Family!

I believe that we are now facing such a serious need with our JETTs, such an urgent problem, that it demands an immediate solution! And I believe that this problem isn't going to go away unless all of you, all of our Family adults, realise that you must personally do something about it! We are pubbing these answers & reactions from the HCS Overseers & JETT Victor Shepherds — Josiah, Mary Mom, Elaine (Morningstar), Ricky, Faithy, John PI & Ginny — & I'm sure that reading their answers will help convince you that if we are going to salvage our JETTs for the Lord's service, you are going to have to be part of the solution!"[3]

My personal interaction with children was limited mostly to the teens who helped me in the kitchen or accompanied me in the van on various errands. Sometimes I was an extra on music video shoots with teens, or drove a group of kids and their overseers on excursions. If there were teens at the HCS singled out for extraordinarily cruel corporal punishments like those in Macau, I wasn't aware of it.

However, I knew that similar mistreatment could've been happening out of sight somewhere in the complex of buildings. The teens I worked more closely with seemed happy, at least superficially. But after they read the "The Last State" and similar warnings, most were probably wise enough to stay silent and suppress any complaints, criticisms and doubts they had with a smile. After all, teens were the target audience of that letter describing Merry's violent exorcisms after she confessed her criticisms and doubts about Berg.

My own doubts were growing while I too kept smiling. I couldn't forget what I had seen in Macau, or another memory that had resurfaced since then. A few years earlier, I heard that a thirteen-year-old boy, Martin, had committed suicide. He and his mother lived in the same Tokyo home that Rachelle and I had lived in before we moved to Beijing. Hezekiah, who supervised that home at the time, told me that Martin had hanged himself, and his mother had taken his body back to Europe. Martin's suicide had been hushed up, so Hezekiah cautioned me not to talk about it.

When I heard that news, I was shocked and confused. As with my uncle's apparent suicide when I was ten, I struggled to comprehend what could've pushed the child to take his own life. I couldn't, so I boxed that tragedy in the back of my mind with other troubling thoughts about problematic practices and disagreeable doctrines. But now, unable to put out of mind the abusive treatment of teens I witnessed in Macau, I reconsidered Martin's suicide in the context of the extreme indoctrination and discipline used to control Family children. I suspected that was what had pushed him to end his life.

I was finally waking up to the fact that inflicting severe spiritual threats and corporal punishments on vulnerable minors who knew no other life caused them greater psychological harm than the manipulations and chastisements that I and other adults experienced. The hypocritically harsh, authoritarian leadership of the Family of Love, under Berg and Zerby's direct dictatorial control, was more mean-spirited and malevolent now than when I had left the Children of God in 1976. I was also questioning some of Berg's bizarre spiritual doctrines, as well as doubting that specific endtime events would soon happen the way he had predicted.

Berg was a Pentecostalist and spiritualist. He believed in a spirit-world afterlife where the dead interact and communicate with the living. Many of Berg's letters describe supposed spirit trips where he left his body, travelled in the spirit to some other location or dimension, including heaven, and interacted with the spirits of biblical, historical, mythical and even fictional characters. He claimed many of them were his spirit helpers who delivered direct messages to him from God.

Many of Berg's letters also describe and analyze his dreams. Citing Acts 2:17, which describes the day of Pentecost when Jesus's first followers were filled with the Holy Spirit, he claimed his dreams were messages from God.

A typical dream was one he called "Strange Truths," in which he and some followers were drinking crystal-clear water springing from a rock.[4] When the water suddenly became filled with tiny, strange creatures, Berg told them it was still safe and nourishing to drink. He analyzed the dream as a metaphor. The rock was God, the water was God's Word, and the strange creatures were Berg's unique biblical interpretations and extra-biblical doctrines. Since Berg's strange truths came from the same source as the Bible, he interpreted, they were equivalent to the Word of God.

In fact, Berg's truths were fictions. Although I swallowed several, I regarded some of his spiritually bizarre beliefs and extreme sexual doctrines as extra-biblical theological theories, so they were not necessarily meant to be taken literally, in the way I understood the Bible. Applying that approach to the more troubling Mo Letters made it easier to rationalize or ignore and store in my compartmentalized mind some of Berg's strangest truths.

The Mo Letters I was most interested in were his analyses of politics and current world affairs. I believed Berg was the endtime prophet, so I did take his prophecies predicting the imminent Second Coming literally, because they were tied directly to many eschatological scriptures scattered through-out the Bible foretelling specific endtime events. Some seemed already fulfilled, which made it easier to accept and believe Berg's divinations of the end of the world.

I was blinded by the belief that we were in the biblical endtime and doomsday was near. Believing that Jesus was coming back in 1993, I had put aside doubts about uncomfortable, questionable aspects of his dogma, hoping all would be revealed after the Resurrection. But one belief I wasn't blind to was the prophet's preposterous claim that heaven is inside the moon. I was certain that couldn't be true, and not just because there is no biblical basis for it.

— — —

In á 1971 letter, Berg hinted that he had taken a spirit trip to Heaven, referring to it as Space City.[5] In a subsequent letter titled "Space City," he describes a fantastical visitation to what he claims is the same heavenly city mentioned in Revelation 21 and 22.[6] In those last two chapters of the Bible, John the Revelator says an angel carried him in the spirit to a holy city "descending out of heaven from God."[7]

Berg's heavenly lunacy required an even greater leap of faith after he published "The Moon—And the Hidden City" in 1985. He said it was "the most shocking revelation that I have ever received."[8] He declared that the biblical heavenly city was actually inside the moon. It was perhaps Berg's strangest "truth" yet, so strange that he acknowledged it would be hard for his followers to believe, and some would think he had "finally lost his mind."[9] In light of his moon theory, he was more of a lunatic than all the people he claimed were insane.

In various Mo Letters before that revelation, Berg had expounded on his original Space City spirit trip.[10] He interpreted the measurements of the holy city provided in Revelation 21 as describing a multi-level, pyra-mid-shaped city. Berg gave very specific descriptions to the artists creating posters of his heavenly vision, which went far beyond the Bible's description.[11] He claimed, for example, that the entire city was enclosed within a crystal sphere, although the Bible makes no mention of that.

While thinking about that crystal sphere, Berg wondered how its size compared with the moon. He did some ad hoc calculations and concluded that the sphere was slightly smaller than the moon. Suddenly, it occurred to him that the sphere, with the city inside it, could fit within the moon. Seeking scriptural confirmation, he found every biblical reference to the moon and unconvincingly twisted his interpretation of them to fit his theory. But Berg was convinced, confidently declaring, without a doubt, that heaven was inside the moon.

Berg not only believed that the moon was hollow and holding a hidden, heavenly city of gold, but that the earth "is also merely a hollow empty shell surrounding the Bottomless Pit & the Lake of Fire"—in other words, hell. He explained that the moon and the earth were different sizes because "there are so many more people going to Hell than to Heaven! There has to be a lot more room for them in the heart of the Earth!"[12]

In two related letters, Berg addresses discrepancies brought to his attention between his mathematics and that of real scientists.[13] He had wrongly measured the size of the moon, but instead of admitting his error and retracting his revelation, he claimed that scientific calculations regarding the moon couldn't be trusted because scientists didn't really know its dimensions and distance from the earth; they were only guessing.[14]

As a young-earth creationist, believing the earth is only about six thousand years old, Berg had always denounced the sciences of evolutionary biology, geology, paleontology, physics and astronomy. Now he was telling his followers that not even the mathematics used by scientists could be trusted, that his uneducated calculations were more accurate than theirs.[15]

So, in order to make his "heaven in the moon" theory fit, Berg confidently claimed the moon was actually larger than what the science showed. Berg also speculated that the Apollo moon landings never happened, citing the 1978 film *Capricorn One*, which depicts a US government conspiracy faking a manned Mars landing in a film studio.[16] But that too was a leap of faith too far for me. When I was thirteen, I watched on TV every moment of Neil Armstrong's "giant leap for mankind." I also saw the next three Apollo missions that landed men on the moon, before I joined the Children of God. Berg's loony theories seemed far more improbable than those moon missions.

— — —

Although I rejected Berg's loony lunar doctrine, I still believed the dogma of young-earth creationism, which claims events in Genesis literally happened as described and the earth is just over six thousand years old. There was at least a biblical basis for that fundamentalist belief. In the mid-1600s, Irish archbishop James Ussher published a detailed chronology of biblical events that concluded the earth was created in 4004 BC. In King James bibles, that date is noted next to the first verse in Genesis declaring the creation of heaven and earth.

Berg insisted the King James version of the Bible was the most accurate English translation, but he used his own method for determining the year of creation. Unlike Ussher, he relied only on the genealogical lists in Genesis, Matthew and Luke, which supposedly show a direct lineage from Adam to Jesus. He produced an Age of the Earth Chart that claimed the date of creation was 4160 BC.[17]

Although I sometimes struggled with the incredibility of many stories in Genesis, I didn't have the necessary critical-thinking skills to overcome my indoctrination and dispute the doctrine of young-earth creationism. I dismissed any doubts I had and simply accepted that account as the true history of humanity. My narrow-minded, fundamentalist belief that the Bible was literally true closed my mind to scientific facts that had thoroughly debunked the biblical account of human origins. But for now I had more practical, immediate concerns than how old the earth was or where heaven was located.

I was convinced that Berg's endtime predictions were true because they too were directly tied to many scriptures. They had kept me going despite my accumulating concerns and doubts, but my faith in his prophecies had been wavering for a while. Certain political events that should've happened by 1991 still hadn't occurred. It was increasingly clear to me that Jesus wouldn't return in 1993 as Berg had predicted. His excuses, explanations and reinterpretations didn't convince me; they increased my doubts.

Berg was constantly searching the news for signs of the end. In 1983, he began to publish a regular series of letters on international current events relevant to his prophecies. For a while, they seemed to support his predictions, but it was also current events that eventually proved the supposed endtime prophet was wrong.

Berg's original endtime chronology specified that "we should begin hearing something about the Antichrist and his rise to power soon, and certainly not later than the early 1980s."[18] According to his interpretation of biblical passages, for Jesus to return in the first half of 1993, as Berg predicted, the Antichrist had to rule the world for the previous seven years. The Antichrist's global takeover by the end of 1985 would be signified by the public signing of an international covenant, which he would break three and half years later, leading to another three and half years of "great tribulation" before Jesus returned.

When the Antichrist didn't show up on schedule, Berg knew that time was quickly running out on his predictions, so he began to revise them. In April 1990, Berg contradicted his long-held belief that the Antichrist would be a well-known public figure who slowly rose to power in the Middle East or Russia, before controlling the world in 1985.[19] He now claimed that "it doesn't really have to happen that way. He could come suddenly, miraculously, and in such a way that everybody would just be astonished!"[20]

In November 1990, Berg was still convinced the Antichrist would show up at any time, and speculated that his public signing of an international covenant would probably be broadcast to the world by CNN. He wrote: "It looks like it's almost time for the Antichrist...It looks like CNN might be a good beginning for the Antichrist, as it's becoming more worldwide & catering to Europeans, Latins & Asians as well now."[21]

In early 1991, Berg continued to expect the Antichrist would soon appear in public, although it was too late to fit within his original prophetic timeline.[22] Then, in June, just days before Boris Yeltsin was elected president of Russia, Berg wrote another warning letter. He cited Russian astrologers who predicted a "time of trouble" for the new Russian federation that would start a few days after that election. Berg wrote:

> Well, this could be the beginning of the End! All that Russia has to do is go into civil war with leaders fighting leaders, to make a perfect open door for the Antichrist! If Russia goes into such turmoil & civil war that it needs a strong leader to pull it out of chaos, it would be the ideal opportunity for the Antichrist to arise.[23]

Berg was now reinterpreting his prophecies regarding the rise of the Antichrist. Most significantly, specific events he had always taught would be known to the whole world, such as the signing of an international treaty, had supposedly already happened in secret. At the end of 1991, Berg wrote a two-part letter proclaiming that 1992 could be the year his prophecies came to pass.[24]

He claimed that the Antichrist was now ruling the world behind the scenes, although the endtime prophet didn't know his identity. Berg was now getting desperate and denied he had ever made absolute claims about those endtime events.

> We have always said that we don't know whether that's going to be a secret Covenant. Sometimes I've said that I don't see how anything that important could be secret. But I'm changing my mind, or the Lord is changing it for me. Do you know what I'm beginning to think now? That it may have already been made, & been secret for probably about three years![25]

Berg no longer had the same absolute certainty about his predictions that he'd had throughout the 1970s and '80s. More and more, he was hedging his prophetic bets.

> "Ah," you say, "but if '92 passes & it doesn't happen, then Dad's a False Prophet!" I'm not saying I know it's going to happen in '92, but right now I don't see how it couldn't happen in '92! So I'm here to tell you that I've come under a greater conviction the last few days, weeks, months & years, but especially in the recent days when I see how things are going! I am more & more convinced that it could be in 1992![26]

I never read that two-part Mo Letter "It Could Happen This Year of 1992," because my life in the Family finally ended in August 1991. Months before that, I had stopped believing in Berg. His revisions of his visions, prophecies and predictions didn't convince me; they just made me more doubtful that he was a true prophet.

I also couldn't reconcile the extreme abuse of Merry and other teens I witnessed in Macau, or Martin's suicide, with what was supposed to be the Family of Love. I had become increasingly resentful of hypocritical leaders living double standards while they manipulated and maltreated people. I was lonely too, after my forced divorce from Rachelle, and had no one I could confide in. All my doubts came to a head when I returned to Japan in 1991.

Although members had to write regular reports revealing not just their activities, but their state of mind, I now knew better than to expose my true thoughts and feelings. I kept my inner turmoil to myself, choosing my confessions carefully, as I had done as a child in the Catholic confession booth. However, some of my angst spilled out occasionally in angry outbursts and quarrels over petty things with co-workers. That forbidden behaviour was very uncharacteristic of me, so I was as surprised as they were when I did that. I wasn't happy, and it was getting harder to hide behind a smile.

One day, I suddenly realized what was happening to me. Like most members, I had a portable cassette player for listening to Family music. Mine, which I purchased in Hong Kong, also had a radio. Most worldly music was forbidden, so at first I self-censored and only listened to the radio for news reports. But now I began to covertly listen to pop music on an American Forces Network radio station while I walked around the HCS compound for exercise. I placed a Family music cassette in the player to conceal what I was really listening to in case anyone asked.

It wasn't unusual for me to interpret a song's lyrics as a divine message directly applicable to my own life. That's what had happened in 1979 when I'd first heard Dylan's song "Gotta Serve Somebody," which prompted me to return to serving God in the Family. Now, another rock song stopped me in my tracks, only it led me in the opposite direction. When I heard "Losing My Religion" by R.E.M., I finally realized that's what was happening to me.

Chapter 18
Should I Stay or Should I Go?

When I heard "Losing My Religion" on the radio in the spring of 1991, it was a current hit that got regular airplay. Each time I heard it, I was mesmerized by the introspective lyrics that reflected my inner turmoil and spiritual confusion. I understood now that I was starting to lose my religion. Months of soul-searching, questioning and doubting Berg's biblical interpretations and bizarre spiritual fantasies finally led to the realization that, as the song described, I was a blinded fool and the life I was living was just a fanciful dream.

Awakening from a dream can be disorienting. I was confused, unsure of what I believed anymore. I had lost faith in Berg's prophetic power and could no longer disregard my doubts and concerns. I wasn't renouncing all Christian dogma, but my faith in the Family's fundamentalist belief system had collapsed, undermined by facts I could no longer ignore. Totally losing my religion would be a longer process over a few years.

Despite my doubts, it wasn't easy making or implementing the life-changing decision to leave the Family. I remembered how difficult it was for me to adjust to the real world when I left the group in the mid-1970s. I had been infantilized by the four years I spent in the Children of God, from the age of sixteen to twenty, which is the vulnerable stage of middle to late adolescence when my brain was not yet fully developed. After I left that time, I remained a believer in their dogma, so it continued to stunt my maturation. I ended up aimless and homeless before returning to the fold as a prodigal son a few years later.

Now, I had spent almost twelve more years in that socially isolated, paternalistic community where all major decisions were made for me, and my basic needs were met as long as I remained faithfully obedient and subservient. I had become as dependent materially, socially and spiritually on my religious Family as an addict is on narcotics.

Their communal lifestyle meant I always had a home with like-minded people almost anywhere I went in the world. It was difficult to give up that familial support and head into the unknown, a thirty-six-year-old with no money or possessions, few skills and little education. And as with addicts, who often don't successfully kick their harmful habits the first time they try, breaking my psychological dependency was very difficult. It required admitting to myself that I had wasted nineteen years of my life on believing a false prophet, the religious "pusher" in this analogy.

My entire worldview had been wrapped up in Berg's warped theology. Though I couldn't yet see too far beyond that narrow-minded perspective, I was no longer certain of God's will for me and didn't trust my own muddled mind. Should I stay or should I go? I didn't know. I had doubts about my doubts. Trapped between two colliding worlds, unsure about where I belonged, I was worried I couldn't survive in either one, but I knew I couldn't continue living in the Family while harbouring deep doubts that kept rising to the surface.

It was getting harder for me to keep up the pretense and hide my conflicted mind behind a smiley, sunny disposition. I had bet my life on Jesus coming back in 1993, and so never made long-term plans. Having lost that wager, I desperately needed a plan now that would help me decide what to do. I had only three options: I could remain in the Family and try to overcome my concerns and doubts; I could leave the Family and try to remain in Japan; or I could leave the Family and return to Canada.

None of those options were easily achievable. It was highly unlikely I could resolve my internal conflicts at this point and remain in the Family. I thought I could probably find an English teaching job that would enable me to remain in Japan, but without sufficient money or external support of any kind it would be very difficult to simply walk away and survive alone long enough to get established. I also couldn't return to Canada without help. I was mired in anxious indecision as I considered my next step. I had to find some way out of my predicament, though. Time was running out.

Three months after I returned to Japan, I extended my visitor's visa a further three months. I had to apply for an alien registration card, so leaders told me to do that at the local government office using the HCS address. I thought that was odd because I had always registered before using a safehouse address that wasn't easily traced to the Family. My visa extension expired in September 1991, so I would have to leave the country by then, and either move on to another one or return to Japan with a new visitor visa. That impending deadline gave me an idea that could help me deal with my dilemma.

All my previous visa trips had been to Korea or the Philippines, but if I went to Canada this time, with a return ticket, I would be forced to choose between worlds—spiritual or secular, east or west. Although the Naritas were funding the HCS's budget, including visa trips, I had to convince the leaders that the far more expensive trip was worth it. Although no Family member was indispensable, it was those same leaders who had brought me back from Hong Kong, so I knew I was somewhat useful to them and hoped that would work to my advantage.

I had easily fit back into my former roles at the HCS, not only as a cook, shopper and driver, but as a likeable liaison to the local community. I had befriended many of our suppliers, such as a supermarket produce manager, a chicken farmer, a baker and several of Mrs. Narita's friends. I also taught English at the community centre in town as a public relations gesture.

I played up those relationships when I presented my plan to Josiah, who was both the overseer of the HCS and the new head of the entire Pacific region. I pointed out that I could get a new passport in Canada, which could help get me back into Japan for another six months, since it wouldn't have my previous visa stamps. My ploy worked. Josiah thought it was a good idea, and his leadership team also considered it an opportunity to bring back certain items that were hard to find in Japan. At the top of their shopping list was a dozen King James Bibles for teens who didn't have their own yet.

I purchased a round-trip ticket between Tokyo and Vancouver, and a one-way ticket from Tokyo to Hong Kong, which would facilitate my re-entry into Japan. The leaders gave me a significant amount of "show money" for that purpose, on top of the money for shopping. Shortly after my trip was booked, something completely unexpected happened that added a welcome wrinkle to my plan. I fell in love.

Wings was a Japanese single mother of a three-year-old daughter, Joy. She worked in the translation home, the same one I had visited occasionally a couple of years earlier. She had come to the HCS with Joy for a week-long "holiday" from her work. We were mutually attracted at first sight, so we spent much of our free time together in the evenings, opening our hearts. Sexual relations between members of different homes were no longer allowed, so without the distraction of sex, we quickly developed a deep connection. The hormonal euphoria of falling in love was a good antidote to the stressful anxiety my doubts and indecision were causing.

After she left, we continued nurturing our relationship, expressing our desire to be together in a few love letters we exchanged before my trip.

Although Wings knew I was going to Canada and might have difficulty getting back into Japan, she didn't know there was a possibility I might decide not to even try to return. In our short time together, I didn't reveal my deepest doubts about Berg or thoughts of leaving the Family, or dare share those things in writing. I needed to proceed cautiously, as I was still uncertain of what to do, but Wings gave me a glimmer of hope that I had found real love again, and a reason to return to Japan.

In a letter I received from Wings a couple weeks before my flight, she wrote that a few months before meeting me the Lord told her there was someone for her at the HCS. She believed I was that person and she wanted to be with me when I returned from Canada. She had already asked leaders for permission to get together with me, at either the HCS or the translation home.

> [sic] August 2, 1991. Dear Mike: How are you? I was so happy to received letter from you. And wanted tell you that I got so encouraged by the verse which you gave me. (Luke 1:45) Because the Lord was telling me about certain person in HCS. And I believe it's you! I don't know much about you, except of that story you gave me that night & I know that you are sweet person & likes to talk & have broken heart & loves my little Joy & me. That's all I know so far. But I have no doubt about you & me....I'm actually hoping for me & Joy to move in to the HCS or for you to join us here....I'll continue to pray for the Lord's timing, and our situation will not going to be as interference for each other, but blessing and fruitful for the Lord's work! I love you & praying for you. Hope to see you soon. Much love, Wings.

Drugged by the love hormone, I was ecstatic that she also desired to be together. But ours was a complicated, crazy love. My emotions were moderated by the knowledge that our leaders had the final say about any potential coupling. If I did return to Japan, there was no guarantee they would let us be together. I also couldn't be certain Wings would share my concerns and doubts, and want to leave the Family with me. But none of that stopped me from writing her back before I left, reassuring her I felt the same way about her and wanted to be with her and Joy too.

— — —

I returned to Port Alberni in the last week of August 1991. I was an emotional mess, knowing I would soon need to make a life-changing decision, but unsure which world I belonged in. The reverse culture shock after almost twelve years in the Family this time, eight of them in Asia, didn't help. I spent the first few days recuperating from jet lag and catching up with my mum, siblings and a few other relatives.

That homecoming was much like my Christmas visit in the year I joined the Children of God. Everyone was happy to see me, but I kept conversations superficial because I thought they couldn't relate to the strangeness of my Jesus-freak life. When anyone asked probing questions, I gave simple explanations or changed the subject. I didn't think my mum or anyone else could understand my situation, so I was unwilling to discuss my life in any detail, or seek advice about my dilemma. I remained unfamiliar to my family, feeling like an outsider, a stranger in my own homeland.

I applied for a new passport and purchased the items on my shopping list, but was still mired in indecision. I didn't trust my own mind, so I was waiting for some kind of sign to direct my path. I knew I couldn't remain in the Family, but I worried I might end up hopelessly trapped in my hometown, working an unfulfilling, dead-end job. I also doubted I could even find a job, since Canada was in the second year of a deep recession with a high unemployment rate.

Ever since joining the Children of God nineteen years earlier, I lived according to Jesus's instruction in Matthew 6:19–34 to "lay not up for yourselves treasures upon earth [and] take therefore no thought for the morrow." My spiritual mission had impaired my practical foresight. Motivated by my belief that the world as we knew it would end in 1993, I had never planned for the future. Years of denigrating indoctrination had also diminished my self-esteem, blinding me to my potential. I couldn't yet see the many possibilities and opportunities open to me if I remained in Canada.

I knew I couldn't stay in an indecisive state of limbo for long. I had to choose one life or another, each with certain obstacles and uncertain futures. This time, there was no song, movie, scripture or other sign directing my path. Instead, in my unstable state of mind, I made a rash decision based on my emotional overreaction to an innocent comment at an extended-family gathering.

My birthday is in September, so initially I thought the gathering was an all-in-one welcome-home/birthday/farewell celebration on my behalf. I was surprised when almost all of my mum's relatives came, as I wasn't close to many of them. But there was another purpose for the party. My mum and aunt told me later in the evening that they had used the occasion to plan a family reunion that their brother would come to.

My uncle had recently been diagnosed with advanced cancer, and they thought this would be the last chance to get all nine siblings together. They knew he would be reluctant to attend a reunion focused on him, so a party for me was the perfect opportunity to convince him to come. I realized that some had probably only come for his sake, and in my highly sensitive, emotional mood I couldn't help feeling slightly used. In that moment, I felt as alienated from my real family as I was from my spiritual family. The only thing I was certain of was my love for Wings. I couldn't get her out of my mind.

Love is a powerful motivator. I had long acted out of a misguided, fearful love for God. Now the fear of missing a rare opportunity to share genuine mutual love was moving me. Re-establishing my life in Canada would always remain an option, but I had only one chance to return to Japan and be with Wings. I knew I wouldn't get another one if I didn't use my prepaid return ticket. I didn't know her real name and had no way to contact her without going through the Family. If I didn't return to Japan now, I would never know if I could've successfully rescued her and Joy, and created a new family with them. So I decided to return, not to remain in the Family, but to persuade Wings to leave it with me.

My plan was to return to the HCS and push the leaders for permission to legally marry Wings. I knew that other foreign members lived in Japan on spousal visas, so I thought they might approve that. It was an all-or-nothing gamble that could backfire and strand me overseas again, but I thought it was a fairly safe bet.

The next step in my plan would be to confide my doubts to Wings and convince her that the Family was not a safe place to raise her daughter. I was confident I could persuade her to leave for Joy's sake once I described the abusive treatment of teens I witnessed in Macau. I also thought my English teaching experiences gave me a good chance of finding a job in Japan. So, after three weeks in Canada, I flew back to Japan with that uncertain, though hopeful, plan.

— — —

I was excited by the thought of being with Wings, but I never saw her again. I didn't even make it out of the Tokyo airport. My plot was interrupted by an immigration official who denied me entry into the country. Initially, I thought everything was fine, because the first agent just asked me the typical questions and confirmed I had another ticket out of Japan. My heart started pounding, though, and my jet-lagged mind jolted into high alert when two officers showed up at the booth moments later and escorted me to an office.

I knew I was in serious trouble, but I wasn't sure what the issue was. They probably didn't have instant access to the paper record from 1974, when immigration officials arrested and threatened to deport me. But I had re-entered Japan and renewed my visas several times since 1985, so they certainly had computerized records of those visits. I had no run-ins with law enforcement during those stays, though, so I didn't think there was anything in my file connecting me to the Family.

They had retrieved my suitcase and broken into it before interrogating me further, so they asked me why I was bringing a dozen Bibles to Japan if I was just a visitor. Taking that many Bibles into a country where only one percent of the population is Christian is not something a legitimate tourist would do. Still, I desperately tried to keep up the pretense, telling him they were gifts for friends of mine. It was pointless. He told me he knew I was connected to the Family.

It wasn't until later, when I had time to think about it, that I connected the dots. I had used the HCS address for my last visa-extension application, three months earlier. The authorities certainly knew that location was a Family operation, so the address and any foreign names associated with it, including mine, were likely on an immigration watchlist.

The official told me I needed to leave the country on the first available flight. An officer brought my damaged suitcase and escorted me to the airline counter. Using my ticket to Hong Kong, I was on standby for the last flight that night. Fortunately, I got on the plane, which saved me from spending the remaining money I had. I would need it. After my seat was confirmed, I had barely enough time to make a frantic phone call to the HCS and ask them to call the Hong Kong home so they could pick me up at the airport. It would be too late to take public transit all the way out to Sai Kung.

Once on board, I slumped in my seat, exhausted. Although I'd always known I could be turned away at the border, I was so overly confident I would pass through with my new passport that I hadn't planned for that possibility. Dazed by this development and unsure of my next step, I was too anxious to sleep, so during the flight I tried to think of ways I could get back into Japan. I wasn't ready to give up on Wings yet, but my ideas were futile. My last hope was that Josiah and his co-leaders knew another way, legal or not, that I could return to Japan.

I lost all hope of being with Wings when I discovered the Sai Kung home had another visitor from the HCS with the same problem as mine. Elaine, who supervised the teens with her lover, Ricky, had also recently been denied re-entry into Japan. We were both desperate to return, for similar reasons. When she told me there was some plan in the works to get her back to the HCS, I knew the leaders would prioritize her situation, since she was higher in the hierarchy. My heart sank when Josiah confirmed that in a short message, saying the Lord must've needed me more somewhere else and that I should pray about where to go next.

I felt abandoned and betrayed by my leaders again when I realized they had manipulated me into using the HCS address on my last visa-extension application. Whatever their purpose for that, it was clear to me now that they had used me as an ignorant, expendable pawn. But that was their final move. No longer oblivious to their machinations and manipulations, I would now decide my own moves.

I had been willing to remain in the Family only for the opportunity to be with Wings and convince her to leave with me. Since I couldn't return to Japan, that chance was gone. With no way to contact her directly other than by letters forwarded through the HCS, I couldn't see any way to overcome the barriers preventing us from being together. My heart broke when I accepted that Wings was lost to me.

After receiving Josiah's message, I had just a brief window to make my move, so I had to act quickly without exposing my intentions to the others in the home. Before I could plan my next step, I needed to go into the city alone to find out if the show money I still had for my return to Japan was enough for a one-way ticket to Canada. As far as the others were concerned, I was just passing through, and so was not a member of their home. They left me alone to do my own thing and didn't schedule me into their activities. I knew that wouldn't last long, but it gave me the opportunity I needed.

Pretending that I was taking orders directly from Josiah, I made up a reason to go into the city and headed to a travel agency I was familiar with in Kowloon where I thought I could find the cheapest deal. It was the same one I had gone to several times before when I was doing World Services business with Pauly, who was still living in the Sai Kung home. To my great relief, I did have just barely enough money left to fly back to Canada. I booked a flight to Vancouver for September 24.

My flight was at 9:30 a.m., which meant I would have to leave the Sai

Kung home secretly several hours earlier if I left that same morning. To ensure I didn't miss it, I needed to give myself an extra day in case something went wrong, so after buying my ticket I reserved a cheap hotel room in Kowloon for the night before, where I could hide out. I had no intention of telling anyone what I was doing, knowing the emotionally intense spiritual peer pressure they would apply to try to change my mind. To avoid that confrontation, I planned to sneak out in the middle of the night and be long gone before anyone woke up.

I had a knot in my stomach for the next few days, pretending everything was fine, while anxiously waiting to flee. When the time came, worried I might sleep through my only opportunity to leave, I stayed awake until 4 a.m., hoping everyone would be dead asleep. I then crept as silently as possible, holding my breath as I tiptoed down the creaky wooden stairs with my suitcase in one hand and shoes in the other. My heart pounded so hard it hurt. Outside, I gasped in relief, then quickly made my way to the main bus route, constantly looking over my shoulder. I kept walking for about twenty minutes before a minibus finally came and took me to the nearest train station.

I went directly to the hotel and stayed there until the next morning. I didn't think they could track me there, but I couldn't really relax until I was on the plane. I intended to check in as early as possible, so about four hours before my flight, I took a taxi to the nearby Kai Tak Airport. I was the first in line when the airline counter opened, and proceeded immediately to immigration, knowing that only those with boarding passes could get into the waiting lounge.

Relieved to board the plane, I finally began to relax a little. However, before the jet took off a flight attendant handed me an envelope with my name on it. She said a friend of mine had given it to the check-in counter to pass on to me. My hands trembled as I took it from her, knowing it could only have come from one of the Family members. The envelope contained a typed letter from Josiah, which he must have sent by modem, with a handwritten message at the bottom from Elaine and Pauly. Their note, which included Pauly's pager number, said they were both waiting at the airline check-in counter until the flight left, in case I changed my mind.

Suddenly, I realized the flaw in my escape plan. They had tracked me through the travel agency. There was just one reason both Pauly and Elaine came looking for me: to talk me out of leaving. They may have missed me by minutes, but they were far too late. Even if it was possible to disembark at that point, my mind was made up.

Josiah's letter assumed Elaine and Pauly would find me before I boarded the plane. It contained exactly the kind of spiritual pressure I expected and didn't want to face in person. He used language I'd become familiar with ever since the Children of God persuaded me to join their revolution for Jesus and indoctrinated me as a spiritual soldier in their endtime army. Josiah emphasized the spiritual battle over my soul:

> The Enemy is staging a raging warfare, but you are a valuable soldier, one worth fighting for…wait 3-4 days, to give us some chance to communicate & see if we can lick the Devil & any doubts or lies he may have whispered to you to cause you to be discouraged to the point that you might even give up your crown.

He said delaying my trip by a few days would give them time to work something out for me, claiming that they had been unable to think of a way to get me back to Japan "in light of your number on your book." He was clearly referring to my passport. However, in the same sentence he added parenthetically: "Ricky might have just come up with a possible suggestion, if you were sure you had the faith for it."

It sounded to me like the suggestion was to forge a passport. Whatever Ricky's idea was, it was originally intended for Elaine, because Josiah's initial message to me was that I had to forget about returning to Japan. Too late now, Josiah was saying they would try to help me in the same way they'd help Elaine. But even if I could've got off the plane, I would be stranded in Hong Kong with no money, and control of my life would be back in their hands. I no longer wanted to surrender that control.

Elaine and Pauly's note also included Josiah's personal phone number and asked me to call him during my two-hour stopover in Tokyo, where I would be confined to the transit lounge. I didn't call him. Many months of indecision had come to an end. I was headed back to the system I had rejected and dropped out of for many years.

After jetting across the Pacific three times in less than a month, I arrived back in Canada for the final time on September 25, 1991. I was a misguided, uneducated thirty-six-year-old with less than a hundred dollars in my pocket and everything I owned in a half-empty suitcase. I would have to start my life over from scratch. The process of losing my religion was just beginning.

Chapter 19
Losing My Religion

My family was as surprised as I was that I had returned to Canada just two weeks after leaving. They knew almost nothing about my life in the Family, so I didn't explain the real reason I had been flying back and forth across the Pacific. Still dazed by this development, I just told them that Japanese border agents had denied me entry for trying to smuggle Bibles into the country. I ignored or deflected any questions about my past or why I'd left the group. They soon stopped asking.

Two weeks after I returned, I received a short letter from Josiah, and two letters and a birthday card from Wings. His letter, dated October 8, implored me to return to the Family, promising "a special place of service if you share your heart with me & all that is bothering you, & your desires & heartaches." My eyes were open now, and my mind made up, so Josiah's words had no spiritual or emotional effect on me. Wings' letters did, though.

The first one was dated September 13, the same day I was denied entry into Japan. She started by welcoming me back. Assuming I had safely returned, she explained that she was so certain we should be together that she had made a formal request to Josiah's leadership team at the HCS for us to work together. Her second letter was dated September 25, the same day I arrived back in Canada. She wrote:

> [sic] I just received message few days ago about your trip to H.K. I cryed enough that night....Please write me when you received this little letter. You still haven't get three or four of my letters. So I sent a message throw my shepherd to HCS to sent them to you....Also I heard that there are still some possibility that you can come back to this country. That made me very happy.

She added a PS: "The other day 23 of September, I was praying for you desperately for some reason against voice of the enemy, discouragement and everything....Did something happen to you that day?" I wept at this confirmation of our spiritual connection. It was uncanny how the dates of her two letters corresponded to the day I was denied entry into Japan and the day I returned to Canada. And her premonition that something had happened to me occurred on a day of high anxiety for me. That was the morning I crept out of the Hong Kong home, completely heartbroken that I would likely never see her again. My heart ached as I read of her heartbreak after she heard that I couldn't get back into Japan.

Wings wrote that second letter while I was still in Hong Kong. She was clinging to the hope that we could be together, but I knew her desperate prayers were pointless. Even if I couldn't get back to her, I hoped we might be able to keep communicating by mail. If there was any chance of that, I knew I couldn't ignore Josiah's letter as I wanted to.

The only way I could get a letter to Wings was to send it to the HCS and have them forward it to her, so I had to assure Josiah I was not an enemy or a threat to them. I wrote him a superficial explanation of some of my general complaints and concerns, careful not to expose my deepest doubts about Berg and his doctrines. I was purposely ambiguous about my intentions, hoping he would get the false impression there was a chance I would return to the Family. I included a letter to Wings, which had my mailing address, and asked him to forward it to her.

The leaders were aware of Wings' request for us to be together, so I knew it was a long shot they would allow us to continue communicating now that I was a backslider who might lead her astray. In case they did forward my letter, I chose my words carefully, knowing that a leader would read it first. It was my last chance to stay connected to her, so I downplayed our romance and emphasized my continued love for Jesus, suggesting we could be Christian pen pals. I hoped the leaders would allow her to keep communicating with me if they thought she could reel me back into the Family, or keep me friendly.

Josiah's reply was mostly an effort to keep me as a financial supporter entitled to Family publications intended for the general public. He didn't directly mention my attempt to communicate with Wings, but I got the message when he said that "for reasons of security" people who chose not to live in Family homes could communicate only with World Services.

It broke my heart to know I had no way of contacting Wings ever again, since I didn't know her real name and had no photograph of her. I wasn't

surprised that I was forbidden to communicate with her, g
an unrighteous backslider. The Family's separation from so
in scriptures like 2 Corinthians 6:14, which commands (
fellowship or commune with unbelievers.

They considered backsliding one of the worst sins,
lead others to doubt and stray from God's will too. Berg
scriptures vilifying backsliders as dogs and pigs (2 Peter 2:20–22) unwor-
thy of God's kingdom (Luke 9:62). He warned his followers in the letter
"Backsliders Beware" that

> the punishment of God in some cases has not only been sick-
> ness & trial & tribulation & chastening, chastisement, spank-
> ings, but if you flatly refuse to repent & make things right, you
> become such a poor testimony & such a bad influence on others
> that God sometimes may take your life!...If you backslide
> against Him, turn against Him, against His service, against His
> Family, against His children & against Him Himself, if you turn
> back, I can see nothing more for you than a fearful looking for
> of judgment & fiery indignation.[1]

— — —

Finding a job in Port Alberni was very difficult in the midst of a recession
and high unemployment. To account for the twelve years since my last job
in Canada, I padded my thin resumé by claiming I spent those years in Asia
as an English teacher and staff member at an international boarding school
for children of missionaries. But without higher education and credentials,
it was difficult to find a job where those experiences were useful.

In the six months before I finally got a job, I spent many hours in the
library, scanning the shelves and selecting any title, on any subject, that
grabbed my attention. After years of reading only the Bible and Berg's
letters, the library was a banquet of books feeding my intellectually
malnourished mind. I wrote in a diary entry: "Reading Plato for the first
time in my life and it is immensely enlightening."

I discovered Plato in the fifty-four-volume *Great Books of the Western
World*. The first volume, *The Great Conversation*, included a ten-year reading list, which I photocopied and began reading. Exposure to knowledge
and ideas in different disciplines was exactly what I needed to overcome
the religious dogma I'd been indoctrinated with since childhood. I didn't
realize it yet, but the recommendations were also excellent preparation for
university.

Although I had stopped praying and reading the Bible, I didn't immediately reject the fundamentalist Christian worldview. It would take a while to change my perspective and fully open my closed mind, but it was ajar enough to realize that Berg's dogma against education, rooted in Adam and Eve's original sin of disobeying God by eating fruit from the tree of knowledge, helped him control his unquestioning followers. I was questioning now, though, and the very knowledge I needed to overcome my indoctrination was the forbidden fruit I was inculcated to reject.

A few months after returning, I attended the twenty-fifth anniversary celebration of E.J. Dunn Middle School, where I spent three years. A comment by my social studies teacher, Mr. Richardson, was exactly the kind of encouraging boost to my self-esteem that I needed to nudge me toward university. He mentioned that my Grade 10 English teacher, Mr. Hay, told him he considered me one of the best students he'd ever had. That surprised me. I remembered getting top marks on every assignment and test, but now I wondered why he never took me aside to mentor me if that's how he felt. Perhaps if he had pointed out the many potential careers where I could use my language skills, I might've chosen a different path.

Better late than never, that encouraging comment helped me overcome self-doubt about my intellectual ability to study at the university level. As much as I enjoyed reading and learning new things, I was still wrestling with ingrained anti-education dogma. In a diary entry dated February 24, 1992, five months after leaving the Family, I wrote: "See how deeply indoctrinated I've been against higher education that I should debate this here on these pages in order to convince myself that it is okay to go to school." However, given the difficulty of finding work, education seemed to be my best option.

Coincidentally, around that time I came across the course calendar for Malaspina University-College, now called Vancouver Island University. I was intrigued by the liberal-studies interdisciplinary humanities program. The course contents corresponded to many of the books on *The Great Conversation* reading list. That was exactly the kind of general education I needed. Before I could focus on a field of study or choose a career path, I had to examine my life and confront long-held beliefs by exposing my mind to a wide variety of challenging information and ideas.

University now seemed less intimidating to me, so in March I met with a student counsellor. She told me that because I only had a high-school equivalency certificate, I had to pass an English proficiency test before I could apply. She also explained that to qualify for partial remission of student loans, I needed to be employed, or a full-time volunteer, during the four months preceding the start of classes.

I scheduled the English test and kept searching for a job. In April, I succeeded at both. When I'd been teaching in Beijing, one of my students had corrected grammar mistakes I'd made, so I was a bit worried about that element of the test, but I passed with a higher mark than required, which increased my confidence. I also found a perfect temporary job with the British Columbia Summer Games, which were held in Port Alberni that year. My university application was approved in June.

Since leaving the Family, I'd spent many introspective hours at the crossroads of my past and future. I felt my former life was too strange and complicated to talk about in casual conversations, so I never did. But I also had a contradictory urge to tell everyone all about it. I had attempted to write my story, but stopped after four flimsy chapters when I realized how little I truly knew or understood about that bizarre life. The more I wrote, the more questions I had that I couldn't answer or research. The World Wide Web had only been introduced to the general public in August 1991, so it was still a novelty with little content yet.

Exactly a year after that, I bought my first computer, but used it mostly for word processing. My new life was beginning, and I needed to focus on my future, and so had no time to dwell on the past. After my first year of school, I stopped writing formal diary entries, but whenever random memories surfaced I captured them in a sentence or two and set them aside in a series of pocket notebooks. I still intended to write my story one day, so I didn't want to lose those memories.

In my first month at university, before I realized I would have little time for extracurricular reading, the title of a book on a library display stand was too intriguing to resist. *God Is Red: A Native View of Religion*, by a prominent Indigenous activist, lawyer, historian and theologian, discusses Christianity in relation to Indigenous traditions and belief systems.[2] It was the first time I'd read anything critical of the Bible. Reading that critique of Christian dogma from a different worldview encouraged me to apply my knowledge of the Bible to essay assignments in various courses.

My familiarity with the Bible was particularly useful for studying Middle English literature, like medieval morality plays and Chaucer, and even more so for studying Milton and Shakespeare, who both wrote in the same early-modern English vernacular that I had read for many years in the King James Bible. That gave me an advantage over classmates unfamiliar with that language and the biblical themes, references and allusions those works contain.

Beyond that academic purpose, I set aside the Bible and no longer read it. I still considered myself a Christian, but the more I learned and allowed myself to question and doubt, the more my faith diminished. My studies eventually led me to reject the fundamentalist interpretation of the Bible, question its historicity, and view it as merely a book of myths, metaphors, poetry and parables. A diary entry during my first year at school reveals my beliefs slowly slipping away: "I once believed in an absolute truth, now I'm no longer sure."

A significant catalyst for that process was reading Charles Darwin's *On the Origin of Species by Means of Natural Selection*. That was the initial *aha* moment for me. I also studied the impact of the Scientific Revolution on religion, especially new developments and discoveries in geology and pale-ontology. Examining the clash between religion and reason during the ensuing Age of Enlightenment put Darwin's work in a cultural context and helped me reach my own enlightenment.

I now had more than just flimsy faith in Berg's uneducated writings on the subject of evolution to base my understanding of the world on; I had solid evidence. The fossil record and a few centuries of observations and experiments have firmly established the foundations of evolutionary science. Once I accepted that fact and understood that geological science was a better gauge for the age of the Earth than biblical myths were, it was a great psychospiritual relief to let go of a belief I had difficulty believing.

I had always struggled with the dogma of young-earth creationism, which was central to Berg's fundamentalist Christianity.

> You're either going to have to believe in six straight 24-hour days of creation from the Bible, or you believe the Bible's a lie!...If paleontology says the world is six billion years old, and the Bible says the world is only six thousand years old, which are you going to believe?...The concrete proof or evidence to Christians or believers of the Bible that they cannot both believe these false sciences of evolution and paleontology and also believe the Bible, is the genealogical chronology of Genesis.[3]

Berg frequently denounced what he called the "Big Lie" of Darwinism, comparing it to Hitler's use of propaganda. Since scientific truth exposed Berg's own big lies, he had to convince his followers that there was abso-lutely no evidence for evolution.[4] It's one of the reasons he insisted Family children didn't need more than a basic sixth-grade education.

My own science education in public school failed to properly prepare me with the knowledge or critical thinking I needed to contradict Berg's anti-science religious dogma. No teacher dared to criticize or compare the creation myth with the evidence of evolution. So the few simplistic science lessons I had were insufficient to supplant my belief in creationism. Berg was able to miseducate ignorant believers like me because we were unable to recognize how he completely misunderstood and mischaracterized the science of natural selection. Contrary to his claims, there is overwhelming evidence from a variety of disciplines, making it one of the most substantiated scientific theories.

Catholic indoctrination had deeply ingrained my belief in God and creationism from a very young age. I didn't read the Bible itself, so I learned all I knew about the stories in Genesis and the Gospels through the lens of catechism lessons and Bible-based movies that reinforced those beliefs. The spectacular opening sequence of *The Bible: In the Beginning* showing the creation of the Earth, followed immediately by the appearance of Adam and Eve, impressed on my naive mind a creationist point of view.

My childhood faith was mainly focused on the life of Jesus and miraculous events retold in films such as *The Greatest Story Ever Told*, which I unquestioningly believed was factual. I wasn't yet aware of the idea of young-earth creationism, but if I could believe in impossible things like the virgin birth, walking on water, restoring sight to the blind, raising the dead and other purported miracles, then why not the creation of the world in six days, six thousand years ago. So it isn't surprising that when I met the Children of God, I easily accepted their literal interpretation of the biblical creation story.

Believing in biblical literalism requires faith that is blind to reality. Squelching doubts becomes essential to maintaining that faith. I quickly learned to ignore, reinterpret or rationalize any facts that didn't fit my faith. Throughout my life in the Family, pushing doctrines I doubted or disagreed with to the back of my mind became a habitual way of dealing with the psychological stress of cognitive dissonance I experienced when trying to reconcile religious dogma with reality.

Berg was wrong when he wrote: "It takes more faith to believe this incredible, fictitious, fairy tale of man's origins than it does to accept God's simple, beautiful, inspired explanation in His Word!"[5] To believe the Bible is literally true requires the kind of irrational faith expressed in the oxymoronic scripture that preposterously claims faith *is* evidence (Hebrews 11:1).

On the other hand, accepting evolution doesn't require blind faith, just a basic understanding of the self-correcting scientific method, which counters criticism and dispels doubt with real, reliable evidence that confirms it as fact.

1 Corinthians 13:11 states: "When I was a child, I spake as a child, I understood as a child, I thought as a child: but when I became a man, I put away childish things." Now that I was no longer a Child of God, and understood as a man, evolution seemed far more reasonable and wonderful than young-earth creationism. As Darwin wrote in the final sentence of *The Origin of Species*: "There is grandeur in this view of life…that, whilst this planet has gone cycling on according to the fixed law of gravity, from so simple a beginning endless forms most beautiful and most wonderful have been, and are being, evolved."[6]

It was a tremendous psychological relief to realize while in university that it isn't evolution, but young-earth creationism, that is an "incredible, fictitious fairy tale." Having reached that conclusion, I didn't go on to consider the question of God's existence. By that time, I had shed all other aspects of my former Christian life, so I consciously decided to put aside that ultimate question. For the next several years, I suspended my belief, neither believing nor disbelieving God existed.

Religion was irrelevant in my new life, interesting intellectually, but not spiritually. In my former worldview, I always filtered everything through my indoctrinated understanding of the Bible. Now clear-eyed, I was able to confront and critique my beliefs from a new perspective. It helped that I could examine biblical and religious themes I encountered in some of my classes, and include my new views in various essays. I had successfully deprogrammed myself from biblical bondage. Although words attributed to Jesus promised his truth would set me free, that dogma bound me in chains.[7] It was the truth I discovered through education that gave me genuine freedom.

On the ultimate question of God's existence, I was wary of being absolutely certain one way or the other because that kind of certitude had misguided me down the dangerous path of religious fundamentalism. I was now skeptical that God existed, but unable to say for certain, so I considered myself an agnostic rather than an atheist. Taking an agnostic position left room for the extremely slight possibility that credible evidence of a supernatural divine entity may yet emerge.

However, as I continued to read more on the subject in the ensuing years, I concluded that "agnostic atheist" is probably a better label for my position. I based that on the "spectrum of probabilities" Richard Dawkins describes in his 2006 book *The God Delusion*. At one end are "strong theists," and at the opposite end "strong atheists." Like Dawkins, I consider myself "agnostic only to the extent that I am agnostic about fairies at the bottom of the garden."[8]

Other books I eventually read by philosophers and scientists such as Carl Sagan, Sam Harris, Daniel Dennett, A.C. Grayling, Victor Stenger and Stephen Hawking provided strong support for my agnostic atheism. Carl Sagan stated, "Extraordinary claims require extraordinary evidence."[9] Since the non-existence of God cannot be proven, proof must come from those who claim that God does exist. And Victor Stenger points out that absence of evidence *is* evidence of absence, so the lack of proof is sufficient to deny the existence of the Judeo-Christian-Islamic God.[10]

Stephen Hawking's books were particularly informative confirmations of my new worldview. In his 2010 book *The Grand Design*, he explains why it isn't necessary to invoke the concept of God to explain the existence of the universe.[11] In a subsequent interview, he said: "One can't prove that God doesn't exist, but science makes God unnecessary. The laws of physics can explain the universe without the need for a creator."[12] In his final book, *Brief Answers to the Big Questions*,[13][14] he responds to the question "Is there a God?" by reiterating that science has a more compelling explanation than one involving a divine creator who directs the universe.

Learning that the grand design of the universe does not require a designer was the final step in the process of losing my religion. The universe and natural world are now much more marvellous to me than any imaginary supernatural world, like the one Berg created in his fictional trips to Space City inside the moon, or any other conception of heaven or an afterlife. Knowing that this life is all we get makes me appreciate it more than I ever did before.

Although I overcame my religious indoctrination, I thought I could simply start my life over with a clean slate, so I tried to move on by focusing on my education and ignoring issues related to my life in the Family. I learned the hard way it doesn't work like that. The past doesn't stay buried. Certain memories haunted me, so I knew I had to eventually acknowledge and deal with my old life. I was too busy trying to overcome twenty lost years and create a new life to do that, though. Putting it off inevitably led to my breakdown.

Chapter 20
Law and Disorder

Losing my religion freed me from the Family's groupthink mindset. Having repudiated my religious identity, I needed to create a new, secular one, but to do that I had to know myself first. University was an ideal place for that. Exposure to different ideas, opinions and perspectives helped me discover my own mind and how I viewed the world, now that I no longer believed it was doomed to end soon. Campus life also offered many opportunities to resocialize after years of separation from society.

While I was getting to know my true self for the first time and creating a new persona, I was hesitant to reveal my past to people. Although I felt unwhole with half of my life hidden from others, I feared they would judge the new me if they knew my old self. I did attempt to tell two people in separate conversations, by awkwardly blurting out that I had been in a cult, but neither responded or asked me to explain. I never mentioned it again to them, or to anyone else.

I found it difficult to unravel the complicated story of my strange Jesus-freak life and understand it myself, let alone briefly explain it to someone else. It was easier to simply tell people I had been an English teacher working and travelling in Asia for a decade. My cover story was at least partly true, and helped me account for my ignorance when someone referred to some aspect of popular culture that I was unaware of.

That less-than-honest explanation of my past kept curious people satisfied, but created anxiety as I constantly guarded against revealing the truth. Fearing failure, and so pushing myself to succeed academically, was also stressful. I needed to prove, to myself most of all, that I was capable and intelligent.

My student loans, bursaries and grants were not sufficient for all my living expenses, so I also worked part-time every semester on top of a full course load. Anxiety and stress began to take their toll on my health during my first year, as educational and financial pressures added to the tension of trying to fit in while feeling like an outsider with a secret. For the first time in my life, I began to experience frequent migraines. I couldn't study when afflicted, which increased my stress.

Although still wary of doctors and pharmaceutical drugs, a hangover from my religious indoctrination, I was desperate for relief, so I attended a walk-in clinic where each doctor I saw prescribed different medications, none of which worked. The last doctor who reviewed my file recommended I try natural alternatives instead. I had one in mind, though I didn't dare discuss it with her because it was illegal.

Soon after returning to Canada, I began smoking cannabis again, but once my studies started I used it only on weekends to help me relax. During the first year, I noticed that migraines often occurred on a Friday, and so seemed to be caused by cumulative stress from studying and working. Knowing that cannabis reduced my stress, I wondered if daily use might prevent them.

I had straight As in every course that first year, and wanted to maintain that success. At the time, there was a fear-based drug prohibition campaign, "Just Say No," that depicted a brain on drugs as a fried egg. That scare tactic seemed absurd to me, but the disinformation effectively created enough doubt that I worried using cannabis daily might dumb me down by diminishing my cognitive skills. I was desperate for relief, though, so I experimented with two small joints each evening after all my homework was done.

Over time, I noticed that the frequency of my migraines reduced to less than once a month. Cannabis also seemed to improve my intellectual creativity by opening doors of perception when I reflected on my studies afterwards. I often gained insights and made connections I hadn't considered in class. Far from dumbing me down, disciplined daily use of cannabis had no negative effect on my cognition. For the next three years, I continued to get straight As in every course, and had the highest grade-point average in the program. Awarded the Liberal Studies medal for high academic achievement, I graduated with distinction.[1]

Cannabis was also a social lubricant that made it easier to meet like-minded people. A co-worker at one of my campus jobs welcomed me into her social circle of mostly married couples around my age. They all smoked cannabis too, so I was soon hanging out at their homes, going to house parties and pubs, and even to three out-of-town concerts to see Bob Dylan, the Rolling Stones and Steve Winwood.

It had taken me over two years after leaving the Family to finally meet people I could relate to on some level and be comfortable socializing with. While I was glad to be a little less lonely now, I didn't let them in on my secret past, so they stayed superficial acquaintances rather than intimate friends. I desired deeper relationships, but my inability to be trusting and truthful hindered my search for authentic intimacy. I longed for female companionship too, but I had never dated, not as a teen or as an adult, and there were no courses at school teaching the rules of romance and relationships.

Although I was comfortable conversing with female classmates and co-workers, I was very shy with women I was attracted to, and uncertain how to approach them. Ignorant of the various signals of interest women give, I made a few clumsy attempts to make the first move, but ended up embarrassing myself, so I stopped trying. I also unsuccessfully looked for love in the impersonal personal ads in newspapers. In those four years at school, I did have three intoxicated one-night stands, each initiated by the women, but I found casual sex very dissatisfying.

When I graduated in the spring of 1996 at the age of 40, I still wasn't sure what to do with my B.A. degree. I hadn't been mentored or motivated to pursue a particular career path, so I decided for practical reasons to become a teacher. It was a profession I could enter quicker than others, and I enjoyed my teaching experiences in Asia, which I thought would benefit me. I enrolled in the teacher certification program at Simon Fraser University in Burnaby, which is part of Metro Vancouver, and moved to a suburban neighbourhood near the campus.

The first semester consisted of educational theory, which I enjoyed, but the second semester practicum in a high school was an abrupt reality check. It was nothing like my experience teaching eager students in China, where teachers are respected. I soon had serious second thoughts, and decided teaching wasn't the right profession for me, at least in the public school system. Both my classroom and program supervisors who assessed my progress told me I was doing well, so they were shocked when I told them I was quitting just six weeks into my second semester.

Soon after I had started that program, I found a part-time job as a private English tutor for high school students from South Korea. Tutoring paid well, more than any job I had before. The migration agent who managed the affairs of those international students was glad I quit university, as I could now teach more of his clients who were scattered around the Greater Vancouver region.

With no reason to remain in my noisy basement suite in a dreary suburban neighbourhood far from entertainment options and opportunities to meet people, I moved to an apartment near Vancouver's vibrant Commercial Drive district. After I'd spent a year as a full-time tutor, a financial crisis spread throughout East Asia in the second half of 1997. All my students depended on money from their parents in South Korea, where the currency depreciated by fifty percent. Most could no longer afford my tutorship.

Fortunately, I was able to find a part-time job assisting senior citizens with special needs at the Lion's Den Adult Day Centre on Commercial Drive, a convenient ten-minute walk away. I was just getting by, though, unsure of what direction to take next, until I got involved in political and social activism.

— — —

All my trusted cannabis contacts were on Vancouver Island, so after I moved to the mainland, my only option was to buy it from strangers on the street. The easiest place to find it was in Vancouver's notorious Downtown Eastside open-air illicit drug market, but that trade was controlled by gangs. I was constantly worried about being ripped off with inferior cannabis, or mugged in an alley. I found a safe supplier known as the Muffin Man who distributed free marijuana muffins to heroin and crack addicts, but when he was brutally beaten by gang members protecting their turf, I decided to grow my own herbal medicine.

I set up a grow light in my bedroom closet and about four months later had my first harvest. One morning, while trimming the skunky-smelling buds from my second harvest, the police knocked on my door. They were investigating a domestic abuse complaint across the hall, but could smell the odour of cannabis coming from my apartment. The Vancouver Police Department had recently deprioritized cannabis possession offences, so I hoped they would leave me alone if I admitted that minor violation. I cracked open the door with the chain attached.

I told them that I had just smoked a joint, but that didn't fool them. They knew the difference between the smell of flowering buds and the smoke from dried ones. They assured me that if I let them in, they wouldn't charge me. So I showed them my closet garden, explaining that I used it to prevent stress and migraines. I also showed them my university transcript with straight As, insisting I was a regular citizen with a job just trying to improve my health while avoiding violent criminals. I told them about the Muffin Man and said confiscating my medicine wouldn't stop me from using it, but would endanger me if I had to go back to the street for my supply.

Although they did confiscate my growing equipment, the plants and the fresh buds I had just cut, they didn't conduct a search, and so didn't find the dried buds I had in a cupboard. They also kept their word and didn't charge me. If they had been officers with the RCMP, Canada's national police force, they would've certainly arrested me.

I don't know if the police notified my landlady, but I decided to move before receiving an eviction notice. I found another apartment nearby and immediately set up my closet garden again. As I learned the best techniques for growing cannabis in a confined space, I soon began producing more than I needed for myself.

By the end of 1997, Canada's first and largest medical cannabis club formally registered with the provincial government as a non-profit advocacy organization called the BC Compassion Club Society. In defiance of laws that prohibited growing, selling or possessing cannabis, the society opened a dispensary on Commercial Drive as a civil-disobedience act of compassion to provide a reliable, safe source for sick citizens. I became a member of the society for the legal cover it provided, and sat on the board of directors for four years. I sold my surplus cannabis to the dispensary about once a year.

Fighting the drug war wasn't the only social justice activism I got involved with. My new apartment had a spectacular view of downtown Vancouver's skyline to the west and the North Shore Mountains on the other side of Burrard Inlet. It also overlooked parts of Vancouver's port lands and a dozen blocks of light industry between my residential neighbourhood and the Downtown Eastside.

That industrial area was a notorious red-light district where vulnerable sex trade workers walked the dark, deserted, dangerous streets at night. One street was known as the "kiddy stroll," where sex-trafficked minors were exploited and abused. I was aware that many street sex workers were disappearing, but I had ignored the problem until I witnessed daily the appalling reality of the situation.

I often found distressed, drug-addicted women smoking crack or shooting heroin in my carport, where they had hidden or slept for safety. More than once, I called an ambulance after discovering a woman passed out, not knowing if she was dead or alive. I was astonished to see that these women were such frequent patients that the paramedics knew them by name. So I began investigating to understand how things had gotten to this point.

For many decades, politicians, police and protesters pushed prostitutes from one Vancouver neighbourhood to another, which just perpetuated the problem. The degradation and shunning of street sex workers by an uncaring society only made them suffer more, without ever addressing the underlying, interconnected issues of trauma-related poverty, pain and addiction. Now that the situation was literally in my backyard, I couldn't look away. I had to do something.

Making a difference required doing things differently, so I got involved with progressive activists in my neighbourhood to support street-involved women and advocate for their safety, health and human rights. We held public meetings, inviting criminologists from Simon Fraser University and advocates with lived experience to educate us on the issues. We also coordinated with similar advocacy groups, and enlisted the help of sociology students from the University of British Columbia to conduct participatory action research with sex workers and other community members.

Our harm reduction approach to the problem created conflict with residents involved with the local Community Policing Centre. They set up vigilante citizen patrols and, with the help of police, pushed prostitutes away from safer, well-lit residential streets into the dark, dangerous industrial area. At one of their public meetings, we argued that sex workers are citizens and neighbours too, who needed help, not hostile harassment. Some shouted us down and mocked us as hooker huggers, but that didn't deter us.

Until I got involved with that volunteer work, I was feeling directionless. I was also still greatly burdened by my secret past and an intense need to tell my story, as this diary note from the beginning of 1998 shows:

> There are still a lot of things I haven't re-evaluated, which shows just how much the past has a hold of me. I need to cleanse myself of it and the only way I know to do that is to empty my soul. By that I mean to tell the truth. Because there is not a single person I ever truthfully discuss my past with, I feel the burden of keeping a secret from everyone....I have so many hangovers from that life I lived. Although I never even discuss that life, I am constantly reminded of the legacy it left me.

Those reminders came in the form of triggered memories that intruded on my thoughts. The image of Merry Berg tied to her bed was particularly disturbing and continued to haunt me in flashbacks. Perhaps I was subconsciously processing past experiences that I had confined to the back of my mind until I was able to deal with them. I was aware enough to know that

I couldn't keep my past buried forever, so I had continued the practice of making a quick note each time a memory surfaced. I eventually filled numerous small notebooks with random memories scattered over four decades. I still wasn't ready to write my story yet, as I was focused on surviving financially, but I knew they would be useful one day.

I was only working part-time, but now making student loan payments, so I was barely getting by. If I defaulted on those loans, I couldn't get another one, so I considered going back to school. Coincidentally, the activism I was engaged in, opposing both pot and prostitution prohibition, pushed me in the same direction. It occurred to me that I could accomplish more if I knew the law. I knew how to break it, but I didn't know how to use it to prevent injustices and change harmful public policies.

It was hard to imagine myself as a practising lawyer, but I knew a law degree would give me knowledge and skills useful in non-legal jobs too. So I didn't worry about my student debt doubling, or the fact I would be almost fifty years old by the time I graduated. I was treading water, about to sink, so I needed to start swimming again, even if it was with sharks. In December 1998, I took the Law School Admission Test. I didn't want to leave Vancouver, so when I received the result, I applied only to UBC's law school. I had no backup plan, so fortunately I did well enough on the test to be accepted. I enrolled in the 1999 fall semester.

While in law school, I worked for eight months in UBC's Indigenous Community Legal Clinic, in Vancouver's Downtown Eastside. I frequently attended the nearby provincial criminal court, sometimes representing the same people I advocated for in my neighbourhood activism. I remained engaged in that volunteer social-justice work, and got involved with Pivot Legal Society, a newly formed human-rights organization working on public policy related to poverty, drug prohibition, sex workers' rights and police accountability.

At that time, Vancouver's Downtown Eastside was the focal point of a national public health crisis. It had the highest rates of HIV and AIDS from injection-drug use in North America. There were also extremely high rates of other communicable diseases spreading from one needle-sharing drug user to another, as well as rapidly rising overdose deaths. In response, the Vancouver/Richmond Health Board, as it was known then, declared a public health emergency.

One of Pivot's first projects was to address that emergency. Working with another new advocacy organization, the Vancouver Area Network of Drug Users (VANDU), they fought for the establishment of harm reduction clinics where addicts could safely inject with clean needles under the supervision of health care professionals. It was a controversial idea, although it shouldn't have been, since the goal was to improve health and save lives. The first few safe injection facilities in Europe and Australia had already proved they were effective at preventing deadly overdoses and the spread of diseases.

One of my professors was on Pivot's board, so for his course assignment he suggested I write a legal analysis exploring the possibility of taking legal action to compel the British Columbia government to establish and fund supervised drug-consumption sites for intravenous drug users. I wrote two separate legal arguments, one for that course and another for a social justice seminar course.

My first analysis concluded that constitutional law and human rights legislation obligated the provincial government to control and prevent epidemics of disease and death related to illicit intravenous drug use.[2] Providing supervised drug-consumption clinics for vulnerable, drug-addicted citizens as part of a program of related health services would fulfill those legal obligations. My second analysis examined how international human rights law supported that argument.[3]

The arguments I presented in those papers played a part in the fight led by VANDU, Pivot and other human rights activists that finally forced the government to act, resulting in the opening of Insite in Vancouver's Downtown Eastside in 2003.[4] It was North America's first official supervised drug-consumption clinic. From Insite's opening to the end of 2019, there were over 3.6 million visits to inject illicit drugs, 48,798 clinical treatment visits, 6,440 overdose interventions by nurses, and no deaths. Moreover, thousands of marginalized street-drug users have been able to access other health care services and addiction treatment through Insite.

— — —

Throughout my three years at law school, and for several years afterwards, I continued my advocacy for sex workers. Street-involved women were continuing to disappear from the Downtown Eastside and the industrial area bordering my apartment. Many people suspected that a serial killer was preying on prostitutes. Advocacy groups and relatives of the missing made repeated pleas for an investigation into that possibility, but were dismissed by police authorities, who insisted there was no evidence of a serial killer.

Finally, in 2002, Robert Pickton was arrested and charged with twenty-seven first-degree murders, though he bragged he killed forty-nine and wanted to make it an even fifty. His killing spree could have been ended a few years earlier, saving many lives, if not for systemic failures, callous attitudes and careless police work. Sex workers were stigmatized, second-class citizens, so prosecutors didn't consider them credible witnesses, and when they disappeared, police didn't take seriously or give priority to missing-person reports filed by relatives, friends and advocates. Negligent police investigations and jurisdictional infighting between police forces also contributed to their failure to catch the serial killer sooner.

In 2003, my federal member of Parliament, whose jurisdiction included Vancouver's East Side, helped establish a parliamentary committee to investigate Canada's prostitution laws. Its mandate was "to review the solicitation laws in order to improve the safety of sex-trade workers and communities overall, and to recommend changes that will reduce the exploitation of and violence against sex-trade workers."[5]

In 2005, that committee held public hearings across Canada. I attended the Vancouver session and described for the MPs my personal experiences of witnessing distraught, desperate women trying to survive on the street, our neighbourhood advocacy group's efforts to protect those women from harm, and the resistance we faced from some residents and police who pushed the women into danger instead of protecting them.[6]

Then, in 2010, as a consequence of the incompetent police investigations exposed in the serial killer trial, the British Columbia government established the Missing Women Commission of Inquiry.[7] One of its terms of reference was to "inquire into and make findings of fact respecting the conduct of the investigations conducted between January 23, 1997 and February 5, 2002, by police forces in British Columbia respecting women reported missing from the Downtown Eastside of the city of Vancouver." Since my experiences trying to protect sex workers directly related to this inquiry, I submitted the transcript of my parliamentary testimony with additional details.

— — —

After I moved to Vancouver, I again attempted to find female companionship through personal ads, this time mostly on new online dating sites that were popping up. I met with about ten women in coffee shops, but there were few commonalities and no emotional connections, so no second dates.

After that frustrating dating game, I decided I preferred playing solitaire. I figured I was just as likely to find a sincere soulmate and end my celibacy by relying on chance instead.

Eventually, I had two separate social circles of people I'd met through work and school, almost all of them women. The first group were the friends of my co-worker at the seniors' day-care centre. Like me, they enjoyed concerts, festivals and dancing at clubs, and often invited me to join them. My other social circle was a few law-school classmates, their partners and friends. They were mostly lesbians or bisexual. We had common intellectual interests and shared opinions on social justice issues. We also enjoyed watching various sports, in pubs or in person.

I preferred the company of women, but I never let my acquaintances get close enough to develop a deeper relationship. I was still very reticent and emotionally guarded when it came to intimacy and revealing my past. The few times I met a woman in one of my classes or jobs whom I was attracted to, I stayed a secret admirer. It wasn't only that I was too shy to make the first move; I was emotionally conflicted. If things got serious, I knew I couldn't continue to cover up my past, but I was hesitant to initiate a relationship that would bring someone I cared about anywhere near the orbit of that mad world I'd escaped.

I was relaxed in those two circles of platonic relationships, since there was no sexual tension, so I wasn't worried about misreading body language. I made that mistake a couple of times in bars after a few too many drinks, thinking a woman was expressing interest in me when she wasn't. If anyone I encountered at work, school or play was flirting with subtle signs of interest, I didn't know how to recognize them. I needed someone to be candidly direct, which is exactly how Janet hit on me.

One evening near the end of summer break before my final year of law school, I was at my favourite nightspot, the Yale pub, which featured blues bands from around North America. It was packed, as usual, and when I returned from the restroom a woman was sitting on my bar stool. I let her keep it, so she insisted on buying me a drink. After a couple of shots of tequila, which I didn't usually drink, she asked me if I wanted to go somewhere quieter. I could hardly believe it. She was making all the first moves males are traditionally expected to make, and I loved it. I needed a straightforward, unambiguous invitation like that.

After a few more drinks in a quieter lounge, I walked her home. Halfway there she suddenly stopped and told me to kiss her. We snogged on the sidewalk for a minute, then stumbled on like two giddy teenagers falling head over heels. We kissed again outside her building and exchanged email addresses before I left. A couple of nights later, I went to her place and we began a torrid sexual affair.

Our summer fling probably should've ended with the season, when my last year of law school started. But for the first time in my life I was enjoying typical teen and young-adult dating experiences I missed out on when I joined the Children of God. I was just living in the moment, not thinking about where this was headed, but Janet was. A couple of months later, she told me she loved me, but immediately said I didn't have to say it back, so I didn't. I needed to tell her about my past first. On our next date, I blurted out that I had been in a cult. Like me, she didn't respond. We simply continued on, as if neither of us had said what we said.

In many ways we were incompatible, and our inability to communicate at a deeper level led to bitter arguments. I had no problem debating different points of view academically, but in my personal life I wasn't used to arguing. I had lived for so many years in a groupthink environment where disagreements were disallowed that my automatic reaction was to walk away each time we quarrelled, rather than try to resolve our differences.

I hadn't dealt with my past, so I couldn't recognize all the ways that my former life affected my present one. Without that self-awareness, it was difficult to honestly communicate and develop a deeper relationship with Janet. But I had to sort out my immediate, uncertain future first, before I could deal with my past. As my graduation neared, with no job prospects and money running low, I was under tremendous stress and anxiety. After another heated argument over something trivial, our ten-month affair finally ended. Janet was my first and, to this day, only romantic relationship outside the Family. I've been celibate since then. My time with her was the closest I ever got to a normal life.

— — —

Throughout law school, I was uncertain if I wanted to practise law or use my degree for some alternative job. If I did practise law, I only wanted to specialize in social justice issues I cared about. To do that, I first needed to find a nine-month apprenticeship with a law firm, and take the bar admission courses and exams. I left that search far too late, though, so as a backup I applied to the master of laws program at UBC. My thesis proposal for that graduate degree was to examine Canada's prostitution laws from the perspective of street sex workers harmed by those laws. When my application was approved, I still hadn't found an apprenticeship, so I prepared to start studying again.

Around that time, one of my professors offered me a weekend job assisting with a human rights conference. Another professor of mine who was at that conference told me he knew of a law firm looking for an apprentice and offered to recommend me to the partners at Mandell Pinder, which specializes in Indigenous rights. When they offered me the position, I had a difficult decision to make.

The master's program offered me an opportunity to work on public policy research that had the potential to make a real difference in the lives of vulnerable, marginalized citizens. But I was unsure where that degree would lead, or whether it would be sufficient on its own, without requiring a PhD as well.

On the other hand, Mandell Pinder offered me a chance for a career that was more personally meaningful. My sister, brother and numerous nieces and nephews are Indigenous, which had motivated me to take many Indigenous-law courses and work in the Indigenous Community Legal Clinic. Now I had a chance to train with some of the top lawyers in that field. It was the perfect situation for me. It had the potential to become long-term employment, and meant I could start earning money immediately, without going further into debt at this late stage of my life. So I accepted their offer and began working within a week.

At the end of my apprenticeship, after passing the bar exams, I was called to the bar as a solicitor of the Supreme Court of British Columbia on my birthday in September 2003. I was forty-eight. Shortly after, my supervisor explained that she would be meeting with her co-partners in a couple of months to discuss the firm's future, and until then she could only offer me a temporary contract to the end of the year. I knew apprentices were not guaranteed a job offer, so I was glad I still had my foot in the door. However, their hesitancy to offer me a longer contract shook my confidence and caused me to rethink my plans.

My time at law school had been extremely stressful, resulting in anxiety and chronic insomnia, worsened by industrial noise from nearby port facilities. On top of everything else I was doing, I got involved with neighbours fighting the Canadian Pacific Railway for causing excessive, unnecessary noise pollution that was harming our health.[8] Although I was able to use that experience of dealing with regulatory bodies for a law course assignment, I continued to suffer serious side effects of extreme sleep deprivation from the nightly noise.

I began to have sporadic, abnormal public outbursts of anger in normal situations. Each incident embarrassed and confused me, as it was uncharacteristic behaviour that belied my soft-spoken personality. I suspected my insomnia, anxiety and angry outbursts were related to my past, but I didn't understand the connections and why certain situations triggered my memories and outbursts. So I continued to suppress my past until I had time to write it down, which was the only way I knew how to deal with it.

In the spring of 2002, I celebrated the last day of law school with three close classmates in one of their homes. Maybe the intimacy of sharing that difficult experience and triumphant outcome made me suddenly decide to reveal to them that I had been in a religious cult. I tried to tell the whole story from the beginning, but soon got sidetracked by questions I couldn't answer, and bogged down in details while trying to explain the inexplicable. Not only was it difficult for them to comprehend, but there were many things about that life I still didn't understand myself.

Since leaving the Family, I'd never heard news about it from media reports or other sources, and hadn't looked for information on the Internet. I was putting that off until I had time to write my story. But my friends' many questions aroused my curiosity, so the next day I did a quick search online and easily found the Family's website and a few ex-member websites. I glanced at the Family's site just long enough to see that they were still going strong, despite all of Berg's failed prophecies.

The Family site didn't interest me, but the websites created by former members contained disturbing developments. Skimming through the various sections, articles and discussions, I quickly understood that they were exposing all kinds of past and current abuses in the group. Clearly, there was much more to my story than I was aware of. I quit reading, unable to deal with those terrible truths while my immediate future was still undetermined. But it was too late. I had opened Pandora's box, which, ironically, was the name of the street I was living on. Suppressing my past became more difficult.

I continued having occasional outbursts of aggressive verbal abuse while apprenticing at the law firm. The worst was during a bar-exam mock trial. When my opponent unfairly violated one of the rules, I broke out of character and dramatically stopped the performance by angrily calling him out. Everyone was stunned, including my instructor and the lawyer who was acting as judge. That was a wake-up call. Although it didn't prevent me from passing the bar, an emotional fit like that while in a real court of law or other legal setting wouldn't be as easily overlooked. It could negatively affect not only the case, but my reputation and ability to continue practising law.

If these spontaneous outbursts were being triggered by my subconsciously suppressed past, as I suspected, then they would continue until I exorcised the memories haunting me. I thought the best way to do that was to simply put those secrets into words on a page, exposed for all to see. However, as I worked on legal cases for nearly two years, in the Indigenous law clinic and at Mandell Pinder, it was obvious to me that I wouldn't have the emotional or mental stamina and cognitive concentration to write a memoir in my spare time. So, when the law firm offered me only a short-term contract, I faced another major life decision.

If my supervisor had offered me a long-term associate contract, I might have accepted it on the spot, simply for the financial security it brought. But now, with my job confirmed only until the end of 2003, I was at another crucial crossroads and had some time to think about which path I would take. I wasn't comfortable letting the firm's partners decide my future. I needed to be in control of my life and make my own decision before they made theirs.

It felt like a now-or-never moment. I had put off writing my story twice before, both times to focus on education. Now the compulsion to write it was overwhelming, and that irresistible need pushed me into a decision that I might not have made had I known how things would turn out. I figured I could survive financially by working just three days a week, or two weeks on two weeks off, which would leave the remaining days free for writing. I hoped the firm would agree to keep me part-time, but if not, my risky plan was to try and find work as a freelance legal researcher.

A few weeks after I accepted the temporary contract, I asked my supervisor if the partners would consider hiring me part-time in the new year. Since the firm already had an associate and a paralegal who both worked part-time, I thought she would at least be willing to present the idea to her partners, but she immediately rejected it as unworkable. So I felt obligated to tell her the reason for my request, and my decision to move on at the end of the year rather than wait for them to decide.

I awkwardly tried to briefly explain my strange cult life, and why I needed to write my story. It was difficult to convey in a few minutes what I meant by *cult*, so she didn't know how to react. She had the same confused look other people had when I tried to tell them, and would later encounter when seeking psychotherapy. She didn't ask me any questions about it, or encourage me to wait for their decision before making mine; she only wished me well. I continued working until the end of the year as if I had never mentioned I was a former cult member.

In the new year, I was eligible for employment insurance benefits, which would support me for most of 2004 until I could establish myself as a freelancer. At least, that was my plan. Mandell Pinder gave me my first research contract, but I was too overwhelmed and distracted by what I was learning about child abuse in the Family to concentrate and do my best work. I never heard from them again, and didn't seek contracts elsewhere either.

I had opened the lid on Pandora's box all the way, delving deep into the articles and archives on the ex-member websites. I was entirely engrossed in the disturbing testimonies and evidence of child abuse I found there, which had a profound effect on me. The more I learned, the more my life fell apart. I knew nothing about mental illness, but it seemed to me that I was having a slow-motion nervous breakdown.

Chapter 21
Tragedy of the Chosen One

Thirteen years after leaving the Family in 1991, I finally began to dig up my buried past and examine the skeleton in my closet. Discovering the whole awful truth behind the lie I had lived for so many years was self-shattering. Unlike losing my religion, which relieved me of dogma-induced existential anxiety and set my mind free, this examination left me feeling shackled with shame as I read shocking, heartbreaking accounts of child abuse on three survivor websites.[1]

Those personal testimonies from around the world confirmed the abuses I had seen, and revealed many others I was unaware of or blind to while I was in the Family. I also learned about new policies and doctrines developed by Karen Zerby and Steven Kelly after Berg's death that continued to subject children and teens to various forms of abuse.

Having discarded my religious blinders, it now disturbed me to see things from the perspective of people raised in the group. Re-evaluating Family life from a child's point of view made me realize that what they had experienced was not a righteous life, but was in fact systemic, institutionalized child abuse.[2] Most children in the Family suffered more than one of the following forms of abuse:

- religious indoctrination that denied them freedom of thought and freedom of religion, which includes the right to be free from religion
- isolation from society
- separation from parents, siblings and other relatives
- educational neglect and intellectual abuse
- medical neglect
- child labour and financial exploitation

- sexual coercion, exploitation, assault and rape
- cruel corporal punishment and extreme physical abuse
- emotional and psychological abuse
- spiritual abuse and threats

In some cases the abuse was tantamount to torture. Two of the websites exposing these abuses have the full text of a family court judicial decision in a 1995 custody case in England involving a child raised in the Family.[3] That professional analysis of Family life from a legal perspective was particularly informative, as it helped me to better understand the issues and assess the level of my own blameworthiness as a member of an abusive organization.

Lord Justice Ward, who oversaw this case, essentially put the entire group on trial, spending many months reading and analyzing Family doctrines and practices revealed in Berg's public writings and internal documents. The judge also heard testimony from several expert witnesses, as well as current and former members, including Merry Berg and some of her second-generation peers who had also left the Family. In Ward's almost three-hundred-page decision, he criticizes the Family's expert witnesses, and says Merry was a far more believable witness than the current Family members who testified, describing them as less than honest.

Ward discusses the issue of the truthfulness of Family witnesses by specifically referring to their "deceivers yet true" doctrine, which instructs members to deceive and lie to further their mission.[4] He states, "I regret to find that in many instances there has been a lack of frankness and a failure to tell the truth, the whole truth, and nothing but the truth." He then gives six specific examples of how the Family's witnesses were less than honest in the proceedings, and states, "These are worrying examples, and they are not the only ones, of the ingrained habit of lying if they have to and of telling half the truth if they can get away with it."[5] Throughout his judgment, Ward provides other examples of Family witnesses "dissembling the truth—deceiving yet true" and withholding incriminating documentary evidence from the court.[6]

Conversely, Ward found Merry's testimony truthful and unembellished, stating he "became more and more convinced by her evidence the longer she gave it. She did not seem to paint the picture blacker than it was." Merry described in detail the abuse she suffered at the hands of her grandfather, Zerby and Kelly, saying, "It all felt like torture and once I fainted, throwing up. They said I was throwing up demons. The exorcising terrified me."[7] After reading the Family's own account of events related to Merry, Ward found that she "had been moderate in her complaint of the indignities heaped upon her."[8]

Part of the Family's evidence that Ward considered was an affidavit from Merry's minder in Macau, Crystal, the woman who instructed me to watch over Merry.[9] In his decision, Ward included the following excerpt from her affidavit:

> After our daily taking care of the said MB for 3½ years, rather than improving and normalising as we had so hoped, regrettably she regressed into a sad state of hysteria, and frenzy, to the point that she had to be daily spoon-fed her meals — only to have her wilfully regurgitate her food after hours of struggling to help her eat. She began to have no control over her bladder and bowel movements and became incontinent. She was pulling her hair out by the handful, laying all over the house, on tables etc. and would frequently disrobe in public. She began running around the house threatening to harm myself or my husband if we failed to control her in any way, throwing articles of clothing out of the window and screaming profanities at the top of her lungs. This extreme display of insanity was causing hours and hours of our time and care to the point that we finally had made a decision to have her committed into the care of the Macau Government Centro Mental Hospital. This was on or about September or October 1990.[10]

When I read that description by Crystal, I immediately flashed back to that fateful night when I saw Merry tied to her bed, a dreadful scene that has haunted me ever since. But now I saw Merry not as a helpless victim, but as an admirably strong survivor who stood up to her abusers and helped to eventually bring down the Family.

Through Ward's judgment and the survivor websites, I was learning how the abuse of so-called delinquent teens in Macau was used as the model for punishing rebellious Family children around the world. Ward laid out in great detail evidence of systemic child abuse, neglect and denial of basic children's rights in the Family, and agreed with Merry that her abusive treatment was torture. He found as matters of fact that Merry

> was physically ill-treated; and she was emotionally ill-treated; she was put in fear; she was humiliated; her self-esteem was denigrated. Maria [Karen Zerby] and Peter [Steven Kelly] stood

> by and watched it happen and approved of what was happening. They showed little more sensitivity and insight than their at times demented leader....In my judgment what MB [Merry Berg] went through was a form of torture.[11]

In addition to reading the personal testimonies in this case and on these survivor websites, I learned damning information from a long-time member of Berg's inner circle, known in the group as James Penn.[12] Berg died in 1994 before the custody case concluded. He was succeeded by his co-leaders, Zerby and Kelly, who sent Penn as their representative to testify in the hearings on their behalf. He presented a letter to Ward from Zerby and Kelly in which they falsely promised that the Family had changed and was now a safe environment for children.

Penn left the Family in 1998, and in a series of whistle-blowing exposés revealed some of the unethical, immoral inner workings of Family leadership. He also exposed the fact that Zerby and Kelly didn't reveal to Ward in their letter that they were planning to introduce two new sexual doctrines: the Loving Jesus Revolution and the Marriage of the Generations.[13] Both further sexualized the second generation, those who were born and/or raised in the Family.

Before revealing that second doctrine, Zerby groomed both generations to become even more sexually active by writing a twelve-part series entitled "Living the Lord's Law of Love," which was required reading and came with special instructions ordering the series to be read by each Family home as a group, not individually, thus increasing the peer pressure to conform.[14]

Zerby introduced the Loving Jesus doctrine to members before the custody case was over, but Ward issued his final decision without being aware of it.[15] He accepted the Family's assurances that it was now a safe environment for children. He ruled that the child in question could remain with his mother in the Family. However, he expressed concern that he didn't have the authority to order mandatory supervision of the boy. I have no doubt Ward would've come to a different decision, and instead granted custody of the boy to his grandmother, who wasn't in the Family, if he'd known what Zerby and Kelly were doing behind his back while lying to his face.

As I awakened to the fact that the Family had harmed a generation of children, and continued to do so, I was determined to understand how I ended up in a harmful cult led by a narcissistic, alcoholic, racist, anti-Semitic, abusive, incestuous pedophile.[16] Why did it take me so long to recognize the abuse I saw and experienced? Why was it so difficult to leave? What specific effects did that life have on me? I had many more questions, so I started reading academic books and articles on the subject. The first, *Cults in Our Midst*, a comprehensive study of a variety of harmful high-demand groups, provided many helpful insights.[17]

Although that book has only two brief references to the Children of God, I recognized elements of my own story on almost every page. After comparing my personal experiences in the Family to the various characteristics associated with joining, living in and leaving cults, I could see very clearly exactly how I was indoctrinated, manipulated and exploited. I was beginning to understand some of the psychological processes that kept me ignorant and blind to much of the abuse, and why I didn't recognize it for what it was until I saw Merry's torture in person, which shocked me out of my stupor and prompted me to leave the Family.

The final chapter of that book, "Recovery: Coming Out of the Pseudopersonality," was especially helpful for understanding the difficulties I'd had in recovering from my life in the Family. My thoughts, behaviours and experiences after I left finally began to make sense to me. After leaving their abusive environments, many survivors of various kinds of cults suffer some or all of these symptoms that I did:

- use of cover stories to hide their past from everyone
- difficulty in adjusting socially, feeling like an outsider in every situation
- emotional detachment and distrust of people
- inability to form deep friendships and intimate relationships
- long-term intentional celibacy
- troubling thoughts and memories of their cult life
- health problems including migraines, anxiety, depression, insomnia, tinnitus and chronic pain

Now that I had fully opened my mind to my past, I couldn't hold off the flood of persistent thoughts, which worsened my insomnia. Overcome with regret and sorrow by everything I was learning about the Family's second generation, my anxiety and depression increased too, though not yet diagnosed. I also began to have constant, chronic musculoskeletal pain, starting in my neck and shoulders, and eventually spreading to every part of my body. I was breaking down psychologically and physically.

In the spring of 2004, a televised press conference by a high-profile British Columbia politician made me realize I needed to get help.[18] He had been arrested for an inexplicable, reckless theft. He struggled to speak as he described being under tremendous stress. He said he was now in therapy for bipolar disorder, which he had never sought help for because of the stigma attached to mental illness. When he referred to "emotional turmoil" and broke down crying, that phrase hit me like a ton of bricks. That was exactly how I felt, although I was unable to cry. Ever since puberty, when I was teased as a crybaby by my dad and classmates, I always suppressed tears. To this day, the only time I've cried was after learning of Rachelle's betrayal in Japan.

My lifetime of bottled-up emotions was cracking open, and I felt barely able to keep it from completely shattering me. I knew nothing about mental illness, or where to go for help. I looked online for something specifically for cult survivors, but only found US therapists. I contacted a couple of local mental-health advocacy organizations, but when I mentioned that the problems I was experiencing were related to a cult, they didn't know where to refer me.

I then turned to the Lawyers Assistance Program, a peer-support, counselling and referral service for BC lawyers dealing with personal problems of all kinds. As I nervously tried to explain to the head counsellor that my distress was related to my life in a cult, an incoherent tangle of words tumbled out of me, making it difficult for him to comprehend my story. He stopped me several times to calm me down with a deep-breathing exercise. He hadn't heard of the Children of God or the Family, and said he considered the Catholic Church a cult, so he asked me what I meant by that word.

I didn't yet understand how some cult characteristics are also found in mainstream churches, so I was confused by his question and didn't know how to answer him. I had hoped he could help me identify how my health problems were related to my cult experiences, but I don't think he'd ever encountered a case like mine before.

The counsellor he referred me to in the same program also didn't give me any specific insights into how my past cult life was affecting my current health. She recommended cognitive-behavioural therapy, which I hadn't heard of. It sounded like I would have to let her manipulate my thoughts, which reminded me of the thought control I was subjected to in the cult. Because I misunderstood it, I was unwilling to try it.

Next, I went to a government mental-health office on Commercial Drive, but they told me I needed a referral to their programs from a doctor. A year and a half earlier, I had finally found a family doctor who had accepted me as a patient. I had never revealed my past to him, so he was treating me in the dark. He was a bit taken aback when I gave him the five-minute version of my cult story and explained the mental distress I was experiencing. He referred me to a psychiatrist at St. Paul's Hospital, and to a neurologist to investigate my chronic pain.

After describing various aspects of my complicated cult life over four one-hour sessions with the psychiatrist, he diagnosed me with post-traumatic stress disorder and referred me to a PTSD group-therapy program at Vancouver General Hospital. Meanwhile, the neurologist conducted a variety of tests at St. Paul's and determined my chronic pain was not a result of a neurological disorder. He suggested I had fibromyalgia, and a rheumatologist confirmed that diagnosis after conducting further examinations and tests.

After I was diagnosed with PTSD and fibromyalgia, I thought it was unethical to hide my health problems from potential employers or clients. I knew I wasn't mentally fit to continue practising law, including free-lance legal research, while I was in the midst of this psychological crisis that completely occupied my mind. So I voluntarily changed my membership status with the BC Law Society to "non-practising lawyer," which still allowed me to do pro bono legal work. For most of 2004, I lived on employment insurance, which was extended for health reasons until my application for disability benefits was approved.

In November, while waiting for my turn in the group-therapy program, which had a long waiting list, I started weekly one-hour sessions with a psychiatrist in Vancouver General Hospital's psychiatric outpatient clinic. It took two months to tell her my entire story, which I had never fully told anyone before. She took copious notes in each session, barely keeping up as the words poured out of me. Occasionally, she would stop my free-flowing, detailed narrative to clarify some point, but otherwise allowed me to talk uninterrupted.

During those two months, I was continuing to learn shocking things about the Family. I was particularly distressed to hear about the suicides of numerous people I had lived with or knew of through Family publications. Sadly, similar tragedies were still occurring. In one of my sessions with the psychiatrist in December, I told her about another suicide of a young man that happened just a few days earlier.

I had known Abe when he was a child.[19] I lived briefly with his mother when I was in Japan in 1974. Like me, she had joined as a young teen and was among the first Japanese members. When I returned to Japan in the 1980s, she had three children, and they were all living at the Heavenly City School during one of my stints there. Abe had been out of the cult for four years when he ended his life.

Just a few weeks later, in January 2005, a murder-suicide made headlines around the world. The horrific tragedy made a mockery of the Family's claims that they had the ideal environment for raising children. Karen Zerby's son, Ricky, knifed to death her assistant, his former nanny, then shot himself in the head. The shocking news had an emotional effect on me similar to what I'd felt about the homicide-suicide involving my two uncles thirty-nine years earlier. Fortunately, I was still seeing the psychiatrist, so I had someone to talk to about it.

— — —

Ricky Rodriguez, known in the Family as Davidito, was Karen Zerby's son.[20] His father was a hotel employee in Tenerife who wasn't in the Family. Ricky was the first Jesus Baby, a child born of the sexual proselytizing practice of flirty fishing.[21] He was chosen and groomed by Berg to be the princely heir to the Family's spiritual kingdom who would lead the Family with his mother during the final years before Jesus returned. Just as Berg claimed to be the fulfillment of biblical prophecies that refer to a prophet David in the endtime, he claimed that Zerby and Ricky were the two witnesses described in Revelation 11, prophets with supernatural powers who would fight the Antichrist in the last days.[22]

Zerby and her child-care assistant, Sara Kelley, documented every aspect of Ricky's childhood, along with those of his half-sister, Techi, and Sara's daughter, Davida, whom he regarded as his sister.[23] Explicit descriptions of their indoctrinated, highly controlled, sexualized lives in Berg's securely secluded household were published as *The Story of Davidito*, which became the authoritative child-training manual for Family parents.[24]

As a teenager, Ricky had a normal reaction to his abnormal childhood in the Family. He rebelled. He grew increasingly resentful of how he and his sisters were raised: not allowed to be children; isolated from other children; unable to plan their own free futures; subjected to spiritual threats and cruel corporal punishment; and encouraged or coerced to engage in sexual activity.

Ricky came to understand how abusive that upbringing was, and hated how his mother and Berg had used him as the poster child for practices presented as childhood sex education, but which led to widespread sexual child abuse. As a young adult, he clashed with his mother when she implemented other sexually abusive policies and practices after Berg's death, such as the Loving Jesus doctrine and her re-emphasis on the Law of Love's sexual permissiveness.

In January 2001, when he was in his mid-twenties, Ricky formally left the Family, rejecting both Berg's teachings and Christianity. Like most of his peers who left the cult without a proper education and worldly experiences, he struggled at first to adjust to society. He eventually learned to adapt and live his own life, but found it difficult to put his past behind him. The abuse he'd suffered and witnessed, coupled with his mother's continual refusal to acknowledge and accept responsibility for systemic abuses of children and teens, weighed heavily on him.

In 2002, Ricky was intent on exposing the truth about Berg and his mother, hoping that would help bring an end to the Family, so he wrote an article for MovingOn, a website for second-generation survivors of the Family.[25] He described in detail what life was like growing up in Berg and Zerby's household, including the horrific sexual, physical and psychological abuse Merry Berg suffered there, confirming her testimony in the British custody case.

Diabolically, the Family had attempted to use Ricky as evidence in that case to show they provided a safe, healthy environment for children. They paid two academics, psychologist Lawrence G. Lilliston and sociologist Gary Shepherd, to conduct psychological evaluations of thirty-two Family children, including Ricky.[26] Their extremely limited, shoddy study concluded that Ricky was "a bright, well-adjusted, and emotionally strong young man," and that "very few kids" in the Family had been abused.[27]

In his judgment, Justice Ward rejected this study as unreliable evidence. After considering the study's conclusion about another young man born in the Family, Ward wrote that Lilliston's observations

> seem to me to be superficial and to lack academic credibility. Likewise his conclusion about Davidito. This was an opportunity to explore exactly what had taken place in Berg's household. He merely touched upon these matters and Davidito made it obvious he was not prepared to talk about it. Nor did they talk about the reasons which impelled that young man to make attempts on his life said by The Family to have been caused by Satanic influences. Because I conclude that Dr Lilliston was not too concerned critically to examine The Family's past, I cannot be sure I get an accurate picture from him.[28]

In August 2004, Ricky posted his last article on MovingOn, titled "Still Around." He explained his two-year absence from the survivor community and updated his situation. He had tried to start a new life, but struggled to move on, writing: "I know now that will never happen. I can't run away from my past, and no matter how much longer I live, the first 25 years of my life will always haunt me."[29]

In that article, he included a desperate final plea for help to find justice by bringing an end to the Family. His message was short on detail, but implied he wanted to take some sort of vigilante action:

> Something has to be done to stop these child molesters, and it would be nice to find some people who think the same way. Every day these people are alive and free is a slap in the face to the thousands of us who have been methodically molested, tortured, raped, and the many who they have as good as murdered by driving them to suicide. It would probably involve a great deal of sacrifice, and would best be accomplished, I think, by people who have nothing to lose, such as myself....I think someone needs to put an end to it because only then can we feel some semblance of justice, and maybe be able to start putting it behind us. I think there are others who feel this way, and I would really like to get in touch with them and exchange ideas.

Just a few months before that last public message from Ricky, I read comments in discussion forums on the survivor websites that indicated a wave of young adults would soon be leaving the cult and needing help. When those from the second generation left the Family, many with children of their own, they were desperate to create new lives for themselves and save their children from the abusive childhood they'd endured. Most left with little or no support of any kind, and many struggled alone with no family or friends to help them make their way in an unfamiliar world.

I was unable to give financial support, but I could provide free legal advice and referrals to resources, so I posted my email address on these discussion forums, offering to help second-generation survivors in any way I could. As a former member who once supported the Family's mission, and so had passively enabled child abuse whether I recognized it or not, I felt responsible to help redress the damage in some way. It was the first time I publicly identified myself as a cult survivor, using my full, real name.

The experiences of those born and raised in the Family were far worse than mine. They were never members, since they'd had no choice. They were conscripts, child soldiers forced to fight their paranoid parents' sham spiritual war. Being exploited and trapped in the only life and worldview they had ever known added a completely different dimension to the abuses they suffered. And when they managed to escape that life, they faced obstacles I didn't have. Still, despite our different experiences, I now had some insight into their plight, and so could empathize with their suffering and the difficulty of recovering from that life.

Ricky's anguish and pain was palpable in his last online message, and I understood his need for justice, but I hoped that his volatile language was just a way to vent his anger in a safe community of peers who suffered and struggled like he did. I was also in a fairly fragile state of mind at the time, as I'd recently been diagnosed with PTSD and was soon to start psychotherapy, so I didn't contact him. I wasn't sure if he had a legitimate plan to bring down the Family, so I was waiting to hear more information before getting involved.

Five months later, on January 8, 2005, Ricky went through with his plan alone, viciously murdering Angela Smith.[30] She was Berg's long-time lover, and Zerby's secretary, one of the first three flirty fishers in Tenerife, with Zerby and Sara Kelley. She was a familiar part of Berg's household, and occasionally one of Ricky's childhood minders, so he knew her well.

Ricky's original plan was to murder his mother and her co-leader Steven Kelly, hoping he could kill the snake by chopping off its head. After posting his last online message, Ricky heard rumours that they were somewhere in the United States. He knew that his mother's parents owned a retirement home in Arizona, and that she had visited them before, so he moved to Tuscon in September 2004. He found work as an electrician and made contact with his relatives, who were never Family members. He maintained a close relationship with one of his aunts and spent Christmas with the family, hoping his mother would show up.

After Berg's death in 1994, Angela hadn't remained on Zerby's personal staff. She had been reassigned to California to help set up and run the Family Care Foundation, a Family front organization ostensibly operating as a charity.[31] She was also involved with the Zerby family's Arizona retirement home and went there at least twice a year for board meetings. While Ricky was visiting his relatives that Christmas of 2004, he learned that Angela would be coming to town in early January. Suspecting she knew where Zerby was, he thought this might be his only chance to track down his mother. He put his plan into action.

Ricky recorded a disturbing, hour-long video on January 7, 2005, the night before the murder.[32] He referred to Angela, without naming her, as his "source" for information about his mother, and explained what he was about to do, and why. He had arranged to meet her for dinner the next night, before she returned to California. He intended to torture her to get information on his mother's location.

The video shows Ricky in his apartment, the scene of the crime, describing the collection of weapons and tools covering the kitchen table. They included a Glock 23 pistol with several bullet magazines, a stun gun, a soldering iron, an electric drill, duct tape, several small knives, and a Ka-Bar combat knife with a seven-inch blade. He explained why that was his weapon of choice for "taking out the scum, taking out the fuckin' trash."

Throughout the video, Ricky calmly loads bullets into the magazines as he talks about how the child abuse he and his sisters experienced and witnessed affected his mental state. Describing the physical beatings Merry Berg suffered during her numerous exorcisms, he says: "Nobody, nobody deserved that. Especially not a kid that age. So I watched every day new bruises on her, big fuckin' fat fuckin' bruises on her."

Ricky also discusses suicidal thoughts he had in his teen years, his ongoing mental-health struggles since leaving the Family, and how he had many times considered just disappearing and quietly ending his life. He partly blames the extreme social seclusion of growing up in Berg's secretive, isolated household for his deeply depressed state of mind.

> I don't think most other Family kids can relate to this, because yeah, they were abused. But one thing I don't think they were that much is secluded. And that really can fuck you over, because if you don't have that, um, mirror, if you will, of other kids your own age, um, even kids older than you, you know, older siblings, whatever, friends, then uh, it really fucks ya up.

Ricky laments that he tried to move on, create a new life and forget the old one, but "I got stuck because there's this need that I have, this need. It's not a want, it's a fucking need. And I wish it wasn't, but it is. It's a need for revenge. It's a need for justice, because I can't go on like this." At the end of the video he states, "They sure fucked with our brains. Used us as slaves… just there for those sick fuckers' pleasure…That's the way it was at Grandpa and Mama's house."

The next evening, Ricky lured Angela to his apartment, where he attacked her with the combat knife, stabbing her five times before cutting her throat. Crime scene investigators said she had been stabbed in her breast and stomach and had defensive wounds on both arms, but they found no evidence Ricky had tortured her. After the murder, he drove several hours to California, found a deserted parking lot outside Blythe, and shot himself in the head.[33]

Chapter 22
Everything Is Broken

Reports of Ricky's shocking tragedy spread quickly in the global survivor community before it hit the headlines. As I tried to make sense of the stunning news, my mind flashed back to Ricky's last online message pleading for help to find justice and bring an end to the Family. When I first read it, I didn't think he was actually making a public appeal for people to join him in a murder plot. However, in his video he says that is exactly what he was referring to in this message.

Ricky's video was posted on one of the survivor sites soon after his suicide, but I hadn't watched it yet when I went to my next session with the psychiatrist. She cautioned that watching it might have a negative effect on me. I knew it would increase my emotional turmoil, but I felt I had to face it full-on if I ever hoped to heal. Now that I had finally started to examine my past, I couldn't turn away from any part of it, no matter how dark, and Ricky's video was very dark indeed. It was gut-wrenching, heartbreaking, mind-messing to realize that the thirteen-year-old cloistered cult kid I'd chauffeured several times in Japan had been deeply disturbed and suicidal at the time, and was now surrounded by weapons, expressing his mental torment and raging need for revenge.

When that tragedy happened, I was still in the process of reading all the articles, documents and survivor stories on the three websites. As I learned new information and followed every conversation in the online forums, often discussing issues late into the night, it was emotionally shattering to see the full picture of the Family's child-abuse legacy emerge while I put the pieces together. Seeing things from the perspective of children raised in the cult helped me recognize the systemic abuses that affected all of them in one way or another.

What started as background research for this memoir turned into a psychological crisis. After immersing myself every day in cult-related information from various sources — websites, books, academic journals, documentary films — I couldn't turn my mind off at night, and so was getting only about four or five hours of broken sleep. I began to dread going to bed and being kept awake by incessant thoughts in my head. As my sleep decreased, my pain increased, eventually spreading throughout my body. I slowly became more anti-social and withdrawn, certain that no one in my family or social circles could understand what I was going through.

After two months of weekly sessions with the psychiatrist, I came to the end of my story. She then informed me that she didn't do talk therapy, only drug therapy, which surprised me. I had assumed all psychiatrists did some form of counselling, and thought that she wanted to hear my full story first so she had the context for discussing specific cult-related issues. Instead, she suggested I try a fairly new antidepressant with sedative properties that might help reduce my anxiety, insomnia and pain.

When my family doctor had previously recommended an anti-seizure medication for my chronic pain, I discovered it was at the centre of a criminal fraud case involving the pharmaceutical company. Also, I could find only weak anecdotal evidence that it was effective for pain, so I refused to take it. But extreme insomnia made me desperate for relief, so I agreed to try the new antidepressant.

While I waited for my turn in group therapy, I started weekly sessions with a psychologist, a recent graduate with limited clinical experience. Although she'd read all the psychiatrist's detailed notes in my file, after a couple of conversations it was clear she knew very little about the kinds of cult-related issues I was dealing with. So I lent her *Cults in Our Midst* and a VHS video of the 1994 documentary *Children of God*. I was teaching her more than she was helping me.

I had a more helpful experience with group therapy, which I started in the summer of 2005. The doctor leading it was one of Canada's top PTSD specialists, Greg Passey, a former military psychiatrist recognized internationally for his trauma research and therapy work with UN peacekeeping forces who witnessed genocidal war crimes in Rwanda and Yugoslavia. Now in private practice, he worked primarily with military veterans, police officers and other emergency first responders.

In weekly sessions, Dr. Passey taught us the basic psychological mechanisms of PTSD and strategies for dealing with the symptoms. None of the other nine people were survivors of an abusive cult, although two of them had been sexually abused by Catholic priests. But while we had different traumatic experiences, we all suffered many of the same symptoms. There was a strange comfort in talking to strangers. We helped each other see behaviours and attitudes we didn't recognize in ourselves until we saw and heard them in one another.

Although it wasn't specifically cult recovery therapy, I began to recognize how much of my mental state and behaviour, both in the cult and after leaving, was caused by undiagnosed complex PTSD. That helped me understand my uncharacteristic reactions in certain situations, how they were connected to past experiences, how those experiences led to ill health, and why I was developing new symptoms after all these years.

I found it helpful to understand my experiences in the Family as a spiritual variation of long-term domestic abuse causing battered-wife syndrome, a subcategory of PTSD. After all, I had been a bride of Christ, according to the Family's version of bridal theology.

— — —

A few months after Ricky's murder-suicide, and before I started group therapy, I travelled to Texas for a weekend conference with about twenty second-generation survivors from around the US, Canada and Europe. I was one of two former first-generation members who were invited. The conference was organized by Julia McNeil, who had created the MovingOn website in 2001 as a safe space for second-generation survivors of the Family to find resources, tell their stories, and offer mutual moral support.[1] Over five thousand of Julia's peers participated on the site.

Knowing personally how difficult it was for anyone raised in a socially isolated cult to create a new life after leaving with few resources, little education and no support, Julia had also helped establish Safe Passage Foundation in 2003 to assist to those in need. The conference was a brainstorming session on ways to raise awareness of SPF's work.

I couldn't provide financial assistance to SPF, but I could be an advocate by corroborating the stories of abuse survivors and helping to amplify their voices, which some scholars were attempting to silence. By now I was aware that there was a division among academics who study groups like the Family.[2] One crucial difference is that some accept cult survivor stories as relevant evidence of harms caused by high-demand groups, while others doubt, dispute or downplay their claims of abuse. The differences between these two camps are reflected in two academic journals, *Cultic Studies Review* and *Nova Religio*.[3] The latter refers to "new religious movements," a term some scholars prefer, as it avoids negative connotations associated with the word *cult*.

I first learned of these academic disputes by reading the book *Misunderstanding Cults: Searching for Objectivity in a Controversial Field*.[4] That anthology of articles by scholars who study the subject attempts to bridge the divide through direct discourse between the two sides. The assertions of some of these scholars insinuate that what I personally experienced and witnessed didn't happen, and that thousands of abuse survivors discussing their experiences on the Moving On website must be exaggerating or lying. That outraged me.

I found it extremely frustrating and infuriating that some scholars attacked the credibility of former cult members, stereotyping and smearing them as self-serving liars, while at the same time accepting the truthfulness of accounts by current cult members as if they had no self-interest in lying to protect themselves and their group.[5] That made no sense to me, and seemed to be academic bias. The author of the next book I read displayed this bias in his study of the Family, so I wrote a detailed response, hoping it would be published in one of these academic journals.

In 1993, the year that Jesus failed to return as Berg predicted, Family leaders reached out to various religious scholars, hoping to find a level of acceptance or tolerance from the mainstream Christian community. One of them was Southern Baptist Theological Seminary professor James Chancellor. A few months after Berg's death in late 1994, he presented Zerby and Kelly with the idea of writing "an oral history of the movement from the perspective of persons who have chosen to remain loyal and committed disciples of Father David [Berg]."[6] In 2000, Chancellor published *Life in the Family: An Oral History of the Children of God*, an account of the cult told entirely from the point of view of active members.

Unfortunately, without accounts from former members who left because of the abuse, especially those born and raised in the Family, who were never members of their own free choice, Chancellor's one-sided approach gives his readers an incomplete history and a distorted self-portrait of the Family. In a review of the book, sociology professor Stephen A. Kent suggested that "social scientists, feminists, and some former members may tell the same story very differently, and certainly they will provide less kind interpretations of many facts."[7]

In the introduction to his book, Chancellor does acknowledge that it is not the whole story; however, in making that point, he mischaracterizes survivors of the Family as a few "hostile career apostates" and "thousands of former Children of God who have little or no stake in the outcome."[8]

Reading that derogatory phrase "career apostates" riled me. It revealed Chancellor's bias against former members who warn the public by expressing valid criticisms of the Family. I could've applied a similarly pejorative epithet to Chancellor and called him a "career apologist" for an abusive cult, since he ignored or downplayed the tremendous harms it caused. In fact, contrary to his claim, thousands were abused in one way or another, especially those in the second generation, and many still live with significant consequences today, so they have always had a "stake in the outcome."

Also omitted from Chancellor's book is any mention of the Family's "deceivers yet true" doctrine. He must have been aware of that doctrine, if not from the Family's publications, then from reading Justice Ward's judgment in the British custody case, which some of his interviewees discuss. It is unreasonable to assume that Family members chosen by leaders to interact and co-operate with Chancellor were more honest than those who were delegated by the same leaders to falsely testify under oath in Ward's court. Yet Chancellor chooses not to inform his readers of that highly relevant doctrine of deceit.

Since its inception, the public face presented by the Family never honestly reflected the group's true nature behind closed doors. Deeply distrustful of non-members, and always fearful of interventions by legal authorities, they had well-prepared public-relations teams to deceive outsiders. They also used special Media Homes, sanitized to deceive government agents, journalists and academics. In a 1998 article, Professor Kent and Theresa Krebs wrote about various deceptive tactics the Family used:

> Part of making "everything look as perfect as possible" at the Media Homes required "mega-preparation" such as moving out crowded children, removing bunkbeds from overcrowded bedrooms, and placing single mothers elsewhere....The Family "only kept the best PR people there"....In order to avoid revealing sensitive information, Family spokespersons underwent intensive rehearsals of questions and answers...and maintained strict security regarding which among its publications members could provide to "Systemites" for perusal.[9]

It wasn't only adults who participated in creating a false image of the Family in those Media Homes. In a 2004 article, Professor Kent describes how the Family set up these special homes after a series of government raids in the late 1980s and early 1990s, when child-protection authorities apprehended Family children in Canada, Argentina, Spain, Australia and France:

> The Family, in response, burned controversial documents, published public denials of sexual impropriety between children and adults, and created media homes containing carefully selected teens who rehearsed probable questions and appropriate answers before reporters or academics arrived….many of those teens observed serious discrepancies between the group's public posture and their own private experiences.[10]

Considering what Justice Ward described as the Family's ingrained habit of deception, I found it difficult to understand why Chancellor thought he could convey a reliable oral history of the Family that excluded the voices of those who'd left it. Interviewing some of them and including their side of the story would have provided a different perspective and painted a more accurate picture of what life was really like in the Family, especially for the children who were born and raised in it.

If anyone should've had a say in telling the Family's history, it was Merry Berg. Her story is significant and essential to any accurate telling of that history, but Chancellor almost completely erases her from it. His only reference to Merry is a single sentence in a footnote: "In the court case, Father David's [Berg's] granddaughter gave testimony that she had been sexually and physically abused by Father David, then subjected to terrifying ordeals of exorcisms."[11]

That footnote doesn't indicate whether Chancellor believed Merry's testimony or not, and ignores the fact that Ward considered her a far more credible, reliable witness than the Family members who testified. Chancellor marginalizes Merry's important role by omitting her voice from his version of the Family's oral history. Clearly, he deliberately decided that Merry's story is irrelevant to that history, unlike Ward, who wrote:

> I have perhaps dealt with MB [Merry Berg] at inordinate length. I do so because of the central role she plays not only in The Family's past but in its present. For The Family to gain the respectability which they now appear to seek, they must acknowledge that what David Berg did to his granddaughter was wrong, not just a mistake, but inexcusably wrong. They must atone for their treatment of her which I find to have been barbaric and cruel.[12]

About a year after Merry was sent from Macau to the United States, she moved in with her Aunt Deborah, who had written a highly critical exposé of her father and his abusive cult. Similarly, Merry began to speak publicly about the horrific, torturous abuses she suffered at the hands of her grandfather, Zerby and Kelly. In 1992, she told part of her story in a newsletter by former members.[13] That same year, Berg and Zerby began maliciously maligning and vilifying her in vile, demonizing attacks.[14]

Berg described a vision he claimed he'd had about Merry: "I got the most gruesome picture of this backslider with her mouth all red & dripping, drooling with blood like a vampire! Of course, she's just a little ignorant nobody, but it shows you how the Devil is using her. Even Deborah is just being used."[15]

Zerby also warned members about Merry in a letter published at the same time as Berg's: "Why would anyone in the Family ever believe Mene [Merry] above the Prophet?…why would you believe this girl who very obviously went completely insane?…why would anyone in the Family accept the word of this crazy girl, who completely yielded herself to the Devil, over Dad's [Berg's] account of what happened?"[16]

The descriptions of Merry's exorcisms, and those dreadful denunciations that depicted her as an insane, blood-drooling, demon-possessed enemy, were used to terrorize Family children and teens into submission and justify their cruel corporal punishments. Merry's court testimony was a pivotal point in the Family's history that flung open the curtain on the wizardly pedophile prophet pulling the puppet strings, fully exposing the evil immorality at the head and heart of the Family. Her truth-telling helped lead to its downfall, so any account claiming to be a history of the Family that deliberately excludes Merry's story is deceptively incomplete.

Although Chancellor's book is certainly useful for religion and sociology scholars trying to understand the mindset of active cult members, I thought his use of the word *history* in the subtitle misled the general public. I was still doing background research and organizing my diary notes in preparation to write my story, but his book so angered me that I put that project off again. I felt compelled to respond to Chancellor by pointing out major omissions in his one-sided history.

Since some scholars tend to disbelieve the accounts of cult survivors, I wrote a well-documented article I thought was suitable for academic journals in that field. Before submitting it to a journal, I contacted Professor Kent, who had published a wide range of studies on various sects, cults and alternative religions.[17] I first became aware of his work on the Children of God through a chapter he wrote in *Misunderstanding Cults*.[18] In journal articles such as "Lustful Prophet: A Psychosexual Historical Study of the Children of God's Founder, David Berg" and "Misattribution and Social Control in the Children of God," I read information about Berg and his cult I hadn't been aware of, or now saw in a different light.[19]

Kent's valuable insights on the cult dynamics operating in the Family concurred with many of my experiences and those of others I was reading about on the survivor websites. I also respected his willingness to consider the accounts and claims of former members, so I asked him by email if he had time to read my article and provide feedback. He generously recommended ways to improve its readability, and suggested my best chance for publication was to submit it to *Cultic Studies Review*.

I agreed with Kent's suggestion, but I was curious to know how academics on the other side of the debate over the credibility of former members would react to my article. So I first submitted it to *Nova Religio*, fully expecting the editor to consider me an unreliable apostate unqualified to challenge the work of a professor of world religions and Christian missions. I hoped, though, that my article wouldn't be rejected outright, but put through the peer review process first so I could at least benefit from any criticisms that would help me improve it, which is what happened.

The editor emailed me a compilation of comments by three anonymous reviewers. She also mistakenly forwarded a private group email discussion that revealed their names, which enabled me to identify through online searches the general position they took in their work as professors of religious studies. With that information, I wasn't surprised their comments on my manuscript were very condescending and dismissive.

One reviewer objected to a passage where I discussed the phenomenon of groupthink, and the controversial concepts of brainwashing and mind control. To avoid that controversy, I removed the passage, and elsewhere used the word *indoctrination* when referring to the process of creating conformity and obedience through the inculcation of doctrines and the repeated reinforcement of dogmatic thoughts, beliefs and behaviours. I also refrained from using the provocative term *mind rape*, which is how I now saw the indoctrination of children before they have developed the critical-thinking skills necessary to ask the right questions, doubt authority and rationally think for themselves.[20]

These reviewers also objected to my personal observations, which I included to contradict some of Chancellor's conclusions and claims by his interviewees. For every issue I disputed, I also provided corroborating evidence from many credible sources and the Family's own publications. So, because my personal anecdotes were unnecessary for my arguments, I removed passages describing my own experiences. I have included them all in this memoir.

The reviewers dismissed my well-documented, valid counternarrative to Chancellor's book as biased, apparently without recognizing their own biases in doing so. All three agreed "that *Nova Religio* is not the appropriate venue" for my article, and the editor gave me this reason in her rejection email: "The methodology of your paper varies too much from the scholarly treatments that are accepted for publication in *Nova Religio*."

I thought they demonstrated a double standard by completely rejecting my experiential expertise on the subject. My insights were as valuable for understanding life in the Family, the purported purpose of Chancellor's book, as the information provided by his interviewees, who were all loyal cult members well trained to deceive and distort facts.

I sent the manuscript to the editor of *Cultic Studies Review*, who accepted it for publication. First, he sent a copy to Chancellor for his response, then gave me an opportunity to reply to that. Both Chancellor's response and my reply were published with the article in 2007.[21]

— — —

After my PTSD group therapy finished at the end of 2005, I had no further mental health support, and no intimate relationships in which I could discuss my experiences. I did tell a few people that I had been in a cult, but no one could easily relate to that, so those uneasy conversations didn't last long. Since my breakdown, I had slowly withdrawn from all the friends I made during my nine years in Vancouver. Depression and widespread chronic pain reduced my desire to socialize, so I stopped most activities I once enjoyed, and isolated myself.

The antidepressant I was taking didn't provide pain relief, as the psychiatrist suggested it might, or decrease my depression much either, considering my socially withdrawn behaviour. I kept taking it for chronic insomnia, though, because its strong sedative effect tranquilized my anxiety and stopped incessant thoughts that caused long, sleepless hours.

I was subsisting on poverty-level disability benefits in what was fast becoming one of North America's most expensive cities. I could no longer afford to live in Vancouver. The rent for my apartment had almost doubled in ten years, and was now eighty percent of my income. The number of homeless in Vancouver more than quadrupled in those years. With no affordable options left, I feared becoming a statistic in this homelessness crisis, so in mid-2007 I moved back to Port Alberni, where my story started, hoping to avoid that ending.

Unfortunately, homelessness was increasing everywhere, even in my small hometown. I couldn't find a place that was both affordable on my disability pension and had the kind of quiet environment I needed for my mental health to improve. For the next ten years, I languished in unsuitable, substandard housing conditions that triggered my PTSD and worsened my health. I moved six times, fleeing unbearably noisy environments, bad neighbours and unethical landlords.

Lack of medical care added to my struggles after I returned to Port Alberni. Before I left Vancouver, my psychiatrist had given me a prescription for the antidepressant, renewable for one year. However, there were no family doctors taking new patients, so when that prescription expired I had no way to get a new one.

A psychiatrist at the BC government's Mental Health and Addiction Services clinic refused to prescribe the antidepressant, supposedly because the dose was too high, although he could've simply reduced the dose. And a nurse there told me they had no services for PTSD patients. When the city's first walk-in clinic opened, a doctor there also refused to treat me. After I explained my situation, he told me the clinic was only for urgent acute care, not for chronic conditions or mental illness. The hospital's emergency ward also would not provide prescriptions for me.

I had no choice but to stop taking the drug I had used for almost four years. I was forced to withdraw from the antidepressant on my own, without medical supervision, which all health authorities strongly advise against. Fortunately, cannabis helped me get through the difficult withdrawal process, but I was extremely angry that several doctors had so easily turned their back on me, refusing to treat me unless I had a medical emergency.

I felt abandoned by the medical system, and endangered by government policies that worsened my health and housing crises. I knew about the causal connection between mental illness and homelessness, and that many vulnerable citizens who face the same systemic barriers I did end up living on the street. Angered by that ongoing injustice, I decided to fight back by speaking out. Over the next few years, I filed formal complaints with four government agencies, the medical doctors' oversight body, and a non-government mental health agency that unethically harmed me and other housing clients.

Filing those complaints gave me some hope that I could help improve things, for myself and for everyone else in similar circumstances. However, I received unsatisfactory, bureaucratic responses to all of my complaints. In each case, some policy or regulation prevented a remedy for me personally, or resolution of the systemic problems I raised.

I remained mired in a deep pit of despair for years, and eventually did become homeless. I spent three months sleeping on my mum's couch, one of the many hidden homeless not counted in government statistics. I had reached rock bottom. Knowing I wouldn't last long in another old, noisy apartment building, I desperately searched for a quiet, affordable alternative. That seemed so hopeless I actually contemplated joining a homeless encampment on the grounds of the courthouse in the province's capital. If I was going to be homeless, then I thought I would at least get in the face of politicians who refused to effectively deal with the issue.

Then, right at that lowest point in my life, I got lucky. I found a very old cottage on a lake fifteen kilometres outside of town. To make the move, I needed some financial assistance from my mum, which, for a man my age, who ought to have been supporting her instead, was embarrassing to admit and ask for. She didn't hesitate, though, despite her own modest means. The rent was barely affordable, so I relied on the food bank for a couple of years, until I reached the age of sixty-five, when I was eligible for old-age security and other supplements.

I had tried to make a difference for others by fighting the systemic issues I faced when seeking suitable housing and health care, but I couldn't save myself, let alone anyone else. So I gave up trying to make the world a better place, and concentrated on writing this memoir. From the moment I moved into the semi-isolated log cabin, I began to relax and recover from over a decade of overwhelming distress. The idyllic environment is the quietest place I have ever lived, ideal for healing and writing.

— — —

I started this story with a Dylan song I heard on the radio. Now, at the end, I'm reminded of another song by him, "Everything Is Broken." My life is broken. There is no happy ending.

Broken family, broken relationships. Gone for years, I was lost to my real family even after I returned. Broken by the fraudulent Family, unable to talk about my experiences, I remained in many ways a stranger to them.

My relationship with my dad never recovered. He remained always sarcastic with me, as he had been throughout my childhood, which pushed me away, so we never had a meaningful, heartfelt conversation. The emotional attachment between us was broken long ago, so when he lay dying in a hospital a couple of hundred kilometres away in 2015, I didn't visit him on his deathbed. I might have if he had asked to see me, but he didn't. I never shed a tear, and still haven't. I don't know if my heart was too hard or too broken for tears.

Broken social scene, broken love. Damaged by lies, betrayals and the Family's tainted love, I've had difficulty even expressing the word *love* to those who care for me. My inability to trust people and be open about my past prevented me from forming intimate relationships. Although I've had many acquaintances since leaving the cult, in those thirty years I've never found deep friendship or true love. I've been almost entirely and intentionally celibate, and have always lived alone.

Broken finances, broken future. Religious manipulators preying on my ignorant teen naiveté convinced me to waste two of the most potentially productive decades of my life. Trying to warn the world of doomsday and save souls for Jesus before he returned was a fool's mission doomed from the start. Following a false prophet left me with nothing but the clothes on my back. To make up for lost time, I invested in eight years of schooling, spending tens of thousands of dollars in student loans, but my life broke down before I could take financial advantage of that education. Unable to pay off those loans, I will likely die in debt.

Broken health, broken hope. Some wounds never heal. Racked with remorse, and emotional and physical pain from a broken brain that broke my body, I've become old before my time. In the beginning, I thought I could save the world with religion. Later, I tried to change the world with protests, politics and law. In the end, I gave up. World-weary, I retreated from it to a life of solitude.

One day, when I was about five or six years old, we discovered our dog hiding under the house. She was injured, probably hit by a car. I remember hearing an adult explain that some dogs do that when they are sick or injured. Sometimes, when the pain caused by my dogmatic past is at its worst, I remember that dog as I'm curled up alone in a semi-secluded log cabin, licking my wounds.

Epilogue

"The Family International's Executive Overseers Address the International CESNUR Conference"

SALT LAKE CITY, UTAH, June 13, 2009/24-7PressRelease/ —Karen Zerby and Steve Kelly, spiritual and administrative leaders of the Family International, presented a paper at the 2009 Conference of the Center for Studies on New Religious Movements, hosted in Salt Lake City, Utah from June 11th to June 13th, 2009. The paper, entitled: "The Future of the Family International: Establishing a Culture of Innovation and Progress," outlined organizational changes and evangelistic goals....[1]

Zerby and Kelly's speech was the final presentation of the conference, and that press release was issued after it ended. Clearly, they didn't want to announce their participation in advance. The official program for the conference listed the schedule of events with details of sessions, including names of presenters and titles of their papers.[2] However, that program schedule makes no mention at all of the Family, Zerby and Kelly, or the title of their paper.

As the *Salt Lake Tribune* newspaper reported, Karen Zerby's appearance at the conference was "her first-ever public address."[3] After four decades of living with Berg in hiding from enemies and followers alike, it isn't surprising that Zerby wanted to keep her participation in the conference a secret until after it was over. It also isn't surprising that they chose to present their paper at the Center for Studies on New Religions (CESNUR) conference, rather than at a similar annual conference held by the International Cultic Studies Association. Professor Stephen Kent described CESNUR as the highest profile lobbying and information group for controversial religions...under the directorship of patent/trademark lawyer and independent scholar, Massimo Introvigne. A persistent critic of any national attempts to identify or curtail so-called 'cults,' Introvigne has spoken out against what he considers to be intolerance toward "minority religions," especially in Belgium, France, and Germany....Many German and French officials working on issues related to religious 'sects' and human rights do not see CESNUR and Introvigne as neutral parties in the ongoing debates (a judgement that certainly flows both ways).[4]

Some members of CESNUR, including Introvigne and cofounder J. Gordon Melton, have faced criticism for defending dangerous cults and downplaying their harms, or for maintaining financial or personal connections to organizations they are studying.[5] They and other CESNUR board members are also involved with the journal *Nova Religio*. Both men were at the conference attended by Zerby and Kelly.

Melton wrote five pages on the Family in the 1986 and 1992 editions of his *Encyclopedic Handbook of Cults in America*. In both editions he concluded: "The sexual manipulation in the Children of God has now been so thoroughly documented that it is doubtful whether the organization can ever, in spite of whatever future reforms it might initiate, regain any respectable place in the larger religious community."[6] However, just two years later Melton was one of the Family's witnesses in the British custody case, and co-edited an anthology of essays favourable to the Family entitled *Sex, Slander and Salvation: Investigating The Family/Children of God*.[7] Melton also contributed an essay to that collection, as did Introvigne.

Melton's co-editor of that book was James R. Lewis.[8] A year later, in 1995, both scholars were invited to Japan by members of Aum Shinrikyo, a doomsday cult that was suspected of releasing deadly sarin gas into the Tokyo subway system, killing thirteen, seriously injuring dozens and harming thousands more. In his rush to defend the religious rights of the group, Lewis relied on biased information from active cult members to wrongly claim publicly that they were not responsible for the attack, but were scapegoats in a government conspiracy.[9]

That situation not only undermined the credibility of those academics who sided with the group, but also more generally discredited the scholarship of religion in the eyes of the public. In "Scholarship, Aum Shinrikyôô, and Academic Integrity," religious studies professor Ian Reader wrote:

The visit [by Lewis and Melton], however, had the unfortu-
nate effect of simply reinforcing the public view that scholars
of religion were naïve support teams for dangerous religious
groups....We need to recognize that when scholars operate
primarily as defenders of religious movements they are following a particular agenda and as such run the risk of compromising their position as objective scholars....It is essential that
we take a critical stance towards the movements we study so
that we can maintain the degree of objectivity that will be most
beneficial to all concerned....Otherwise there remains the
danger that scholars of religion will continue to be seen more
as apologists than as analysts of the movements they study.[10]

Lewis's defence of that deadly doomsday cult before knowing all the facts
exemplifies the problem of cult apologists siding with harmful groups and
accepting their accounts as truthful while rejecting credible accusations
from critics.[11] They do a disservice to the public when they only consider
anecdotes and evidence provided by leaders and members of groups to be
credible, while disbelieving disaffected dissidents and former members.
This academic bias paints a skewed, one-sided portrait.

In their article, "When Scholars Know Sin: Alternative Religions and
Their Academic Supporters,"[12] Professor Stephen A. Kent and Theresa
Krebs discuss that problematic issue of some cults co-opting the scholars studying them, who then write sympathetic reports, essays or books,
or defend them in legal cases. This article starts with an account of how
James Lewis co-operated with the Family's attempt to prevent Kent from
publishing a critical study that examines David Berg's psychosexual history.[13] The Family's lawyer threatened to file a lawsuit against the publisher
of the journal series *Research in the Social Scientific Study of Religion*, which
had intended to publish Kent's article. The threat worked, and the
publisher withdrew the article. However, it was later published in the journal *Cultic Studies Review*.

Kent and Krebs explain that a couple of months before Lewis tried to kill
Kent's article, the Family had contacted Lewis for public relations advice on
how to counter negative press. One result of that request for advice was the
favourable anthology Lewis and Melton edited. So, at the same time Lewis
was attempting to prevent Kent from publishing a negative article about
the Family's founder, he was also engaged in helping the cult "cultivate a
positive public image," along with several of his academic associates.

As Kent and Krebs describe in their article, the Family not only funded that anthology, but also restricted these academics to sham homes, and controlled who they spoke to and the information they received. The Family was able to influence their conclusions, resulting in a book of positive essays so advantageous that they promoted it to the press and on their website as proof of their legitimacy.

Several years later, in 2000, the Family gave Melton a donation of $10,065.83 USD.[14] In 2004, Melton wrote a concise overview of the group's history in *The Children of God: The Family*.[15] In her review of this book, University of Alberta professor Susan Raine identified instances where "Melton uses language to minimize the atmosphere of child sexualisation" and downplays other controversial aspects of the Family's sexual doctrines and practices.[16] Just three months after Melton's book was published, Karen Zerby's son Ricky Rodriguez murdered her assistant and killed himself.

— — —

In the *Salt Lake Tribune*'s report on the 2009 CESNUR conference, one of the conference sponsors described Zerby's speech as "part of the Family's coming-out party." The title of that newspaper article more accurately refers to the major organizational and doctrinal changes discussed by Zerby as an "image makeover."[17] Among the most significant changes was the abandonment of most of Berg's extreme teachings, extra-biblical beliefs, and endtime predictions that made the group unique.

The Family's evangelism had always been motivated by the belief that we are living in the endtime. Even after Berg's prophecies predicting Jesus would return in 1993 proved to be false, they continued to believe the Second Coming was imminent. But now Family leaders no longer expect Jesus to return soon. Instead, as the *Tribune* reported, they are "looking 30 to 50 years into the future," which Zerby said in her speech was "a monumental shift for these believers to contemplate, but an essential one." Zerby and Kelly referred to the radical reversal of many of the Family's doctrines, policies and practices as the "Reboot."[18]

In 2010, about a year after Zerby and Kelly announced the Family's Reboot at the conference, Gary and Gordon Shepherd, both professors of sociology, published the book *Talking with the Children of God: Prophecy and Transformation in a Radical Religious Group*.[19] It is primarily focused on the role of prophecy in the group after the death of their so-called endtime prophet in 1994. The final chapter of this book refers to Zerby's presentation at the conference, but the Reboot, which the Shepherds later called "a startlingly sweeping change of direction,"[20] was still in progress, so they don't discuss those comprehensive changes.

In 2013, the Shepherds provided details of those fundamental changes in their journal article "Reboot of the Family International."[21] They summarize the radical reorganization of the Family in the opening paragraph:

> The changes…shifted TFI from being a closely regulated, exclusive communal society requiring uniformity, high commitment levels, and collective decision making to becoming a loose, inclusive, and amorphous cyber community that emphasizes personal choice of individuals pursuing their own spiritual paths as ordinary citizens within the secular societies in which they reside. Virtually all the organizational and cultural structures of TFI were subsequently dissolved, and many previously accepted beliefs and practices modified, downgraded, or simply jettisoned…pushing it almost to the threshold of dissolution.…TFI could simply fade away altogether as a distinct organizational entity.

In 2018, long-time Family spokesperson Claire Borowik wrote an article published in *Nova Religio* that discussed the dramatic impact the Reboot had on the Family. Interestingly, the editor of that journal who rejected my critical article about the Family had no similar concern of bias about Borowik, and failed to inform readers that former members and legal authorities have accused her of committing various child abuse crimes when she was a Family leader in Argentina.[22]

Borowik reports that the Family's core membership was less than seven thousand around the time the Reboot was announced in 2009. By 2018, only about nineteen hundred remained, but they no longer thought of themselves as members. She uses the word *affiliates* to describe them. Borowik and some of her interviewees paint a pessimistic picture of the group in its death throes, essentially concluding that the Family has no future as an unstructured community connected only online:

> The Reboot represented a profound redirection of TFI's religious practice and worldview, and the virtual dismantling of the communal households that had been central to TFI's religious identity construction and the perpetuation of its culture and belief system.…the aftermath of the Reboot [has]

rendered the sustainability of the movement and its future viability uncertain.[23]

Zerby and Kelly intended the Reboot to be the Family's road to the future, but it turned out to be a dead end. The ex-member community—especially the second generation, many of whom consider themselves survivors rather than ex-members, since they were never members of their own free choice, deserves a lot of credit for this ending. Like the academic cult apologists who discredit and denounce accounts by critical former members, Borowik blames them for making it impossible for the Family to whitewash its past, rewrite history and create a new public image for itself:

> Efforts to modernize and reinvent its public image were met with heightened public opposition in the early 2000s due to the development of three adversarial former member websites (exfamily.org, xfamily.org, and movingon.org), which rapidly gained prominence in search engine rankings of information featured about TFI. A murder/suicide in 2005 perpetrated by Karen Zerby's estranged son, Ricky Rodriguez (1975–2005), further increased tensions and placed the movement once again at the center of controversy and stigmatizing media.... The permanence and visibility of counter-narratives on the internet...[hindered] its efforts to distance the movement from past controversies and reinvent itself as a legitimate contemporary movement.[24]

The Family is now an unrecognizable shadow of its former self, thanks to the heroes of this story: Merry Berg, Julia McNeil and their second-generation peers who spoke out, defiantly pushing back against Family leaders who denied their claims of abuse and denounced them as lying apostates. Those who gave evidence of child abuse in the British custody case delivered some of the first deadly blows.

Merry's willingness to testify against her grandfather exposed the extreme immoralities that lay at the heart of the Family, undermining its very foundation, which is why Berg, Zerby and Kelly so viciously vilified and demonized her. Merry bravely bared the naked truth that "the emperor had no clothes." It was a fiction that David Berg was the Love Prophet, as he was referred to in a Canadian documentary.[25] Instead, he was the Lustful Prophet, as Professor Kent referred to him in his study.

Like many of her peers, Merry struggled at times to recover from the various extreme abuses she suffered in the Family. While working on my article about Chancellor's book, I considered reaching out to her to apologize personally for my failure to help her or speak out against her mistreatment when I was in Macau. Because I included parts of her story in the article, I also wanted to let her read the draft before I submitted it, if she was interested. However, a 2005 *Rolling Stone* article on Ricky's murder-suicide reported that Merry was homeless and addicted, and according to her mother had "given up on life."[26] It felt inappropriate to try and contact her at that time.

Merry had successfully recovered from addiction and homelessness by the end of 2006, and was making a new, happier life for herself with the help of friends and family. I was greatly relieved to hear this news, but decided again to put off contacting her to avoid the risk of interfering with her recent recovery by triggering traumatic memories. Instead, I planned to wait until I finished a draft of this memoir, and then to contact her through her close friend, Amy Bril, another outspoken advocate, to ask if she was interested in reviewing the passages I'd written about her.[27] I also still wanted to apologize personally, but I waited too long. Sadly, on December 16, 2017, Merry Berg died in her sleep from respiratory failure at the age of forty-five.[28]

Like Merry, Julia McNeil, another influential activist who helped bring down the Family, also died too young. After a decade of advocacy work compassionately supporting her fellow cult survivors, Julia died of cancer on June 5, 2012, at the age of thirty-seven.

Many others too numerous to name also deserve credit for helping to kill the cult by exposing its abuses and inner workings, making it impossible for the Family's sanitized image makeover to succeed. They include: everyone who contributed to the ex-member websites; everyone who gave interviews to journalists and academics, appeared in documentaries or published memoirs;[29] and everyone who endured systemic and personal abuses until they were able to defiantly resist their maltreatment and rebel against their abusers by escaping to the real world.

Most of those in the second generation have managed to survive and make new lives despite deficiencies in their upbringing that may have hindered or delayed their progress in some ways. Many have even thrived, but most still bear psychological scars or suffer various heath problems from the trauma of adverse childhood experiences.[30] I continue to hear many sad stories of broken families, poverty, homelessness and addiction. Tragically, overwhelming psychological injuries have led many to commit suicide.

A list of suicides and premature deaths created in a private Facebook group of survivors contains around one hundred names as of this writing, the most recent in April 2023. While most are confirmed suicides, other causes of death linked to child abuse in the cult include drug-addiction poisonings, risk-taking accidents and various health problems related to childhood medical neglect. Those listed deaths are only the ones known by the eight hundred or so people participating in that Facebook group, so the actual number is likely much higher.

The Family expected their children to be the vanguard of Christian soldiers in Berg's endtime army, and leaders of the world during the millennium, Christ's thousand-year reign on Earth. They raised them to be shining examples to the world of the group's godliness, the fruit that proved the tree was good. Instead, turning on its head a Bible passage members often cited as proof of their moral goodness (Matthew 7:15–20), the experiences suffered by the second generation show that Berg was a false prophet who grew a corrupt tree.

Family members also frequently cited Proverbs 22:6 in support of their Bible-based, fundamentalist education: "Train up a child in the way he should go: and when he is old, he will not depart from it." But almost all their children did depart from the Family's way of life and beliefs by revolting against Berg's Jesus Revolution. Many are no longer even Christians. Through their mass defections, legal testimonies and personal accounts in website forums, media reports, documentaries, academic studies and memoirs, the children of the Children of God have shown the world that the Family tree was rotten to the core.

In the 2006 British documentary *Cult Killer*, Ricky Rodriguez's wife, Elixcia, told the interviewer: "He was searching for his meaning in life. He really was. And I think he finally came up with the conclusion that his reason for living was to make right his mother's wrongs."[31] Ricky felt a responsibility to act on behalf of his peers, but had given up hope that justice could be achieved through the legal system, so he resorted to revenge instead.

Though his crime can't be condoned, Ricky's frustration over the lack of justice is echoed by his second-generation peers.[32] An FBI agent working the murder-suicide case was looking for any relevant information former members had, so there was some initial hope that the investigation might go beyond Ricky's crime to examine the child abuse crimes he described in his writings and suicide video. Many former members gave personal interviews or affidavits to the FBI, describing the abuse they suffered in the Family.

I also contacted that agent, who told me the FBI was well-aware of the Family's long history of child abuse. However, she implied a broader investigation of the Family was unlikely, even though Zerby, Kelly and other top leaders were living in the US at the time of Ricky's tragedy. The FBI's continued refusal to investigate Zerby and Kelly for their role in instigating child abuse crimes in the group is extremely disappointing for survivors.

In hindsight, I regret not contacting Ricky after he posted his final message on the Moving On website, asking for help to obtain some kind of justice. Perhaps if I had, I could have persuaded him against violent revenge by convincing him to personally take legal action against his mother as the best chance to bring Zerby to justice. I certainly would have helped him with that.

Sadly, the lack of justice for those who suffered child abuse in the Family is an additional emotional scar many bear. There have been numerous legal actions taken against Family members in various countries, but I am only aware of eight individuals who have been convicted of child abuse crimes.[33] The two most recent convictions occurred in Scotland in 2018 and 2020. The second-generation survivors who fought for justice in those cases, Verity Carter and Hope Bastine, along with Celeste Jones, tell their stories in the five-part documentary *Children of the Cult*. I appear briefly in the first three episodes.[34]

There are several obstacles in the way of abuse survivors who hope to see criminal charges, or want to take civil actions, against perpetrators and Family leaders. Alberta lawyer Andrea Willey and sociology professor Stephen A. Kent identify some of the barriers to prosecuting child sexual abuse in religious cults. These include overcoming a defence that relies on constitutional religious freedom, the difficulty of establishing necessary evidence given the secrecy of most cults, and various tactics such groups use to avoid legal accountability.[35]

At the 2015 conference of the European Federation of Centres of Research and Information on Cults and Sects, sociology professor Janja Lalich discussed four factors faced by cult survivors seeking justice through the US legal system:

> As I see it, presently, four main issues affect cult-related court cases in the United States. These are (1) not enough attorneys who will take these cases; (2) not enough qualified experts to testify on behalf of victims; (3) the unwillingness of the courts to touch anything related to "religion" because of the omnipotent

First Amendment of the US Constitution (the so-called "freedom of religion" amendment); and (4) the confusion wrought by cult apologists—that is, the confusion about cults vs. religion, and the confusion about free will vs. what I call "bounded choice"—which may also be regarded as a confusion about brainwashing vs. indoctrination. These factors can affect both criminal and civil cases, including divorce and custody cases and settlements.[36]

Survivors of child abuse in the Family face additional difficulties specifically related to the cult's lifestyle and practices purposely designed to thwart legal actions. The use of aliases and legal name changes, constant moving and secret locations make it difficult to identify and find perpetrators and establish the locus of their crimes.[37] Jurisdictional issues can also hinder justice if perpetrator and victim are in different countries, as can time limits for taking legal actions.

Those wishing to take legal action against Zerby and Kelly for encouraging and enabling institutional child abuse must also overcome the hurdle of proving that, as leaders of the organization, they are liable for crimes committed by their followers. Even if they could be flushed out of hiding and a legal case was successful, financial compensation would be difficult to collect. If any of the millions made by members over the years remains, that money, or any asset secretly purchased with it, is certainly well-protected against seizure. However, despite the various legal barriers they must overcome, some second-generation survivors continue to explore ways to hold their abusers accountable and bring them to justice.

— — —

Most children of the Children of God refused to stay children, and rejected the fraudulent Family, thereby practically killing the cult. But while this one is effectively dead, cults are everywhere. There are thousands around the world.[38] Millions of people have been involved with cults in recent years, and new cults of all kinds continue to be created by charlatans or zealots.[39] There is now more information than ever about the characteristics of cults and how to identify their harmful aspects, but people still get sucked into them.[40]

Some of the same social, political and environmental factors that led to the counterculture movement and a new wave of cults in the 1960s have worsened since then. Young people today face an even greater existential crisis.[41] Since 1947, the Bulletin of the Atomic Scientists has maintained a metaphorical "Doomsday Clock." Midnight represents a global catastrophe. The time on the clock, which was initially set to seven minutes to midnight, is determined primarily by the risks presented by nuclear war and climate change. In January 2018, scientists set the clock to two minutes to midnight. The only other time it got that close was in 1953, after the US tested its first thermonuclear device.

Then, in January 2020, the revised time on the clock was announced in seconds for the first time. They set it at one hundred seconds to midnight, the closest it's ever been, because of the increasing possibility of a deliberate or accidental nuclear war, and the world's failure to effectively combat climate change. Those double threats to humanity, the scientists said, "are compounded by a threat multiplier, cyber-enabled information warfare, that undercuts society's ability to respond."[42] In January 2023, these scientists moved the hands of the clock to ninety seconds to midnight.[43]

Just a couple of months later, the COVID-19 global pandemic started to upend almost every aspect of life as we knew it. Catastrophic changes included the collapse of international trade and travel, and widespread national lockdowns, causing a financial crisis for individuals and the global economy. In the background, drums of war were beating, heating up the New Cold War between the US and China. During troubled times of great social upheaval, people can be even more susceptible to cultic manipulations. Taking advantage of all this turmoil and uncertainty, and millions of deaths, were fearmongering fundamentalists, religious proselytizers, spiritual charlatans, con men, conspiracists and political extremists, each peddling all kinds of harmful beliefs, quack cures, conspiracy theories, Bible-based apocalyptic predictions, propaganda and disinformation. Meanwhile, the Doomsday Clock's change to ninety seconds to midnight after Russia's invasion of Ukraine, and speculation about the use of nuclear weapons, indicated that the real danger of global catastrophe caused by a world war or a warming climate continued to be an existential threat.

Many people wrongly assume that only stupid people fall prey to cultists, and that they themselves would recognize a cult, and so could never be enticed or tricked into joining one.[44] Those are myths and misconceptions.[45] No one joins a cult. Potential followers of charismatic cult leaders are recruited and indoctrinated in ways that prevent the unwary from recognizing the true nature of a harmful group, and how they are being deceived and manipulated, until it's too late. It's too late for me, but let my story be a cautionary tale. Beware of blindly believing and being misled by persuasive proselytizers of all kinds. Don't allow yourself and your children to be *misguided*.

Acknowledgements

First, I must offer my deeply sincere, unequivocal apology to every person who was born and/or raised in the Children of God/the Family International for the systemic child abuse you all suffered in many ways. No matter how misguided, misinformed and indoctrinated I was, my membership in the cult makes me partly to blame for that institutionalized abuse. I am forever remorseful for not recognizing during my involvement with the cult that its doctrines, policies and way of life violated many of your rights as children and were extremely harmful to your childhood and adolescent development. Only after I discarded my religious indoctrination that blinded me to the abuses you suffered, and began to re-evaluate Family life from a child's point of view, was I able to recognize that what you all experienced was not a righteous life, but was in fact systemic, institutionalized child abuse. Once I awakened to that fact, I dedicated myself to supporting you child-abuse survivors. Words alone are inadequate to express how sorry I am for the abuses and crimes perpetrated against you all, so I continue to speak out publicly to confirm the experiences you suffered, expose the cult in various media, and advocate on your behalf in any way I can.

I am grateful to the following people for their feedback on my manuscript. Amy Bril was born in the Children of God, is an activist for survivors of abuse and human trafficking, and has participated in many media reports and documentaries. Natacha Tormey, author of the memoir *Born into the Children of God*, has also actively exposed child abuse in the cult by participating in media interviews, documentaries and social media campaigns. Sandy Ellis was a first-generation member of the Children of God who was instrumental in exposing the organization's abuses to Australian authorities after escaping with her children, which she discusses in the documentary series *Children of the Cult* that Amy and I also appear in. Lorinda Stewart was also a first-generation member of the Children of God. Her memoir *One Day Closer* tells the story of her efforts to rescue her daughter from Somali kidnappers.

I also want to thank New Star Books publisher Rolf Maurer for recognizing the importance of my book, his managing editor, Melissa Swann, for her work bringing it to market, and Brian Lynch for his excellent editing of my manuscript.

Notes

In the event you encounter URLs that no longer work (dead links) in the notes below, you can enter them into the Internet Archive's Wayback Machine at web.archive.org/ and read archived copies.

Photographs of many of the people mentioned in this book can be found at: perry-bulwer.blogspot.com/p/photos-of-people-mentioned-in-my-memoir.html.

Chapter 1 – Gotta Serve Somebody

1. Catechism of the Catholic Church, section 1250, www.vatican.va/archive/ENG0015/__P3K.HTM

2. Catechism of the Catholic Church, section 1022, www.vatican.va/archive/ENG0015/__P2L.HTM

3. Catechism of the Catholic Church, sections 1849–64, www.vatican.va/archive/ENG0015/__P6A.HTM

4. Catechism of the Catholic Church, section 1295, www.vatican.va/archive/ENG0015/__P3R.HTM

Chapter 2 – California Dreamin'

1. In 2021, former members born and raised in the group began to speak out about the various forms of child abuse they experienced and referred to it as a cult. Ryan Burns, "Escaping Outreach: Former Members of Eureka Church Say It's a Cult with a History of Hiding Sexual Abuse,"; *Lost Coast Outpost*, August 25, 2021, lostcoastoutpost.com/2021/aug/25/escaping-outreach-former-members-eureka-church-say/

2. Gospel Outreach Lighthouse Ranch played a major role in the Jesus People movement throughout the 1970s and '80s, establishing one hundred communal churches around the world. See: Randall Herbert Balmer, *Encyclopedia of Evangelicalism* (Baylor University Press, 2004)

Chapter 3 – He's Leaving Home

1. Karen M. Staller, *Runaways: How the Sixties Counterculture Shaped Today's Practices and Policies* (Columbia University Press, 2006), cup.columbia.edu/author-interviews/staller-runaways

2. Stephan A. Kent, *From Slogans to Mantras: Social Protest and Religious Conversion in the Late Vietnam Era* (Syracuse: Syracuse University Press, 2001), 1–5

3. Spencer R. Weart, *Nuclear Fear: A History of Images* (Cambridge, Massachusetts: Harvard University Press, 1988), 265

4. See Stephen A. Kent note above. In Chapter 6 of Kent's book, he discusses how the Children of God "rapidly attracted countercultural youth into its fold. Some of the recruits were wayward hippies; others, such as former members of the Jesus People Army in Vancouver, British Columbia, already were involved in Christian missionary activities; and a few of the converts were or had been antiwar activists and radicals....[Their founder] Berg offered American youth a new means for achieving their desired goal of revolution: through the lives that they would live within COG after they had been born again....In essence, Berg's rhetoric resonated with the attitudes of his youthful followers by the manner in which it transformed anti-Americanism into theology....Idealistic youth, sometimes propelled by the perceived shortcomings of their own generation, and always compelled by promises of dramatic social change, chose to commit themselves to high-demand beliefs that always rested upon supernatural claims....These new faiths gave to their converts what direct political protest no longer could provide, hope for the appearance of a purified world."

5. A year after I joined the Children of God, their founder, David Berg, compared his group to the Franciscan order in his review of Franco Zeffirelli's 1972 film *Brother Sun, Sister Moon*, based on the life of Saint Francis. See: David Berg, "Brother Sun," April 1973, www.exfamily.org/pubs/ml/b4/ml0225.shtml

Chapter 4 – Revolution for Jesus

1. All four *Vancouver Sun* stories are by Lisa Hobbs, published under the following headlines: "Teen Menace Feared: Amid Religious Sect Rivalry," January 7, 1972; "B.C. Pays Jesus Army Grant: Courses Never Got Started," January 8, 1972; "Radical U.S. Children of God Sect Think It's Just Great: B.C. Gov't Fund for Jesus People's Army," January 10, 1972; "Scripture Cards Back Breaking With Family: Children of God Provided with Instant Answers," January 11, 1972.

Another article on the same page, titled "Jesus Freaks Authentic," is a Canadian Press news agency report from Ontario. It states: "The moderator of the United Church of Canada says churches should open their doors to the 'Jesus revolution' now popular with many North American young people. Rev. A.B. Moore...advised against criticizing 'Jesus freaks'. 'You ought to realize that here is a fresh, articulate, authentic approach to Jesus Christ of the 20th century,' said the moderator."

On January 14, 1972, the *Sun* published a brief article without a byline, titled "Sect Denies Forcible Detention: Children of God Members Speak," which quotes three Vancouver leaders who rejected criticisms and allegations. One of them stated: "We are conservative Christians. We believe in the literacy of the Bible." See: perry-bulwer.blogspot.com/p/1972-newspaper-reports-about-children.html

2. "The Alternative Jesus: Psychedelic Christ", *Time*, June 21, 1971, content.time.com/time/magazine/article/0,9171,905202,00.html

3. David Berg, "Jesus People? Or Revolution!", June 1971, www.exfamily.org/pubs/ml/b4/ml0148.shtml. David Berg's writings, which are transcripts of audio recordings made of his sermons and personal conversations, contain unusual grammar and style. Almost every sentence ends with an exclamation mark, and those that don't often end with a question mark. Also, words in the first sentence, or part of it, in every paragraph are capitalized. In all the quotations I provide, I've changed these all-caps sentences, but I've kept all the other odd grammar and text styles

4. "Whose Children?" *Time*, January 24, 1973, www.xfamily.org/index.php/Time_Magazine:_Whose_Children%3F

5. *NBC Evening News*, March 5, 1972, www.xfamily.org/index.php/NBC_Evening_News:_Children_of_God

6. With increasing controversies caused by teens joining the Children of God, the group started requiring written permission from parents of minors. Lorinda Stewart, whom I lived with in communes in Burlington, Washington, and Tokyo, Japan, wrote about her parents providing written permission for her to join at the same age I was. "When I was sixteen years old, my parents, thrilled to put me in the care of what they thought were good Christians, signed legal documents that handed me over to my 'colony shepherd' [commune leader]." Lorinda Stewart, *One Day Closer: A Mother's Quest to Bring Her Kidnapped Daughter Home* (Simon & Schuster, 2017), 57.

Chapter 5 – Indoctrination

1. David Berg, "The Revolutionary Rules," March 1972, www.exfamily.org/pubs/ml/b4/ml0000S.shtml

2. Ibid, paragraph 9.

3. See: www.xfamily.org/index.php/Mo_Letters

4. David Berg, "Diamonds of Dust," October 1970, paragraphs 6, 11, www.exfamily.org/pubs/ml/b4/ml0003.shtml

5. Shibley Culpin, "Sect Members Tell Their Side: Under Some Criticism," *Alberni Valley Times*, May 24, 1972, perry-bulwer.blogspot.com/p/1972-newspaper-reports-about-children.html

6. My reference to "a doctor or lawyer" in the Mother's Day card is directly related to lyrics in the 1960s folk song "Little Boxes," a satirical song about middle-class conformity, with specific references to university, doctors and lawyers. We often sang it at school in music class, and I absorbed its nonconformist attitude along with other countercultural influences of the time.

7. Two Mo Letters written less than a year before I joined the Children of God contradict Japheth and Hannah's claim that the group was not deliberately encouraging young people to leave their families. David Berg believed that the legendary character, the Pied Piper, was a real person and one of his spirit helpers. He considered himself a modern-day Pied Piper, calling youth to leave their parents and follow him. See: David Berg, "The Pied Piper Prophecy," September 7, 1971, paragraphs 7–11, www.exfamily.org/pubs/ml/b4/ml0102.shtml; and David Berg, "Question and Answers," September 15, 1971, paragraph 10, www.exfamily.org/pubs/ml/b4/ml0111.shtml

8. David Berg, "Advice on 10:36ers," August 1971, paragraph 4, www.exfamily.org/pubs/ml/b4/ml0091.shtml

9. Bertrand Russell, "Why I Am Not a Christian," Watts & Co., for the Rationalist Press Association Ltd., 1927, users.drew.edu/~jlenz/whynot.html

Chapter 6 – The Endtime Prophet

1. "The Revolutionary Rules," paragraph 9, www.exfamily.org/pubs/ml/b4/ml0000S.shtml

2. David Berg, "David," June 1971, paragraphs 2 and 4, www.exfamily.org/pubs/ml/b4/ml0077.shtml

3. Matthew 3:3 and 11:10, Mark 1:1–3, and John 1:23 claim that John the Baptist's ministry was foretold in Isaiah 40:3 and Malachi 3:1, though he is not mentioned by name in those scriptures.

4. David Berg, "Survival," June 1972, www.exfamily.org/pubs/ml/b4/ml0172.shtml; "Our Shepherd, Moses David" (compilation), January 1976, www.exfamily.org/pubs/ml/b4/ml0351.shtml; "David Verses and Letters" (compilation), January 2005, www.xfamily.org/index.php/David_Verses_and_Letters.

5. David Berg, "Survival," June 1972, paragraph 94, www.exfamily.org/pubs/ml/b4/ml0172.shtml

6. David Berg's first child, Deborah Davis, exposed the deliberate deception regarding her grandmother's paralysis in Chapter 2 of her book *The Children of God: The Inside Story* (Zondervan, 1984), which is available to read for free at: www.exfamily.org/art/exmem/debdavis/debdavis00.shtml. The facts about Virginia exposed by Deborah are briefly summarized in the section titled "Virginia Brandt and Hjalmer Berg" in "History of The Family International/Children of God," www.exfamily.org/hist/

7. David Berg, "The Key of David," June 1971, paragraph 40, www.exfamily.org/pubs/ml/b4/ml0078.shtml

8. David Berg, "Our Shepherd," paragraphs 39–42, www.exfamily.org/pubs/ml/b4/ml0351.shtml

9. "Fred Jordan," XFamily, www.xfamily.org/index.php/Fred_Jordan

10. David Berg, "Our Shepherd," paragraphs 44 and 45.

11. Matthew 24:21, 29-30.

12. Virginia Berg, "Warning," 1965, www.exfamily.org/pubs/ml/b5/ml0655.htm

13. David Berg, "Our Shepherd," paragraph 49.

14. David Berg,"The 70-Years Prophecy of the End," March 1972, paragraphs 2 and 3, www.exfamily.org/pubs/ml/b4/ml0156.shtml

15. Ibid., paragraph 9.

16. Ibid., paragraph 24.

17. David Berg, "The Laws of Moses," February 1972, paragraphs 30–32 and 49, www.exfamily.org/pubs/ml/b4/ml0155.shtml

18. John 20:24–29

Chapter 7 – Fleeing Babylon the Whore

1. David Berg, "Bye, Bye, Pie," May 1973, paragraphs 22–27, www. exfamily.org/pubs/ml/b4/ml0232.shtml. Berg interprets the references in Revelation 17 and 18 to Babylon as a metaphor describing the global capitalist system led by America.

2. David Berg, "America the Whore," March 1973, paragraphs 26–27, www.xfamily.org/index.php/America_The_Whore!

3. David Berg, "Diamonds of Dust," 1970, www.exfamily.org/pubs/ml/ b4/ml0003.shtml

4. David Berg, "Mountain Men," 1969, www.exfamily.org/pubs/ml/mlB. html

5. David Berg, "Wonder Working Words," February 1973, paragraphs 23–32, www.exfamily.org/pubs/ml/b4/ml0207.shtml

6. David Berg, "Shiners? — or Shamers!," June 1973, paragraphs 2–11, www.exfamily.org/pubs/ml/b4/ml0241.shtml

7. David Berg, "Are We Catholics or Protestants?" September 1972, paragraphs 54–56, www.exfamily.org/pubs/ml/b4/ml0184.shtml

8. David Berg, "The Great Escape," April 24, 1972, paragraphs 17 and 18, www.exfamily.org/pubs/ml/b4/ml0160.shtml

9. David Berg, "Statistics," November 1971, paragraph 8, www.xfamily. org/index.php/HomeARC_ML_0141

10. "Children of God," *NBC Evening News*, March 5, 1972, www.xfamily.org/index.php/NBC_Evening_News:_Children_of_God

11. Berg, "Statistics."

12. David Berg, "Persecution," November 1971, paragraphs 12–18, www.exfamily.org/pubs/ml/b4/ml0125.shtml

13. "Caleb Dietrich," XFamily, www.xfamily.org/index.php/Caleb_Dietrich

14. "Comet Kohoutek," en.wikipedia.org/wiki/Comet_Kohoutek

15. David Berg, "The Christmas Monster," September 8, 1973, www.exfamily.org/pubs/ml/ml269.html; "More on Kohoutek — The Coming Comet of the Century!" November 4, 1973, www.exfamily.org/pubs/ml/ b4/ml0278.shtml

16. David Berg, "40 Days!" November 12, 1973, www.exfamily.org/ pubs/ml/b4/ml0280.shtml

17. David Berg, "The Comet Comes," December 20, 1973, paragraphs 3

and 33, www.exfamily.org/pubs/ml/b4/ml0283.shtml

18. David Berg, "The Comet's Tale," January 24, 1974, paragraph 34, www.exfamily.org/pubs/ml/b4/ml0295.shtml

19. "The Message of Jeremiah" song lyrics can be found at www.nubeat. org/audio/1ad/dm-btb/LYR15.html

Chapter 8 – Revolutionary Sex

1. Brother Sun with Deborah, whom he met on the final leg of our road trip and later married: www.flickr.com/photos/146761602@ N04/32857987363/in/album-72157680396692341/

2. "Little Sisters of Jesus," en.wikipedia.org/wiki/Little_Sisters_of_Jesus

3. "Papal Audience—Faith's Audience with Pope Paul and His Speech That Day!" October 1972, paragraphs 1–3, www.exfamily.org/pubs/ml/b4/ ml0192.shtml, Faith Berg, www.xfamily.org/index.php/Faith_Berg

4. David Berg, "Revolutionary Sex," March 27, 1973, www.exfamily.org/ pubs/ml/b4/ml0258.shtml

5. David Berg, "Scriptural, Revolutionary Love-Making," August 1969, www.exfamily.org/pubs/ml/b4/ml0000N.shtml

6. David Berg, "Revolutionary Love-Making," Summer 1970, paragraphs 53, 111, 114–116, www.exfamily.org/pubs/ml/b4/ml0259.shtml

7. Berg, "Revolutionary Sex," paragraphs 15 and 16. However, by 1980, Berg had changed his mind and no longer criticized promiscuity—he encouraged it: "As far as God's concerned, there are no more sexual prohibitions hardly of any kind, except he sure seemed to hate sodomy and I don't see where He withdrew that....there's nothing in the world at all wrong with sex as long as it's practised in love, whatever it is, whoever it's with, no matter who or what age or what relative or what manner!...There are no relationship restrictions or age limitations in His law of love." David Berg, "The Devil Hates Sex," May 1980, paragraphs 35, 67–69, 110, www.exfamily. org/pubs/ml/ml999_main.shtml

8. Berg, "Revolutionary Sex," paragraph 59.

9. Ibid., paragraph 54.

10. Ibid., paragraph 67.

11. David Berg, "Beauty and the Beasts," April 1974, paragraphs 20–25, 36 and 37, www.exfamily.org/pubs/ml/b4/ml0309.shtml

12. David Berg, "The Old Church and the New Church—A Prophecy of God," August 1969, www.exfamily.org/pubs/ml/mlA.html

13. Karen Zerby has used many pseudonyms over the years, including Maria David, Maria Berg, Maria Fontaine, Mama Maria and Queen Maria. She legally changed her name to Katherine Rianna Smith in 1997. See: www. xfamily.org/index.php/Karen_Zerby

14. "Jane Miller Berg," XFamily, www.xfamily.org/index.php/Jane_Miller_Berg

15. See Chapter 6, note 6. Deborah discusses the events surrounding her father's affair with Karen Zerby and the prophecy he used to justify it in chapters 4 and 5 of her book

16. Berg, "Old Church," paragraph 20.

17. Ibid., paragraphs 11, 13 and 25.

18. David Berg, "One Wife," October 28, 1972, paragraphs 9, 20, 22, 23 and 27, www.exfamily.org/pubs/ml/b4/ml0249.shtml

19. David Berg, "Survival," June 1972, , paragrasphs157–62, www.exfamily.org/pubs/ml/b4/ml0172.shtml

20. John 15:13, I John 3:16, Acts 2:44, Acts 4:32.

21. David Berg, "The Law of Love," March 21, 1974, paragraphs 3, 18, 24 and 26, www.exfamily.org/pubs/ml/b4/ml0302C.shtml

22. David Berg, "God's Only Law Is Love—What the Bible Says about True Free Love!" July 29, 1977, paragraphs 25 and 30, www.exfamily.org/pubs/ml/b4/ml0592.shtml

23. London Poorboy Club photographs: www.flickr.com/photos/146761602@N04/albums/72157679414192391

24. "Jeremy Spencer," XFamily, www.xfamily.org/index.php/Jeremy_Spencer

25. David Berg, "The Little Flirty Fishy," January 3, 1974, paragraphs 17, 19, 99 and 100, pubs.xfamily.org/text.php?t=293. An illustrated version of that letter was published in the *True Komix* series of comics intended for children and teens: "Little Flirty Fishy," www.xfamily.org/index.php/True_Komix_-_Little_Flirty_Fishy

26. David Berg, "Beauty and the Beasts, paragraphs 8 and 9.

27. Ibid. paragraph 5.

28. Matthew 22:35–40.

29. Berg, "Beauty and the Beasts," paragraph 40. And in a later letter Berg declares: "That's the whole basic doctrine of FFing, that sex proves love! Sex proves the existence of Love, that these girls are willing to go to bed with these men to prove they love them." Berg, "Devil," paragraph 126.

30. Berg used the phrase "hookers for Jesus" in more than one of his letters on flirty fishing. However, those and many others on the subject are not available on the two websites where most Mo Letters are archived. The phrase was used in media reports on their sexual escapades in Tenerife. See: *Time*, "Tracking the Children of God," August 22, 1977, www.xfamily.org/index.php/Time_Magazine:_Tracking_the_Children_of_God

31. Former member Miriam Williams wrote about her experiences as a "sacred prostitute" in *Heaven's Harlots: My Fifteen Years in a Sex Cult* (Eagle Brook, 1999).

32. See David Berg, "The Wrath of God—On Tenerife and Its System's Ugly Face of Tyranny!" March 5, 1977, www.exfamily.org/pubs/ml/b4/ml0577.shtml. I've written in more detail about Berg and Zerby in Tenerife and their clash with Catholic authorities there in the blog article "Secret Letter Claims Family International Leader Caused Deadliest Air Crash in History," November 2, 2011, chainthedogma.blogspot.com/2011/11/secret-letter-claims-family.html

Chapter 9 – I Felt the Earth Move

1. Many years later, when I returned to Japan in the mid-1980s, the leader of a commune I briefly stayed in knew me because of that hotel incident. Ben remembered reading about it when he was at the head office in England, where regional leaders around the world sent their reports. He told me those who read or heard about Brother Sun's flirty fishing tale didn't understand why leaders reprimanded him for it, but some were enticed to go to Japan because of that and similar stories.

2. Thomas Moore, "Where Have All the Children of God Gone?" *New Times*, October 4, 1974, www.xfamily.org/index.php/New_Times:_Where_have_all_the_Children_of_God_gone%3F

3. David Berg, "Shiners?—or Shamers!" June 1973, paragraphs 21 and 30, www.exfamily.org/pubs/ml/b4/ml0241.shtml

4. The following photo of the members of an early Children of God home in Japan in 1973 includes these four leaders. Shiloh is in the foreground, Laadah is in the centre, Medad is behind her in the back row, and Abby is next to him on the right: www.flickr.com/photos/146761602@N04/33630354116/in/album-72157680396692341/

5. "Vietnam: A Thrilling Account of the First Team in the Far East," 1972, media.xfamily.org/docs/fam/bor/bor-v2-pg183-185.pdf

6. "Texas Soul Clinic," XFamily, www.xfamily.org/index.php/Texas_Soul_Clinic

7. David Berg, "Faith and Healing," August 1970, paragraphs 15–18, 43–52, and 58, www.exfamily.org/pubs/ml/b4/ml0000M.shtml

8. Billy Graham Evangelistic Association, "A Look Back at Billy Graham's Largest Ever Crusade," billygraham.org/story/seoul-south-korea-a-look-back-at-billy-grahams-largest-ever-crusade/

9. Campus Crusade for Christ International, "About—History of CRU—1974: More Than 300,000 Delegates Attend EXPLO '74 in Seoul, South Korea," www.cru.org/us/en/about.html

10. "Explo '72," en.wikipedia.org/wiki/Explo_%2772

11. Kang Hyun-kyung, "'Ridiculous' 1970s: Book Lampoons Park Chung-hee Era," *Korean Times*, February 22, 2019, www.koreatimes.co.kr/www/culture/2019/02/142_264236.html

12. David Berg, "Israel Invaded", November 25, 1973, pubs.xfamily.org/text.php?t=281

Chapter 10 – Welcome to the Jungle, or The Guest Who Wouldn't Leave

1. The following photograph is of Zichri and Shalisha on their way to set up the first Children of God commune in the Philippines. Zichri is second from the left and Shalisha is next to him. The man on Zichri's left is Caleb, David Berg's second disciple and the leader of the Burlington commune when I lived there: www.flickr.com/photos/146761602@N04/32820607454/in/album-72157680137412630/

2. The following photograph shows Daniel and Ruth in the first Children of God commune in the Philippines. Daniel is on the left in the back row and Ruth is in front of him. Zichri and Shalisha are also in the back row: www.flickr.com/photos/146761602@N04/32850376133/in/album-72157680137412630/

3. David Berg, "The Love of Christ," July 1984, paragraph 10, www.exfamily.org/pubs/ml/b5/ml1806.shtml

Chapter 11 – The Prodigal Child Returns

1. It was hard to accept that my dad steered his truck directly at me. I wanted to doubt he did it deliberately, but that is how I experienced it. Over twenty years later, I learned he did the same thing to someone else he had a dispute with, directly driving his car at them in a fit of rage. His girlfriend called me for legal advice about it because I was in law school at the time. She told me that my dad did not want her to tell me about the incident, but she called me anyway because she wanted to understand the restraining order filed against him.

2. David Berg, "The Re-organisation Nationalisation Revolution," January 1978, paragraph 20, www.exfamily.org/pubs/ml/b5/ml0650.shtml

3. David Berg, "Dear Friend or Foe," January 1979, paragraphs 7 and 8, www.exfamily.org/pubs/ml/b5/ml0754.shtml

4. Berg, "Re-organisation," paragraph 28. Also see: Ed Priebe, "The Children of God's Name Change to 'The Family,'" 1993, web.archive.org/web/20080214132018/http://www.excult.org/namechg4.html

5. David Berg, "To the Media—From a Guru—About the Sects," May 1979, paragraphs 2, 8, 11 and 19, www.exfamily.org/pubs/ml/b5/ml0800.shtml

6. "World Services," XFamily, www.xfamily.org/index.php/World_Services

7. David Berg, "Have Faith, Will Camp! Part One," July 1979, www.exfamily.org/pubs/ml/b5/ml0807_01.shtml

8. David Berg, "Have Trailer—Will Travel!—Part 1: Fires!" July 1979, www.exfamily.org/pubs/ml/b5/ml0812_01.shtml

9. John 15:20: "If they have persecuted me, they will also persecute you;" 2 Timothy 3:12: "Yea, and all that will live godly in Christ Jesus shall suffer persecution;" Matthew 10:23: "But when they persecute you in this city, flee ye into another."

10. David Berg, "No Lit? No Letters!" August 1979, paragraph 16, www.exfamily.org/pubs/ml/b5/ml0814.shtml

Chapter 12 – On the Road Again

1. Berg, "Revolutionary Rules," paragraph 12, pubs.xfamily.org/text.php?t=S

2. David Berg, "The Education Revolution," November 1975, paragraphs 71 and 72, www.exfamily.org/pubs/ml/b4/ml0371.shtml. Also see the

Introduction to the Childcare Handbook, vol. 2: www.xfamily.org/index. php/Category:Education#Introduction

3. David Berg, "The End Is Here!", May 1980, paragraphs 13, 15, 25 and 28, www.exfamily.org/pubs/ml/b5/ml0906.shtml

4. David Berg, "Keep Your Caravans at Home!", July 1980, www.exfamily.org/pubs/ml/b5/ml0921.shtml

5. "Ted Patrick," XFamily, www.xfamily.org/index.php/Ted_Patrick.

6. Jeff Goldberg, "From the Archives: Mind Control U.S.A. (1979)," *High Times*, April 9, 2022, hightimes.com/culture/from-the-archives-mind-control-u-s-a-1979/.

7. Thomas Moore, "Where Have All," www.xfamily.org/index.php/New_Times:_Where_have_all_the_Children_of_God_gone%3F

8. "FreeCOG," XFamily, www.xfamily.org/index.php/FREECOG. Parents who did not see the Children of God as a harmful group set up a counter-organization called Thankful Parents and Friends of the Children of God (ThankCOG). They challenged FreeCOG claims and negative publicity with a newsletter supporting the group. My mother received some of their material.

9. Ted Patrick and Tom Dulack, *Let Our Children Go!* (Ballantine Books, 1979). The first chapter of the book can be found here: web.archive. org/web/20080929120346/http://ocmb.lermanet.us/discussion/viewtopic. php?t=432

10. David Berg, "Jimmy Carter—America's Last Chance?" June 1976, paragraph 23, www.exfamily.org/pubs/ml/b4/ml0520.shtml

11. David Berg, "The Reagan Reaction!" November 5, 1980, paragraphs 40 and 73, www.exfamily.org/pubs/ml/b5/ml0946.shtml

12. David Berg, "Operation P.A.C.C." May 1972, paragraph 5, www. exfamily.org/pubs/ml/b4/ml0164.shtml

13. David Berg, "Refuges," April 1981, paragraphs 28, 51 and 52, www.exfamily.org/pubs/ml/b5/ml1003.shtml

14. David Berg, "Go East! And Grow Up with the Golden Triangle!" January 1982, www.exfamily.org/pubs/ml/b5/ml1088.shtml

15. David Berg, "War in 1983?" November 1982, paragraphs 1 and 2, www.exfamily.org/pubs/ml/b5/ml1341.shtml

16. Ian Mulgrew and Mark Budgen, "B.C. Officials Seize 13 Children after Claim that One Molested," *Globe & Mail*, February 24, 1983, www. xfamily.org/index.php/Globe_and_Mail:_B.C._officials_seize_13_children_after_claim_that_one_molested

17. UPI, "Ministry Will Seek Custody of Cult Children," March 23, 1983, www.xfamily.org/index.php/UPI:_Ministry_will_seek_custody_of_cult_children

18. The following article from that period involves a Family couple who fled England to Vancouver with their two children after a judge awarded custody of the kids to the wife's parents. It is an example of the kinds of custody disputes many Family members were facing. "Transatlantic Custody Battle

Continues," *Globe & Mail*, January 11, 1982, www.xfamily.org/index.php/ Globe_and_Mail:_Transatlantic_custody_battle_continues

19. David Berg, "Guard Your Children!" December 1983, paragraphs 23, 27 and 61, www.xfamily.org/index.php/Guard_Your_Children!

20. David Berg, "Revolutionary Sex," paragraph 25, www.exfamily.org/ pubs/ml/b4/ml0258.shtml

Chapter 13 – Pearls of the Orient

1. David Berg, "Views on the News! World Currents No. 72!" March 1994, paragraphs 30 and 31, www.exfamily.org/pubs/ml/b5/ml2916.shtml

2. "Louris Nielson," XFamily, www.xfamily.org/index.php/Louris_May_ Yamaguchi

3. Keda, "What a Liberation!" June 1978, www.xfamily.org/index.php/ What_a_Liberation!_by_Keda

4. David Berg, "Revolutionary Sex," paragraph 24, www.exfamily.org/ pubs/ml/b4/ml0258.shtml. Berg ignores Romans 1:26-27, which does equate lesbianism to male homosexuality.

5. David Berg, "Women in Love," December 1973, paragraphs 2 and 5, www.exfamily.org/pubs/ml/b4/ml0292.shtml

6. David Berg, "The Girl Who Wouldn't," June 1978, paragraphs 4, 5, 7, 25 and 31, www.exfamily.org/pubs/ml/ml721.html

7. David Berg, "Law of Love," paragraph 14, www.exfamily.org/pubs/ml/ b4/ml0302C.shtml

8. David Berg, "Jealousy," September 1973, pubs.xfamily.org/text. php?t=287. See also: David Berg, "FFing and Jealousy!" July 1977, paragraphs 1, 2 and 40, www.exfamily.org/pubs/ml/b5/ml0603.shtml

9. "Louris Nielson," XFamily.

10. "Jonathan Berg," XFamily, www.xfamily.org/index.php/Jonathan_ Berg

11. A memoir by Ruthie's daughter includes descriptions of her life growing up in that commune. See: Faith Jones, *Sex Cult Nun: Breaking Away from the Children of God, a Wild, Radical Religious Cult* (William Morrow, 2021).

12. "World Services," XFamily, www.xfamily.org/index.php/World_Services

13. See: Proverbs 19:18; 23:13-14. David Berg's views on corporal punishment can be found in "Lashes of Love," August 1975, www.xfamily.org/ index.php/Lashes_of_Love!; and in "Dad's Guidelines for Teen Discipline," compiled and edited by Karen Zerby from the Mo Letters, October 1985, pubs.xfamily.org/text.php?t=2066

14. David Berg, "Guard Your Children," paragraph 76, www.xfamily. org/index.php/Guard_Your_Children!

15. David Berg, "Obedience in Little Things," 1984, paragraph 13, pubs. xfamily.org/text.php?t=1781

16. For a first-person account of flirty fishing, see: Miriam Williams, *Heaven's Harlots: My Fifteen Years in a Sex Cult* (Eagle Brook, 1999), www.xfamily.org/index.php/Miriam_Williams_Boeri

17. David Berg, "Make It Pay," March 1978, paragraphs 9 and 10, pubs.xfamily.org/text.php?t=684

18. "Bought with a Price! A How-To Manual for Escort FF'ers!" *Heavenly Helpers*, vol. 4, June 1983, 377–92, www.xfamily.org/index.php/Heavenly_Helpers

19. "Escort Servicing," XFamily, www.xfamily.org/index.php/Escort_Servicing. Family women describe their escort experiences. Maria Rousse, the author of one those testimonies, was one of the women in the Kowloon home I overheard talking about escorting.

20. John D.: "It turned out in Hong Kong, from what I can speak of from my own personal experience, that The Family had a friend in an escort agency who made it possible for the Family girls to meet people at hotels on an invitation basis. There was a situation with my wife where she accompanied business people for a whole weekend for several thousand dollars." Transcript of the 1998 documentary *The Love Prophet and the Children of God* (DLI Productions, in association with TVOntario, CFCF 12 and the Knowledge Network), www.xfamily.org/index.php/The_Love_Prophet_and_the_Children_of_God

21. James D. Chancellor, *Life in the Family: An Oral History of the Children of God* (Syracuse University Press, 2000), 127.

22. "Flirty Fishing—Discontinuation," XFamily, www.xfamily.org/index.php/Flirty_Fishing#Discontinuation

Chapter 14 – I Shook Hands with the Butcher of Beijing

1. David Berg, "Combos—The 7-Purpose National Centers!" February 1982, paragraphs 1, 2 and 21, pubs.xfamily.org/text.php?t=1115

2. "Open Heart Report," XFamily, www.xfamily.org/index.php/Open_Heart_Report

3. Jude 1:14–16

4. David Berg, "The Advantages of Having Children", May 1978, paragraphs 34, 38 and 51, pubs.xfamily.org/text.php?t=688

5. "Chris" was the alias of Thomas Hack, a long-time high-ranking leader of the Family, and the person Berg paired Keda/Magadalene with after he condemned her lesbianism. See: www.xfamily.org/index.php/Thomas_Hack

6. I did purposely destroy my passport once. A leader told me to pour coffee on it while I was on a trip to Korea and apply for a new one at the embassy in Seoul. A clean passport without all the visitor visa stamps showing my previous stays in Japan made it easier to get back into the country.

7. Here is a photograph of me (wearing sunglasses) outside the Beijing Friendship Store with a member visiting from Harbin: www.flickr.com/photos/146761602@N04/33327540110/in/album-72157680396692341/

8. David Berg "Happy Endings," June 1979, paragraphs 5, 9 and 12, pubs.xfamily.org/text.php?t=802

9. David Berg, "Are You a Sight-seer, or a Seer-sighter?" November 1970, paragraph 12, www.exfamily.org/pubs/ml/b4/ml0007.shtml

10. Jonathan Watts, "'Butcher of Beijing' Tries to Clear His Name," *Guardian*, August 19, 2004, www.theguardian.com/world/2004/aug/19/china.jonathanwatts

11. "English Corner: China's Free Speech Zone," *The Face of China*, web.archive.org/web/20210115140956/http://thefaceofchina.com:80/2014/01/09/english-corner-china%E2%80%99s-free-speech-zone/

12. Ruth Cherrington, *Deng's Generation: Young Intellectuals in 1980s China* (Palgrave Macmillan, 1997), chapter 1, endnote 5.

Chapter 15 – Mr Big. in Japan

1. "Regional Offices: PACRO," XFamily, www.xfamily.org/index.php/Category:Leaders#Regional_Offices

2. David Berg, "The Law of Love," paragraphs 14 and 16, www.exfamily.org/pubs/ml/b4/ml0302C.shtml

3. "Heavenly City School," XFamily, www.xfamily.org/index.php/Heavenly_City_School

4. "Naritas," XFamily, www.xfamily.org/index.php/Naritas

5. Video of the Japan Teen Training Camp held from August 27, 1986, to October 14, 1986, can be found at: www.xfamily.org/index.php/Japan_Teen_Training_Camp

6. "Teen Training Camp," XFamily, www.xfamily.org/index.php/Teen_Training_Camp. A Basic Training Handbook based on these camps was required reading for all members aged ten and over. See: www.xfamily.org/index.php/Basic_Training_Handbook

7. David Berg, "Mo's Pointers for Health," April 1975, paragraphs 317, 318 and 333, www.exfamily.org/pubs/ml/b4/ml0353.shtml

8. David Berg, "Pyramid Power," January 1975, pubs.xfamily.org/text.php?t=630

9. "Steven Douglas Kelly," XFamily, www.xfamily.org/index.php/Steven_Douglas_Kelly

10. David Berg, "Obedience in Little Things," pubs.xfamily.org/text.php?t=1781

11. David Berg, "Jesus' Babies: A Child of Love for Jesus' Sake!" June 1976, paragraphs 1, 82 and 83, www.exfamily.org/pubs/ml/b5/ml0739.shtml

12. "Christina Teresa Zerby," XFamily, www.xfamily.org/index.php/Christina_Teresa_Zerby. See also: "Sara Kelley," XFamily, www.xfamily.org/index.php/Sara_Kelley

13. David Berg, "Ban the Bomb–Inter-Home Sex!" March 1983, paragraphs 16 and 17, pubs.xfamily.org/text.php?t=1434

14. "Arthur Lindfield," XFamily, www.xfamily.org/index.php/Arthur_Lindfiel.

15. "King Arthur's Nights," XFamily, www.xfamily.org/index.php/King_Arthur%27s_Nights!

16. "Jeremy Spencer," XFamily, www.xfamily.org/index.php/Jeremy_Specer.

17. The Family's music albums: www.xfamily.org/index.php/Category:Music_Artists#Bands.2C_groups.2C_and_albums

18. "Music with Meaning," XFamily, www.xfamily.org/index.php/Music_With_Meaning

19. "Family Videos," XFamily, www.xfamily.org/index.php/Category:Family_Videos#Publicly_Distributed

20. Margaret Thaler Singer, *Cults in Our Midst*, revised edition (Jossey-Bass, 2003), 114.

21. Joshua 10:12-13.

22. Isaiah 38:8.

23. "Grant Cameron Montgomery," XFamily, www.xfamily.org/index.php/Grant_Cameron_Montgomery

Chapter 16 – The Exorcism of Merry

1. "Michael Hawron," XFamily, www.xfamily.org/index.php/Michael_Hawron

2. Perry Bulwer, "Former Cult Leader, Michael Hawron, Hiding in Plain Sight in New Boston, Texas," Religion and Child Abuse News, August 12, 2019, religiouschildabuse.blogspot.com/p/former-cult-leader-michael-hawron.html

3. David Berg, "You Must Obey the Least of These Commandments! — A Personal Talk on Our Family Rules at Dad's Home!" 1983, paragraphs 33, 34 and 37, www.exfamily.org/pubs/ml/b5/ml1827.shtml

4. David Berg, "Whose Slave Are You? — God's or Mammon's," September 1962, paragraphs 57 and 58, pubs.xfamily.org/text.php?t=1332

5. American Bible Society, "Slaves and Servants in the Time of Jesus," bibleresources.americanbible.org/resource/slaves-and-servants-in-the-time-of-jesus-history-and-culture: "The word in the New Testament usually translated as 'servant' actually means 'slave,' and referred to someone who was owned or controlled by someone else, not just a servant hired to do a certain job. Some slaves performed menial household tasks."

6. "Peter Bevan Riddell," XFamily, www.xfamily.org/index.php/Peter_Bevan_Riddell

7. "Steven Riddell Abduction Case," Xfamily, www.xfamily.org/index.php/Steven_Riddell_Abduction_Case. For other abduction cases involving children in the Family see: Child Abduction https://xfamily.org/index.php/Category:Child_Abduction

8. A whistle-blowing defector using the alias James Penn, who worked in World Services for twenty years, wrote articles exposing various abuses and crimes committed by Berg, Zerby, Kelly and other top leaders. He described how Berg had to suddenly flee Canada one step ahead of the police. In 1989, Maggie, the top leader who instructed members to forge university degrees, was arrested in Montreal and convicted of forging passports for members

of Berg and Zerby's staff. That investigation led police to Berg's door near Vancouver, British Columbia. Penn revealed that Berg and Zerby had been using fake Australian passports for years, and wrote: "Can you imagine how much it cost Mo, Maria, Peter and their staff to flee on a moment's notice to Europe, and then travel from country to country there for several months before settling down?...The head of WS Finances told me that they had left behind about 500 one-ounce gold coins, worth about US$200,000." James Penn, "All of These Things Moved Me," February 2001, www.xfamily.org/index.php/All_of_These_Things_Moved_Me. Elsewhere, Penn revealed that WS units kept $20,000 USD or more in gold coins as emergency reserves, and that at one point he held "nearly $40,000 in cash and gold coins in my own safety deposit box for WS." James Penn, "A Few Replies," August 2004, www.xfamily.org/index.php/Penn_-_A_Few_Replies

9. "Michael Gambrill," XFamily, www.xfamily.org/index.php/Michael_Gambrill. See also: "Kathy Farrell," XFamily, www.xfamily.org/index.php/Kathy_Farrell

10. "Merry Jolene Berg," XFamily, www.xfamily.org/index.php/Merry_Jolene_Berg

11. "Paul Brandt Berg," XFamily, www.xfamily.org/index.php/Paul_Brandt_Berg

12. Judy Helmstetler (aka Shulamite), Merry Berg's mother: web.archive.org/web/20090401200405/https://www.newdaynews.com/openhouse/index.cgi/read/21793

13. "Jane Miller Berg," XFamily, www.xfamily.org/index.php/Jane_Miller_Berg

14. David Berg, "The Last State—The Dangers of Demonism," March 1987, paragraph 55, www.xfamily.org/index.php/The_Last_State.

15. "Alfred Strickland Kelley," XFamily, www.xfamily.org/index.php/Alfred_Strickland_Kelley

16. Berg, "The Last State," paragraph 114.

17. Ibid., paragraph 1.

18. Ibid., paragraphs 46, 47, 54 and 55.

19. David Berg, "A Father Applies the Rod!—Dad's Phone Call with Ho," December 1980, paragraphs 17, 18 and 20, pubs.xfamily.org/text.php?t=952-8

20. "Open Heart Report," XFamily, www.xfamily.org/index.php/Open_Heart_Report

21. Berg, "The Last State," paragraphs 244–46, 249.

22. "Macau Victor Camps," XFamily, www.xfamily.org/index.php/Macau_Victor_Camps. See also: "Victor Program," XFamily, www.xfamily.org/index.php/Victor_Program

23. See the sections "Alleged Child Abuse" and "Writings" in "Michael Hawron," XFamily, www.xfamily.org/index.php/Michael_Hawron

24. "Contend for Our Teens! The Story of Teen James!" July 1988, page 4, archive.xfamily.org/docs/fam/fsm/teen-james-fsm104.pdf

25. "Family Mythology," XFamily, www.xfamily.org/index.php/Category:Family_Mythology#Legendary_Spirit_Helpers

26. Faith Jones, *Sex Cult Nun: Breaking Away from the Children of God, a Wild, Radical Religious Cult* (William Morrow, 2021), 41.

Chapter 17 – Heavenly Lunacy

1. "Junior End Time Teen," XFamily, www.xfamily.org/index.php/Junior_End_Time_Teen

2 "Techi" refers to Christina Teresa Zerby, Karen Zerby's daughter. As a young teen, she was the subject of the Techi Series, which led to mandatory Open Heart Reports for Family children. See: www.xfamily.org/index.php/Christina_Teresa_Zerby

3. Josiah's real name is Paul Péloquin (www.xfamily.org/index.php/Paul_Peloquin). Mary Mom is Linda Perfilio (www.xfamily.org/index.php/Linda_Perfilio). Elaine (Morningstar) is an Australian who is the subject of the Mo Letter "Frustrated? Your Children ARE God's Full-time Service" (September 1979, www.xfamily.org/index.php/HomeARC_ML_0835_01). Faithy is Faith Berg (www.xfamily.org/index.php/Faith_Berg). John PI is Samuel Charles Perfilio (www.xfamily.org/index.php/Samuel_Charles_Perfilio). Ginny is one of the leaders in Maggie's office home, which I lived in with Rachelle, and is the mother of Amber, one of the teen girls I saw being abused in the Teen Detention Home in Macau around the time Zerby wrote this letter ("JETT/Teen Discipleship Revolution Needed Now!" Maria no. 136, October 1990, www.xfamily.org/index.php/HomeARC_ML_2658)

4. David Berg, "Strange Truths!" July 1975, www.exfamily.org/pubs/ml/b4/ml0360.shtml

5. David Berg, "Dear Rahel," June 6, 1971, paragraph 35, pubs.xfamily.org/text.php?t=76

6. David Berg, "Space City," June 1971, pubs.xfamily.org/text.php?t=75A

7. Revelation 21:2, 10.

8. David Berg, "The Moon—And the Hidden City," November 1985, paragraph 7, pubs.xfamily.org/text.php?t=2110

9. Ibid., paragraph 42.

10. "Space City," XFamily, www.xfamily.org/index.php/Space_City

11. "Gallery of Posters," XFamily, www.xfamily.org/index.php/Gallery_of_Posters

12. Berg, "Moon," paragraph 33.

13. David Berg, "More on the Moon," November 1985, pubs.xfamily.org/text.php?t=2111. See also: David Berg, "The City of the Future," November 1985, pubs.xfamily.org/text.php?t=2112

14. Years later, a former member wrote a rebuttal, explaining the errors in Berg's calculations and the science disproving the prophet's impossible claims: www.exfamily.org/pubs/ml/ml2110-ml2111.html

15. Berg, "City of the Future," paragraphs 6, 7 and 10.

16. David Berg, "Science Falsely So-Called," February 1992, paragraph 24, www.exfamily.org/pubs/ml/b5/ml2847.shtml

17. David Berg, "The Big Lie—Exposed!" April 1977, paragraphs 66–8, www.exfamily.org/pubs/ml/b5/ml0736.shtml

18. David Berg, "The 70-Years Prophecy," paragraph 24, www.exfamily.org/pubs/ml/b4/ml0156.shtml

19. In the early 1970s, Berg said he received prophecies indicating that Muammar Gaddafi, who had recently taken control of Libya, was either the Antichrist or preparing the way for him. In 2011, as Gaddafi's dictatorship was collapsing, I wrote the following blog article several months before his death: "Gaddafi, the Family International and the Antichrist," February 2011, chainthedogma.blogspot.com/2011/02/gaddafi-family-international-and.html

20. David Berg, "World Currents—No. 49," April 1990, paragraph 23, www.exfamily.org/pubs/ml/b5/ml2616.shtml

21. David Berg, "World Currents—No. 53," November 1990, paragraphs 1–3, www.exfamily.org/pubs/ml/b5/ml2667RV.shtml

22. David Berg, "World Currents—No. 55—More on the Gulf War!" February 1991, paragraph 15, www.exfamily.org/pubs/ml/b5/ml2674RV.shtml

23. David Berg, "Warning—Be Prepared!" June 1991, paragraph 7, www.exfamily.org/pubs/ml/b5/ml2696.shtml

24. David Berg, "It Could Happen This Year of 1992—Part 1," December 1991, www.exfamily.org/pubs/ml/b5/ml2738.shtml

25. David Berg, "It Could Happen This Year of 1992—Part 2," December 1991, paragraph 45, www.exfamily.org/pubs/ml/b5/ml2739.shtml

26. Ibid., paragraph 106.

Chapter 19 – Losing My Religion

1. David Berg, "Backsliders Beware," June 1981, paragraphs 71 and 135, www.exfamily.org/pubs/ml/b5/ml1045.shtml

2. Vine Deloria Jr., Review of *God Is Red: A Native View of Religion*, second ed. (Golden, Colorado: North American Press, 1992), www.journals.uchicago.edu/doi/abs/10.1086/489553

3. David Berg, "The Big Lie," paragraphs 7, 66 and 68, www.exfamily.org/pubs/ml/b5/ml0736.shtml

4. Ibid., paragraphs 1, 2, 5 and 7.

5. Ibid., paragraph 57.

6. Charles Darwin, *The Origin of Species by Means of Natural Selection, or the Preservation of Favoured Races in the Struggle for Life*, sixth ed. (London: John Murray, 1872).

7. John 8:31-32.

8. Richard Dawkins, *The God Delusion* (New York: Houghton Mifflin, 2006), 50–1.

9. "Sagan standard," *Wikipedia*, en.wikipedia.org/wiki/Sagan_standard.

10. Victor Stenger, "Absence of Evidence Is Evidence of Absence," *Huffington Post*, August 14, 2010, www.huffingtonpost.com/victor-stenger/the-evidence-against-god_b_682169.html

11. Stephen Hawking and Leonard Mlodinow, *The Grand Design* (New York: Bantom Books, 2010), 180.

12. Nick Watt, "Stephen Hawking: 'Science Makes God Unnecessary,'" *ABC News*, September 6, 2010, abcnews.go.com/GMA/stephen-hawking-science-makes-god-unnecessary/story?id=11571150

13. Stephen Hawking, *Brief Answers to the Big Questions* (John Murray Press, 2018).

14. "Stephen Hawking Claims 'No Possibility' of God in Last Book," NBC News, October 18, 2018, www.nbcnews.com/mach/science/stephen-hawking-claims-no-possibility-god-last-book-ncna921806

Chapter 20 – Law and Disorder

1. "Malaspina University-College Awards 134 Baccalaureate Degrees," *Vancouver Island University*, June 11, 1996, news.viu.ca/malaspina-university-college-awards-134-baccaulaureate-degrees

2. Perry Bulwer, "Safe Injection Facilities: Compelling Government to Act," December 2001, perry-bulwer.blogspot.com/p/safe-injection-sites-bc.html

3. Perry Bulwer, "International Law and the Right to the Highest Attainable Standard of Health Care: Using Safe Injection Facilities to Control and Prevent Epidemics," April 2002, perry-bulwer.blogspot.com/p/safe-injection-sites-international.html

4. Vancouver Coastal Health, "Supervised Consumption Service at In-site," www.vch.ca/locations-services/result?res_id=964

5. Report of the Standing Committee on Justice and Human Rights, "The Challenge of Change: A Study of Canada's Criminal Prostitution Laws," December 2006, www.ourcommons.ca/DocumentViewer/en/39-1/JUST/report-6

6. Perry Bulwer, "Parliamentary Presentation on Prostitution," perry-bulwer.blogspot.com/p/parliamentary-presentation-on.html

7. Missing Women Commission of Inquiry: missingwomen.library.uvic.ca

8. Perry Bulwer, "Racket on the Rails," July 2006, perry-bulwer.blogspot.com/p/racket-on-rails_9.html

Chapter 21 – Tragedy of the Chosen One

1. ExFamily, a "source of truthful information about The Family" (www.exfamily.org/index.htm); Xfamily, "a collaboratively edited encyclopedia about The Family International/Children of God cult" (www.xfamily.org/index.php/Main_Page); and Moving On, a website for second-generation survivors that no longer exists, but that has been partly archived at www.xfamily.org/index.php/MovingOn

2. Perry Bulwer, "Respecting a Child's Point of View," December 14, 2011, chainthedogma.blogspot.com/2011/12/respecting-childs-point-of-view.html

3. "The Judgment of Lord Justice Ward," exFamily.org, www.exfamily. org/art/misc/justward_ver1.html. See also: "Complete Judgement of Lord Justice Ward," XFamily, www.xfamily.org/index.php/Complete_Judgment_ of_Lord_Justice_Ward

4. David Berg, "Deceivers Yet True," 1979, www.exfamily.org/pubs/ml/ b2/1248.shtml. A condensed, illustrated version of "Deceivers Yet True" taught children and teens that it is necessary to deceive and lie to outsiders in order to protect the Lord's work: www.exfamily.org/pubs/tk/deceivers_yet_ true.html

5. "Complete Judgment," part 4.8: "The Family's Attitude to Lies and Deception."

6. Former member Ed Priebe compiled a detailed analysis of the Family's deceitful policies and practices in the article "Official Policy on Lying & Deception": www.exfamily.org/the-family/policy-on-lying-and-deception.shtml

7. "Complete Judgment," part 6: "Medical Neglect."

8. "Complete Judgment," part 5.19: "Sexually Inappropriate Behaviour—Incest—The Oral Evidence."

9. "Kathy Farrell," XFamily, www.xfamily.org/index.php/Kathy_Farrell

10. "Complete Judgment," part 6: "Medical Neglect."

11. "Complete Judgment," part 6: "Medical Neglect" and part 8: "Impairment of Emotional, Social or Behavioural Development."

12. "James Penn," XFamily, www.xfamily.org/index.php/James_Penn

13. "Loving Jesus," XFamily, www.xfamily.org/index.php/Loving_Jesus. See also: James Penn, "No Regrets," in the section "Law of Love and the Marriage of the Generations": www.xfamily.org/index.php/No_Regrets#Law_of_Love_and_the_Marriage_of_the_Generations

14. Karen Zerby (Maria), "Living the Lord's Law of Love," 1998. The individual letters are numbered 3199 to 3212, and censored versions are available at www.exfamily.org/cgi-bin/pubindex.pl?3201

15. Months after issuing an interim order requiring the mother to meet certain conditions to keep custody of her son, Justice Ward considered her reaction and the Family's official response before issuing his final decision. He wrote a lengthy addendum to his judgment titled "The End Result," which is at the end of this PDF version of his decision: media.xfamily.org/ docs/legal/uk/ward-judgment/ward-judgment-v2.pdf

16. See: Ed Priebe, "The Alcoholic Prophet," March 2003, www.exfamily.org/articles/alcoholic-prophet.htm; and Perry Bulwer, "What Do Pat Robertson and the Family International Cult Have in Common?" January 18, 2010, chainthedogma.blogspot.com/2010/10/what-do-pat-robertson-and-family.html. David Berg declared his own anti-Semitism: "Yes, I'm an anti-Semite, because God is! Yes, I'm a racist, because God is!" (See: www. exfamily.org/art/exmem/anti-semitism-hate-the-family-international.htm.) On the subject of pedophilia: "At least seven women, including both his daughters, his daughter-in-law and two of his granddaughters, have publicly alleged that Berg sexually abused them when they were children." (See: www.xfamily.org/index.php/David_Berg#Alleged_sexual_abuse)

17. Margaret Thaler Singer and Janja Lalich, *Cults in Our Midst*, revised ed. (San Francisco: Jossey-Bass, 2003).

18. "MP Svend Robinson Admits Theft, Takes Stress Leave," *CBC News*, April 16, 2004, www.cbc.ca/news/canada/mp-svend-robinson-admits-theft-takes-stress-leave-1.518412

19. "Abe Braaten," XFamily, www.xfamily.org/index.php/Abe_Braaten.

20. "Ricky Rodriguez," XFamily, www.xfamily.org/index.php/Ricky_Rodriguez

21. "Jesus Baby," XFamily, www.xfamily.org/index.php/Jesus_Baby

22. David Berg, "The End-Time Witnesses," May 1978, paragraphs15 and 16, pubs.xfamily.org/text.php?t=707

23. "Davida Kelley," XFamily, www.xfamily.org/index.php/Davida_Kelley

24. "Story of Davidito," XFamily, www.xfamily.org/index.php/Story_of_Davidito

25. "Life with Grandpa—the Mene Story," XFamily, www.xfamily.org/index.php/Life_with_Grandpa_-_the_Mene_Story

26. "Lawrence Lilliston," XFamily, www.xfamily.org/index.php/Lawrence_Lilliston

27 . Lawrence Lilliston and Gary Shepherd, "Psychological Assessment of Children in The Family," web.archive.org/web/20210419082907/https://www.psywww.com/psyrelig/family.htm. Carol C. Buening (PhD, LISW, Ohio State University College of Social Work, adjunct faculty) wrote the following response to that study: "Critical Commentary on 'Psychological Assessment of Children in The Family,'" www.exfamily.org/art/ext/critical_commentary.shtml

28. "Complete Judgment," part 9.8.1: "The Psychological and Psychiatric Evidence: Dr. Lawrence Lilliston."

29. "Still Around," XFamily, www.xfamily.org/index.php/Still_Around

30. "Angela Smith," XFamily, www.xfamily.org/index.php/Angela_Smith

31. "Family Care Foundation," XFamily, www.xfamily.org/index.php/Family_Care_Foundation

32. "Ricky Rodriguez Video Transcript," XFamily, www.xfamily.org/index.php/Ricky_Rodriguez_Video_Transcript

33. Those details are described in the book about Ricky's life by religion journalist Don Lattin, *Jesus Freaks: A True Story of Murder and Madness on the Evangelical Edge* (San Francisco: HarperOne, 2007).

Chapter 22 – Everything Is Broken

1. "Julia McNeil Biography," Safe Passage Foundation, safepassagefoundation.org/is/juliamcneil

2. Michael D. Langone, "The Two 'Camps' of Cultic Studies: Time for a Dialogue," *Cultic Studies Journal*, 2000, 17, 79–100, articles2.icsahome.com/articles/the-two-camps-of-cultic-studies-langone

3. *Cultic Studies Review* was the journal of the International Cultic

Studies Association at the time. See: www.icsahome.com/icsa-publications. See also: *Nova Religio: The Journal of Alternative and Emergent Religions*, nr.ucpress.edu/

4. "Academic Disputes and Dialogue," International Cultic Studies Association, www.icsahome.com/elibrary/topics/academic-disputes-and-dialogue. See also: Benjamin Zablocki and Thomas Robbins, eds., *Misunderstanding Cults: Searching for Objectivity in a Controversial Field* (University of Toronto Press, 2001), www.jstor.org/stable/10.3138/9781442677302

5. Stephen A. Kent and Kayla Swanson, "The History of Credibility Attacks Against Former Cult Members", *International Journal of Cultic Studies* 8, no 2 (2017), www.icsahome.com/articles/the-history-of-credibility-attacks-against-former-cult-members-docx. This article contains an analysis of two important court cases, one being the British child-custody case involving the Family that pitted the testimonies of former members against those of current group members. The researchers "found that most of the apostates' information was credible, while current members often lied." See also: Carmen Almendros et al., "Reasons for Leaving: Psychological Abuse and Distress Reported by Former Members of Cultic Groups," *Cultic Studies Review* 8, no. 2 (2009), 111–38, articles2.icsahome.com/articles/reasons-for-leaving-almendros. This study found that negative experiences reported by former cult members were accurate and credible. It concludes that it may constitute a secondary victimization to presume inaccuracy in former members' reports of their experiences.

6. James D. Chancellor, *Life in the Family: An Oral History of the Children of God* (Syracuse: Syracuse University Press, 2000), xviii.

7. Stephen A. Kent, "Book Reviews," *Nova Religio* 8, no. 1 (2004): 108–12, skent.ualberta.ca/wp-content/uploads/2020/07/Life-in-The-Family-An-Oral-History-of-the-Children-of-God.pdf

8. Chancellor, *Life*, xxii.

9. Stephen A. Kent and Theresa Krebs, "When Scholars Know Sin: Alternative Religions and Their Academic Supporters," Skeptic 6, no. 3 (1998), in the section "Biased Studies," www.xfamily.org/index.php/When_Scholars_Know_Sin

10. Stephen A. Kent, "Generational Revolt by the Adult Children of First-Generation Members of the Children of God/The Family," *Cultic Studies Review* 3, no. 1 (2004): 56–72, in section E, "The Cover-Up and Its Impact upon the Teens," www.xfamily.org/index.php/Generational_Revolt_by_the_Adult_Children_of_First-Generation_Members_of_the_Children_of_God/The_Family

11. Chancellor, *Life*, 137.

12. "Complete Judgment," part 6: "Medical Neglect."

13. "Merry's Story, XFamily, www.xfamily.org/index.php/Merry%27s_Story

14. "Merry Jolene Berg," XFamily, in the section "Vilification," www.xfamily.org/index.php/Merry_Jolene_Berg#Vilification

15. David Berg, "Persecution & Backsliders," July 1992, paragraph 18, pubs.xfamily.org/text.php?t=2817

16. Karen Zerby, "False Accusers in the Last Days!" July 1992, paragraphs 79–81 and 89, www.exfamily.org/pubs/ml/b2/2820.shtml

17. For examples of Stephen A. Kent's publications on the Children of God/the Family, see: skent.ualberta.ca/contributions/children-of-god/

18. Stephen A. Kent, "Brainwashing Programs in The Family/Children of God, and Scientology," *Misunderstanding Cults: Searching for Objectivity in a Controversial Field*, eds. Benjamin Zablocki and Thomas Robbins (Toronto: University of Toronto Press, 2001), 349–78, skent.ualberta.ca/wp-content/uploads/2014/06/Scientology-Brainwashing-in-RPF-and-The-Family.pdf

19. Stephen A. Kent, "Lustful Prophet: A Psychosexual Historical Study of the Children of God's Founder, David Berg," *Cultic Studies Journal* 11, no. 2 (1994): 135–88, skent.ualberta.ca/wp-content/uploads/2014/07/COG-Lustful-Prophet.pdf. See also: Stephen A. Kent, "Misattribution and Social Control in the Children of God," *Journal of Religion and Health* 33, no. 1 (spring 1994): 29–43; reprinted in *Spirituality in East and West* no. 1 (1997): 16–22, skent.ualberta.ca/wp-content/uploads/2014/07/Misattribution-in-COG.pdf

20. Maureen Griffo, "Spiritual Abuse Across the Spectrum of Christian Environments," *ICSA Today* 9, no. 1 (2018): 2–5, www.icsahome.com/articles/spectrum-of-spiritual-abuse-doc. "Dr. Joost Meerloo's *The Rape of the Mind* (Merloo, 1956) examined how mental coercion exploits empathy and perception to steal a person's autonomy. In abusive religious environments, what might be called a rape of the soul and also the mind occurs."

21. Perry Bulwer, "A Response to James D. Chancellor's Life in The Family: An Oral History of the Children of God," *Cultic Studies Review* 6, no. 2 (2007): 101–59, articles1.icsahome.com/articles/a-response-to-james-d-chancellor-s-life-in-the-family-an-oral-history-of-the-children-of-god. A copy on my blog has easier-to-access footnotes instead of endnotes: perry-bulwer.blogspot.com/p/response-to-james-d-chancellors-life-in.html. For Chancellor's response, see: James D. Chancellor, "A Response to Perry Bulwer's Evaluation of Life in the Family," *Cultic Studies Review* 6, no. 2 (2007), articles1.icsahome.com/articles/a-response-to-perry-bulwer-s-evaluation-of-life-in-the-family. And for my reply, see: Perry Bulwer, "A Rejoinder to James Chancellor's Response to My Article," *Cultic Studies Review* 6, no. 2 (2007): 167–72, articles1.icsahome.com/articles/a-rejoinder-to-james-chancellor-s-response-to-my-article

Epilogue

1. "The Family International's Executive Overseers Address the International CESNUR Conference," 24-7 Press Release, June 13, 2009, www.24-7pressrelease.com/press-release/the-family-internationals-executive-overseers-address-the-international-cesnur-conference-104165.php

2. The 2009 International Conference of the Center for Studies on New Religions (CESNUR): www.cesnur.org/2009/slc_prg.htm

3. Peggy Fletcher Stack, "Once Dismissed as 'Sex Cult,' Tiny Church Launches Image Makeover," *Salt Lake Tribune,* June 25, 2009, religiouschildabuse.blogspot.com/2010/11/family-international-aka-children-of.html

4. Stephen A. Kent, "The French and German Versus American Debate over 'New Religions', Scientology and Human Rights," *Marburg Journal of Religion* 6, no. 1 (January 2001): 15, 16, archiv.ub.uni-marburg.de/ep/0004/article/view/3742/3559

5. "J. Gordon Melton," XFamily, www.xfamily.org/index.php/J._Gordon_Melton

6. J. Gordon Melton, *Encyclopedic Handbook of Cults in America*, revised and updated edition (New York: Garland Publishing, 1992), 224–31.

7. James R. Lewis and J. Gordon Melton, eds., *Sex, Slander, and Salvation: Investigating the Family/Children of God* (Stanford, CA: Center for Academic Publication, 1994), www.exfamily.org/pubs/misc/sex_slander_salvation.shtml

8. "James R. Lewis," Apologetics Index, www.apologeticsindex.org/l33.html

9. Ian Reader, "Scholarship, Aum Shinrikyôô, and Academic Integrity," *Nova Religio* 3, no. 2 (April 2000): 372, nr.ucpress.edu/content/3/2/368.full.pdf+html

10. Reader, "Scholarship,": 372, 378.

11. "Apologetics and Academic Supporters of The Family," XFamily, www.xfamily.org/index.php/Jules_-_Apologetics_and_Academic_Supporters_of_The_Family

12. Stephen A. Kent and Theresa Krebs, "When Scholars Know Sin: Alternative Religions and Their Academic Supporters," Skeptic 6, no. 3 (1998), in the section "Biased Studies," www.xfamily.org/index.php/When_Scholars_Know_Sin

13. Stephen A. Kent, "Lustful Prophet: A Psychosexual Historical Study of the Children of God's Founder, David Berg," *Cultic Studies Journal* 11, no. 2 (1994): 135–88, skent.ualberta.ca/wp-content/uploads/2014/07/COG-Lustful-Prophet.pdf. See also: Stephen A. Kent, "Misattribution and Social Control in the Children of God," *Journal of Religion and Health* 33, no. 1 (spring 1994): 29–43; reprinted in *Spirituality in East and West* no. 1 (1997): 16–22, skent.ualberta.ca/wp-content/uploads/2014/07/Misattribution-in-COG.pdf

14. "Payment Received from the Family," XFamily, www.xfamily.org/index.php/J._Gordon_Melton#Payment_received_from_The_Family

15. J. Gordon Melton, *The Children of God: "The Family* (Signature Books, in cooperation with CESNUR, 2004).

16. Susan Raine, "The Children of God/The Family: A Discussion of Recent Research (1998–2005)," *Cultic Studies Review* 5, no. 1 (2006): 29–72, articles2.icsahome.com/articles/the-children-of-godthe-family-raine

17. Stack, "Makeover."

18. "Reboot Documents," XFamily, www.xfamily.org/index.php/Reboot_Documents

19. Gary Shepherd and Gordon Shepherd, *Talking with the Children of God: Prophecy and Transformation in a Radical Religious Group* (University of Illinois Press, 2010).

20. Gary Shepherd and Gordon Shepherd, "Reboot of the Family International," *Nova Religio* 17, no. 2 (February 2013): 74–98, nr.ucpress.edu/content/17/2/74.full.pdf+html

21. Ibid.

22. "Susan Claire Borowik," XFamily, www.xfamily.org/index.php/Susan_Claire_Borowik

23. Claire Borowik, "From Radical Communalism to Virtual Community: The Digital Transformation of the Family International," *Nova Religio* 22, no. 1 (2018): 59–86, nr.ucpress.edu/content/22/1/59

24. Ibid.

25. "The Love Prophet and the Children of God" (documentary transcript), XFamily, www.xfamily.org/index.php/The_Love_Prophet_and_the_Children_of_God

26. Peter Wilkinson, "The Life and Death of the Chosen One," *Rolling Stone* 977/978 (June 30–July 14, 2005), www.xfamily.org/index.php/Rolling_Stone:_The_Life_and_Death_of_the_Chosen_One

27. Amy Bril has been interviewed in many media reports and documentaries, including *Children of the Cult* and the A&E series *Cults and Extreme Belief:* www.aetv.com/shows/cults-and-extreme-belief/season-1/episode-3

28. "Merry Jolene Berg—Memorial and Eulogies," XFamily, www.xfamily.org/index.php/Merry_Jolene_Berg#Memorial_and_Eulogies

29. "Books about the Children of God, aka the Family International," Religion and Child Abuse News, religiouschildabuse.blogspot.com/p/books-about-children-of-god-aka-family.html

30. "Trauma and Adverse Childhood Experiences (ACEs)," US Department of Health and Human Services, eclkc.ohs.acf.hhs.gov/publication/trauma-adverse-childhood-experiences-aces

31. "Cult Killer: The Rick Rodriguez Story," XFamily, www.xfamily.org/index.php/Cult_Killer:_The_Rick_Rodriguez_Story

32. Bethany Rielly, "We Feel Forgotten—Children of God Cult Survivors Demand Justice for Decades of Abuse," *Morning Star Online*, March 7, 2022, morningstaronline.co.uk/article/f/we-feel-forgotten-children-god-cult-survivors-demand-justice-decades-abuse

33. A partial list of legal actions: www.xfamily.org/index.php/Category:-Legal_Action

34. For more on Verity Carter, Hope Bastine and Celeste Jones, see the following: Marion Scott, "Police Probe Children of God Sex Cult as Survivor Breaks Silence on Childhood Torment and Abuse," *Sunday Post*, March 18, 2018, www.sundaypost.com/fp/my-hell-on-earth/; Sharon Hendry, "How I

Escaped the Children of God Cult That Destroyed My Childhood," *Sunday Times*, August 9, 2020, dialogueireland.wordpress.com/2020/08/10/how-i-survived-the-children-of-god-cult/; and Celeste Jones, Kristina Jones and Juliana Buhring, *Not Without My Sister: The True Story of Three Girls Violated and Betrayed* (Harper Element 2008).

35. Andrea Willey and Stephen A. Kent, "Prosecuting Child Sexual Abuse in Alternative Religions," *International Journal of Cultic Studies* 8 (2017): 16–36, skent.ualberta.ca/wp-content/uploads/2017/11/Prosecuting-Child-Sexual-Abuse-ICSA.pdf

36. Janja Lalich, "Perspectives on U.S. Cult-Related Court Cases," JanjaLalich.com, May 16, 2015, janjalalich.com/blog/perspectives-on-cult-related-court-cases/

37. "Pseudonyms," XFamily, www.xfamily.org/index.php/Category:Pseudonyms

38. Herbert L. Rosedale and Michael D. Langone, "On Using the Term 'Cult,'" *ICSA Today* 6, no. 3 (2015): 4–6, www.icsahome.com/articles/onusingtermcult

39. Janja Lalich, "Cults Today: A New Social-Psychological Perspective," JanjaLalich.com, January 17, 2022, janjalalich.com/blog/cults-today-new-social-psychological-perspective/

40. Janja Lalich and Michael D. Langone, "Characteristics Associated with Cults," JanjaLalich.com, janjalalich.com/help/characteristics-associated-with-cults/. This article is an excerpt from a book by Janja Lalich and Madeleine Tobias, *Take Back Your Life: Recovering from Cults and Abusive Relationships* (Richmond, CA: Bay Tree Publishing, 2006).

41. Caroline Hickman et al., "Climate Anxiety in Children and Young People and Their Beliefs about Government Responses to Climate Change: A Global Survey," *The Lancet 5*, No. 12, December 1, 2021, www.thelancet.com/journals/lanplh/article/PIIS2542-5196(21)00278-3/fulltext

42. Bulletin of the Atomic Scientists, "Closer Than Ever: It Is 100 Seconds to Midnight," January 23, 2020, thebulletin.org/doomsday-clock/2020-doomsday-clock-statement/

43. Bulletin of the Atomic Scientists, "A Time of Unprecedented Danger: It Is 90 Seconds to Midnight," January 24, 2023, thebulletin.org/doomsday-clock/current-time/

44. Radio New Zealand, "Janja Lalich: How Normal People End Up in Cults Like NXIVM," February 27, 2021, www.rnz.co.nz/national/programmes/saturday/audio/2018785404/janja-lalich-how-normal-people-end-up-in-cults-like-nxivm

45. International Cultic Studies Association, "Common Myths and Misconceptions about Cults and Cultic Groups," www.icsahome.com/articles/common-myths-and-misconceptions-about-cults-and-cultic-groups